Wendy Constant.

CW01584370

Revision for Science

KEY STAGE 4

with answers

Revision for Science

KEY STAGE 4

with answers

JOE BOYD AND WALTER WHITELAW

JOHN MURRAY

First published in 1994
by John Murray (Publishers) Ltd
50 Albemarle Street, London W1X 4BD

Typeset by Litho Link Ltd, Welshpool, Powys, in 11/12½pt New Century Schoolbook
Printed in Great Britain by St Edmundsbury Press Ltd, Bury St Edmunds

Line drawings: Art Construction

A catalogue entry for this title can be obtained from the British Library

ISBN 0 7195 5394 6

Contents

Introduction

During the last few years, you have gained a great deal of important knowledge and understanding from the National Curriculum for Science. You have probably forgotten some of the work. This work must be revised and relearned for your examinations. Unfortunately, revision is hard work and it is easy to avoid. Some of the most common ways are shown in the cartoons below.

First, get organised!

Plan

It is always a good idea to plan your revision. The plan below is an example of a revision timetable. Each box represents 2 or 3 hours of work. There is one box for a school day, and two for weekend and holiday days. Make up something like this for your own revision, and stick it on your wall.

Study/Revision planner

1. Plan all your revision before you begin it.
2. Each box represents 2 or 3 hours of work.
3. Try to keep to your plan, but don't be afraid to change it.

Mon	Tues	Wed	Thurs	Fri	Sat am	Sat pm	Sun am	Sun pm
AT2 levels 4,5,6	AT2 levels 4,5,6	AT2 levels 4,5,6	Look up words in bold	20 March	AT 2 levels 7,8	AT 2 levels 7,8	Day off	Day off
Look up words in bold	AT 3 levels 4,5,6	AT 3 levels 4,5,6	etc	27 March				
				3 April				
				10 April				

Be an active learner

Try to be an active learner. Rather than just reading through notes, make sure that you write or draw or underline as you read through them. Make summaries and answer questions. Use spider diagrams and revision summaries (examples of these are given below).

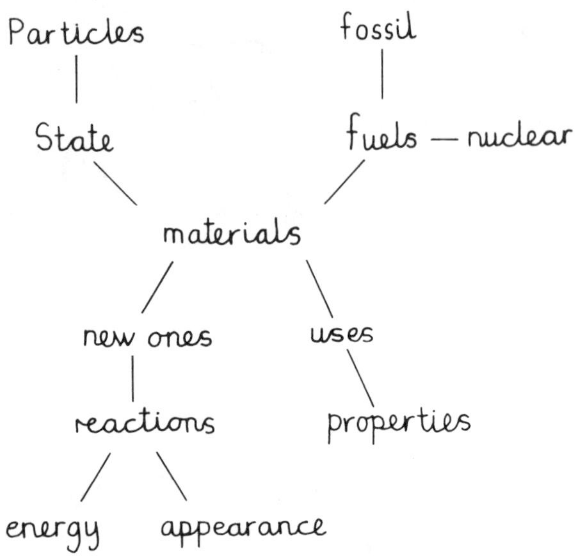

Example of a spider diagram

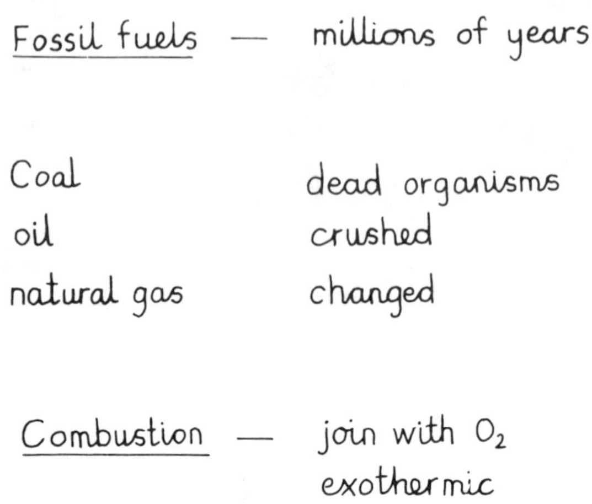

Example of a revision summary

Next, use this book!

Get your own copy

This book contains the main ideas of the whole Science course, Key Stage 4, Levels 4–10. Your teacher will suggest which level you should aim for. Learn the levels in order, from 4 upwards, until you reach your own target. If you are aiming for Level 8, begin with Levels 4, 5 & 6, then learn Levels 7 & 8.

Write all over it

1 Each section starts by listing the main 'big' ideas. Read these and make sure you understand the sense of the work. The paragraph letters link with each big idea.
2 Read each paragraph and underline the key phrases.
3 Continue with the other paragraphs. Complete any diagrams when asked.
4 At the end of each double page, read over your work. Tick the boxes when you know and understand the work.
5 Check your answers at the back of the book. (See your teacher about anything you still do not understand.)
6 Make a list of any words in **bold** and look these up later in your class notes and textbook.
7 Have a short five-minute break.
8 Start the next double page of work.

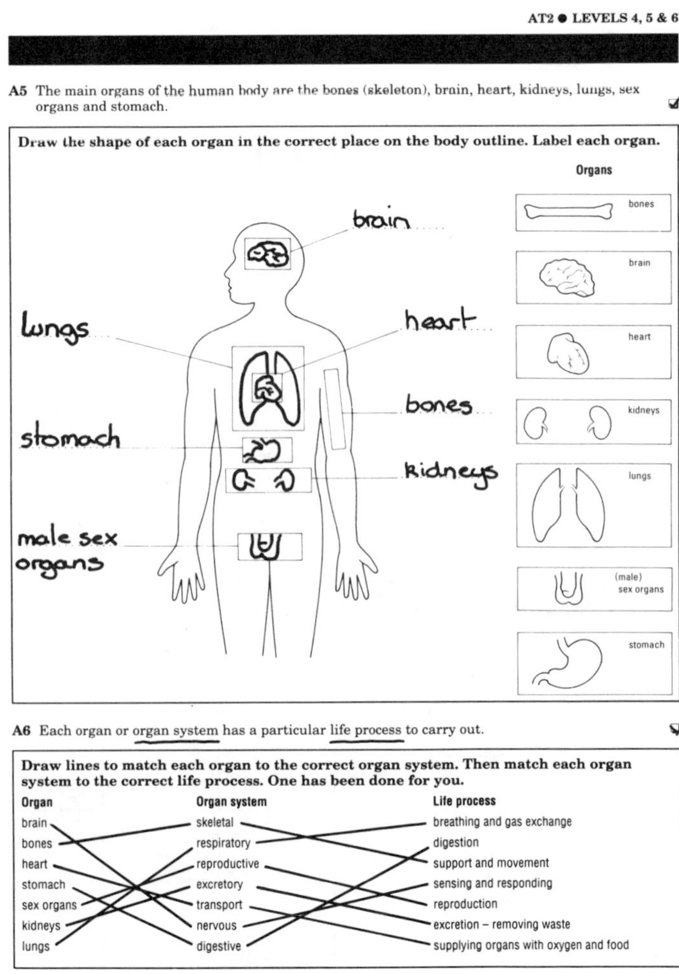
AT2 ● LEVELS 4, 5 & 6

A5 The main organs of the human body are the bones (skeleton), brain, heart, kidneys, lungs, sex organs and stomach.

Draw the shape of each organ in the correct place on the body outline. Label each organ.

A6 Each organ or organ system has a particular life process to carry out.

Draw lines to match each organ to the correct organ system. Then match each organ system to the correct life process. One has been done for you.

Organ	Organ system	Life process
brain	skeletal	breathing and gas exchange
bones	respiratory	digestion
heart	reproductive	support and movement
stomach	excretory	sensing and responding
sex organs	transport	reproduction
kidneys	nervous	excretion – removing waste
lungs	digestive	supplying organs with oxygen and food

An example of a completed page

Finally, record your revision

Complete this record sheet after each revision session. It will help you to plan your work.

Attainment Target		**Session 1** Date completed	**Session 2** Date completed	**Session 3** Date completed
1 Scientific investigation	Levels 4, 5, 6			
	Levels 7, 8			
	Levels 9, 10			
2 Life and living processes	Levels 4, 5, 6			
	Levels 7, 8			
	Levels 9, 10			
3 Materials and their properties	Levels 4, 5, 6			
	Levels 7, 8			
	Levels 9, 10			
4 Physical processes	Levels 4, 5, 6			
	Levels 7, 8			
	Levels 9, 10			

ATTAINMENT TARGET 1

Scientific investigation

Big ideas

You should be able to plan and carry out investigations in which you:

A ask questions, predict and hypothesise;
B observe, alter variables and measure changes;
C record and interpret results and evaluate evidence.

Investigations are practical exercises. You can revise your investigations by reading over your reports about practical work and by remembering what you did, and why you did it.

During this reading, think about the meaning of the words and phrases shown in **bold** on the following pages.

A1 **Predict** means *work out what will happen.* ❑

Predict which container will be hottest after 5 minutes (tick your answer).

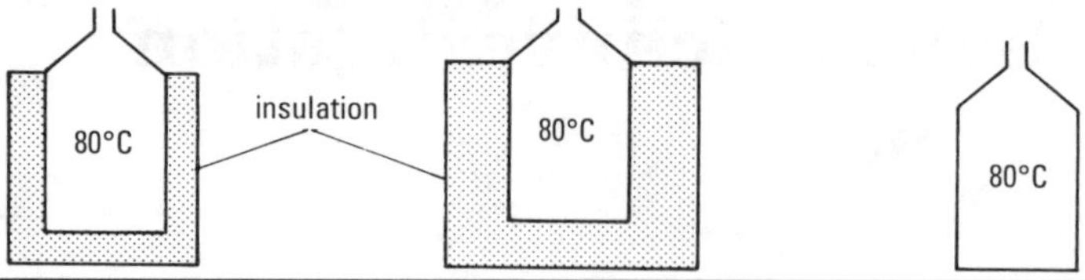

A2 Use **prior knowledge** means *use what you already know.*

For example, you wear clothes made from warm materials in winter. ❑

Use this prior knowledge to name two materials that could be used to insulate this container of hot liquid.

1 ....

2 ....

A3 Formulate a **hypothesis** means *make a prediction that can be tested in an experiment.*

For example, a baker notices that dough rises by different amounts on different days. His hypothesis is that dough rises best at 35 °C. ❑

Describe how you could test this hypothesis fairly.

A4 **Cause and effect (causal link)** means that *you use scientific knowledge or theory to explain why things have happened.*

For example, the dinosaurs disappeared from the Earth millions of years ago. Three possible causes for this effect are that

- a big meteorite hit the Earth
- epidemic diseases killed them
- the climate changed suddenly. ❑

A5 **Theory** means *a system of ideas that can explain observations and measurements.*

For example, the rate of reaction of chalk with acid increases when the concentration of acid is increased. ❑

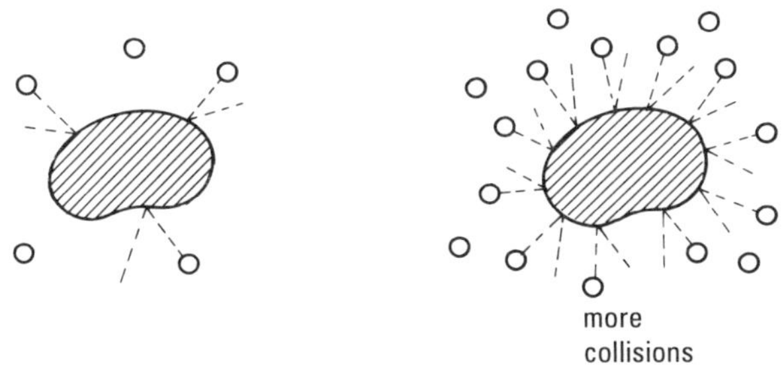

With the aid of another drawing, use the particle theory to explain how the rate of reaction would change if the chalk was broken into small pieces in acid.

B1 **Observe** means *look carefully at what happens.* ❑

What would you observe in the reaction between acid and chalk?

B2 **Variable** means *something that affects the result of an experiment when it changes.* ❑

Underline the variables that affect the rate of reaction of chalk and acid.

volume of acid   temperature   time of day   size of chalk pieces   sex of experimenter   colour of beaker

B3 **Range** of a variable means *using values between sensible lowest (minimum) and highest (maximum) values.* ❑

If you wish to measure the effect of temperature on a living thing whose normal body temperature is 37 °C, then the temperature variable should range between .... and ....

B4 **Fair test** means *changing one variable in an experiment and keeping all others the same so that the comparison is fair.* ❑

Circle the two beakers that can be used as a fair test of the effect of temperature on the rate of reaction.

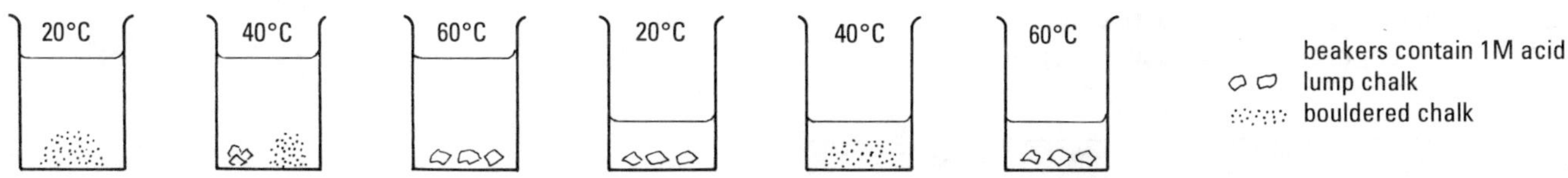

B5 **Key variable** means *a variable that must be taken into account in the design of an experiment, or else the results will not be useful.*

A control means that *one experiment is used to compare with the others; each of the other experiments will have a different key variable changed.* ❑

Examine this control.

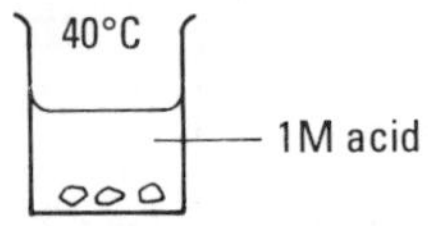

Write down the key variables that are being tested when each experiment below is compared with the control.

....

B6 Qualitative means that *you describe distinct changes.*

Using your senses you can make qualitative descriptions of colour, cloudiness and taste. ❑

Name three more factors that can be described qualitatively.

1 .... 2... 3 ....

B7 Quantitative means that *you measure changes accurately and use numbers to indicate any differences.*

Using instruments you can make quantitative measurements of changes in temperature, volume and length. ❑

Name three more factors that can be described quantitatively.

1 .... 2... 3 ....

B8 Fine discrimination in measurement means that *you read the smallest part of the scale of the measuring instrument.*

Using fine discrimination, the length of this object is 52 mm, not 5 cm. ❑

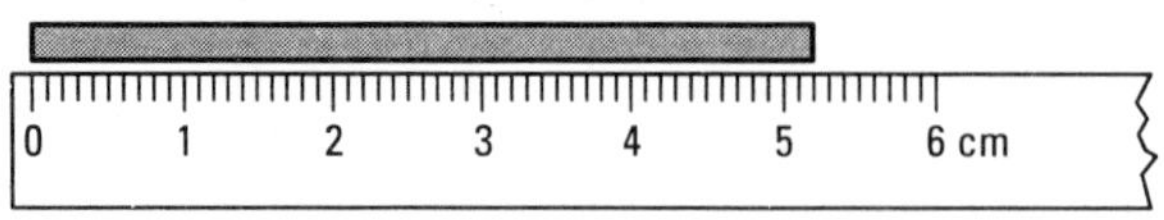

C1 Conclusion means *working out what the results mean.* ❑

Write two conclusions from this table of results.

Time (min)	Temperature with nylon cover (°C)	Temperature with woollen cover (°C)
0	80	81
30	63	74
60	48	67
90	33	61
120	25	55
150	25	50

1 ....
....
....
....

2 ....
....
....
....

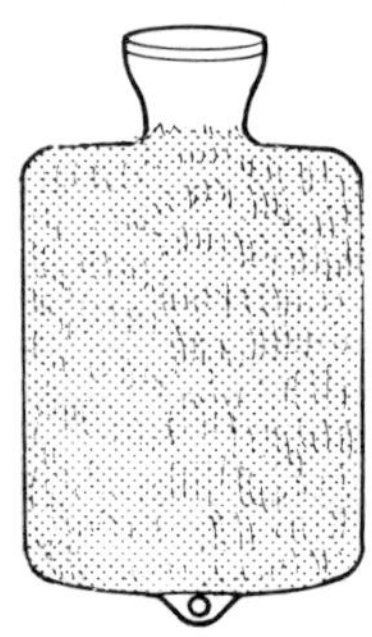

C2 Evaluate means *thinking about how likely it is that a conclusion is correct.* ❑

Evaluate each explanation given below, giving each one a star rating from ★ (poor) to ★★★ (very good).

Dough might rise faster at higher temperatures because:

a) the yeast makes more carbon dioxide gas ....

b) the yeast breathes in and out more quickly ....

c) the carbon dioxide gas bubbles expand when hot ....

d) the water in the dough boils ....

C3 Using a **model** means *representing an idea or a theory with something that you can see and think about easily.* ❑

Draw the model of the particle theory that you used in class.

C4 A **relationship** between variables means that *the variables change together.*

For example, this graph shows that variable x goes up when y goes up. ❑

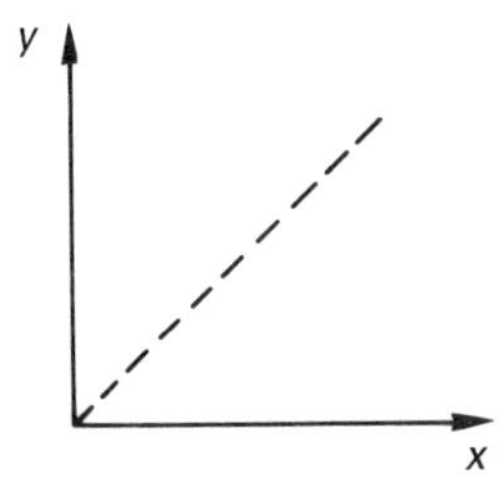

Draw a similar graph to show variable *x* going down as *y* goes up.

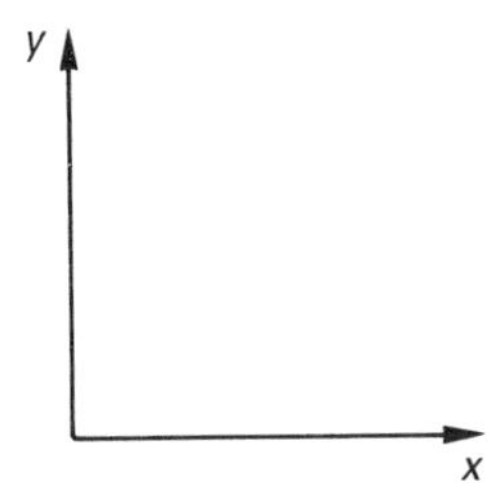

C5 Results can be **recorded** in different ways, such as:

a table which has
- *columns*
- *with titles*

a bar graph which has
- *a title*
- *two labelled axes with units*
- *bars of same thickness*
- *straight lines for axes*

a line graph which has
- *a title*
- *two labelled axes with units*
- *numbers on axes*
- *straight lines for axes* ❑

Thickness of insulator (mm)	Temperature after 10 mins (°C)
2	60
4	63
6	67
8	70
10	74

effect of thickness

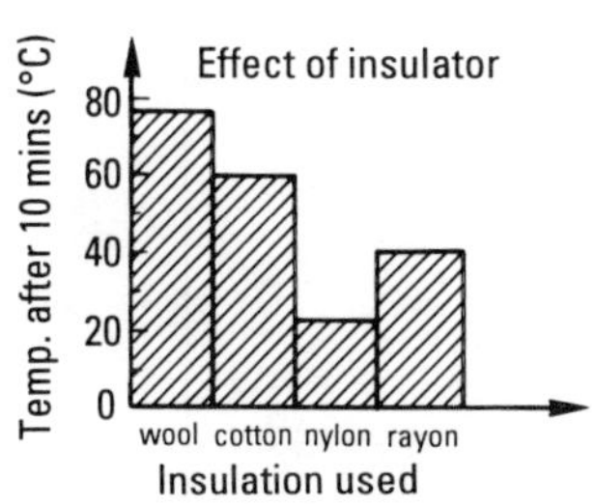

effect of insulator

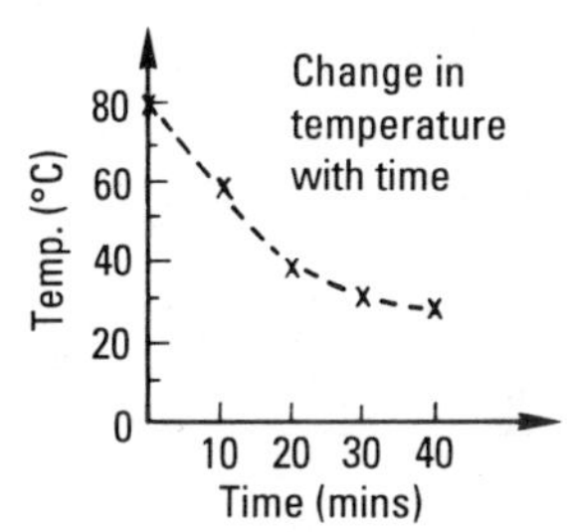

change in temperature

Write a conclusion from each set of results given above.

....

....

....

A1 A **strategy** for investigations means that *you should work out a plan.*

For example, you are investigating the best conditions for growing plants in a greenhouse. Your strategy should include:

- setting up a control plant
- identifying key variables that might affect the growth of the plants (these could be worked out from prior knowledge of photosynthesis, for example, light, temperature, CO_2 level)
- setting up batches of experimental plants to measure the effect of changing each key variable. ❑

Draw up an outline plan for such an investigation.

A2 The **relative effect** of variables means that *the variables are being compared; some will have a bigger effect on the result than others.* ❑

Animals of the same species in different places have bodies of different sizes. To show the relative effects of the key variables below on human body size, write (1) next to the most important, (2) next to the second most important and so on.

population density	light intensity	air pollution ......
amount of food	type of government	education ......

A3 **Optimum conditions** mean *the conditions that are best or most favourable.* ❑

Write in the optimum conditions for human life.

B1 Manipulate means *to change in a pre-planned way.*

For example, in the greenhouse investigation (A1, on page 6), you can manipulate the amount of light by covering all the windows with black paper and installing an electric lamp that you can switch on and off. Otherwise your results will be affected by the weather; there is more light on sunny days than on cloudy days. ❑

Describe how you could manipulate temperature in the greenhouse investigation.

B2 An **independent variable** means that *the value is chosen by the experimenter.*

A **dependent variable** means that *its value depends on the value of the independent variable.*

The rate of many reactions increases with temperature. In an experiment, you can change the temperature and measure the time that the reaction takes. This graph shows the kind of result you might expect. ❑

Label one axis as the independent variable and the other as the dependent variable.

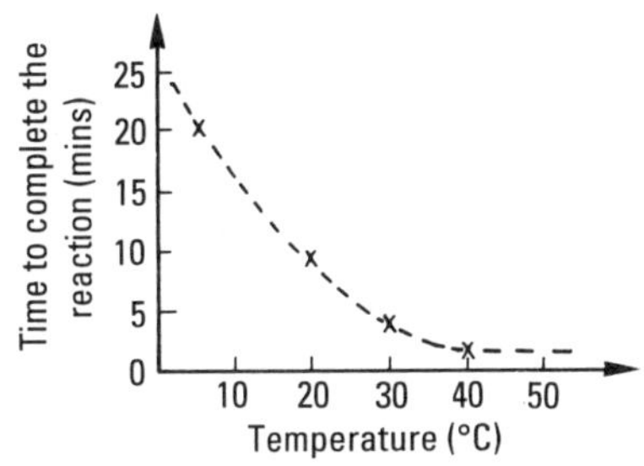

B3 A suitable **degree of accuracy** means *the accuracy of the measuring instrument should be matched to the kind of measurement it has to make.* ❑

Draw lines to match the kind of measurement with the instrument needed to achieve a suitable degree of accuracy.

height of a pot plant	micrometer
height of a fir tree	30 cm ruler
length of a leaf	metre stick
thickness of a leaf	10 m tape

C1 Limitations of evidence means that *any experiment has shortcomings and weaknesses, and experimental results must not be relied on completely.*

For example, in the greenhouse investigation (A1, page 6), the experimental evidence is limited by uncontrollable factors like the effect of insects on individual plants, the health of individual plants or the draft of air which is different in different parts of the greenhouse. ❑

C2 Sources of error means *the defects in an experiment that cause inaccuracies in the results.* ❑

What is the major source of error in experiments carried out in school laboratories?

C3 Justify means *to give a good reason for something.*

If you have to justify aspects of your investigation then be prepared to explain why you did something in a particular way. ❑

A1 **Valid** data means that *the data measures what it is supposed to measure.*

For example, in an investigation of the corrosion of aluminium pots, it would be valid to study the reaction of aluminium with acids and alkalis between pH 4 and pH 11, the range of pH found in foods. It would not be valid to measure the corrosion at pH 1. ❏

Tick the other valid measures of aluminium corrosion in this investigation.

amount of corrosion in used saucepans ...... amount of corrosion on light aircraft wings ......

amount of corrosion on kitchen foil ...... amount of corrosion at temperatures in the range 200 – 400°C ......

A2 **Reliable** data means that *the data has been collected scientifically and is accurate.*

For example, in the aluminium investigation above, the data would be reliable if the amount of corrosion was estimated from conductivity measurements. It would not be reliable if you asked your friend to hit the aluminium with a hammer and to describe the noise. ❏

A3 **Scientific law** means that *a theory has given many predictions that have always been proved correct.*

Mendel's ideas about heredity were worked out from his studies of pea plants. ❏

Look at these results. Which law of heredity do they support?

Parents	Round seeds	Wrinkled seeds	

F_1 generation	all round	(none)	....
F_2 generation	5474	1850	....
	(ratio 2.96 : 1)		

A4 **Secondary sources** means that *the knowledge is learned from a description of someone's original work.*

For example, the significance of Gregor Mendel's work was only recognised after his death, when several biologists read his original paper and included his ideas and results in their own writings. ❏

A5 A **mechanism** means *the way in which something happens.*

For example, the mechanism of inheritance is thought to involve chromosomes. The chromosomes carry two alleles for each characteristic. During meiosis, these two alleles are separated and a gamete is formed with only one set of alleles. ❏

Complete the diagram to show how this mechanism explains why there is an equal chance of humans having a baby girl or boy.

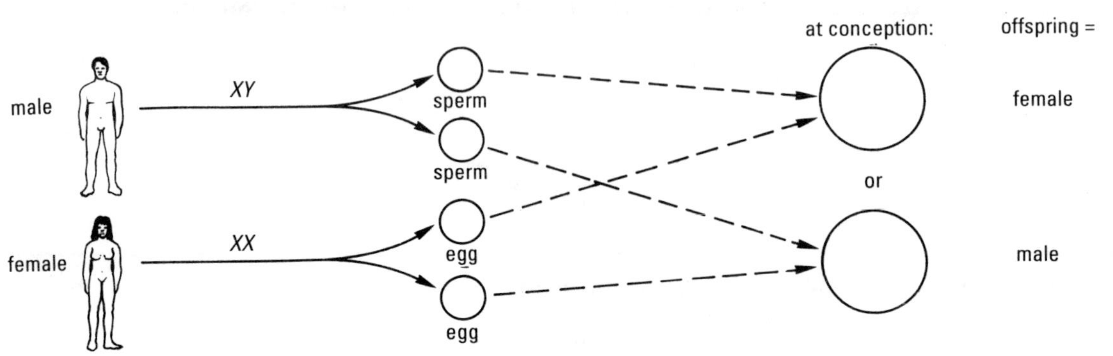

A6 Abstract concepts means *ideas that are theoretical and do not deal with real objects or substances.* ❏

Underline the abstract concepts:

corrosion atom oxygen acid hydrogen ion pH

B1 Systematically means *to do something in an orderly and methodical way.* ❏

Describe how you would systematically investigate this prediction about the inheritance of normal wings in *Drosophila* (fruit fly):

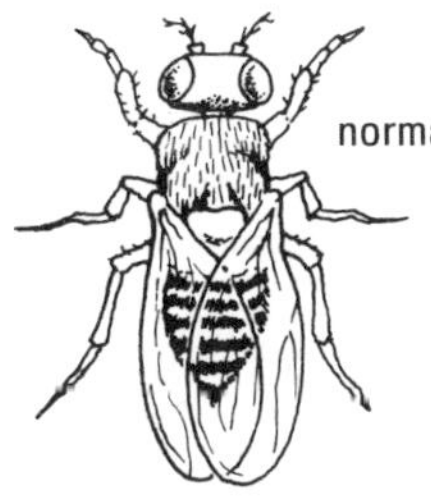

Hypothesis:

Normal wing(W) dominant over miniature wing(w).

Prediction:

Given parent populations of WW and ww, all F_1 offspring will be Ww. F_2 offspring will be WW, Ww and ww in the genotypic ratio 1:2:1.

Investigation:

B2 Critically evaluate means *to find fault with something and work out how it might be improved.* ❏

Critically evaluate this study of smoking conducted by an expensive 'youth' magazine.

All readers were asked to return a questionnaire which asked them about their personal smoking habits. 2000 did so. From this, the magazine concluded that only 15% of British teenagers smoked, and none had health problems.

B3 Precision means *to be exact and thorough.* ❑

Describe two ways in which the precision of the smoking investigation (B2, page 9) could have been improved.

1 ……………………………………………………………………………………………………

……………………………………………………………………………………………………

……………………………………………………………………………………………………

2 ……………………………………………………………………………………………………

……………………………………………………………………………………………………

……………………………………………………………………………………………………

B4 Showing **creativity** and **invention** means *inventing your own ways of doing things.* ❑

How would you investigate the link between smoking and ill-health?

C1 Analyse means *to examine your results closely to find out what they mean.* ❑

Analyse these results which show the amount of corrosion of aluminium at different pH values. (No written answer required.)

pH	2	3	4	5	6	7	8	9	10
corrosion of Al	✓✓✓	✓	✓✓✓	✓✓	✓	✓	✓	x	x

C2 Interpret means *to explain the meaning of your results.* ❑

What is your interpretation of the results given in C1 on the previous page?

C3 Anomalous result means *a result that is atypical and does not fit the pattern of the other results.* ❑

Circle the anomalous result in C1 on page 10.

C4 A generalisation is *a statement that applies to many similar instances.* ❑

Tick the statements that are true generalisations.

living cells contain water ......

people have hairy heads ......

sickle-cell anaemia is inherited ......

metals corrode in air ......

C5 Scientific **controversy** means that *scientists disagree about something.*

For example, the theory of evolution has always been controversial. ❑

Write down two examples of modern scientific controversies (maybe from a newspaper article or a TV programme).

1	2 ....
....	....
....	....
....	....
....	....

C6 Probability means *the chance or likelihood of something happening.*

For example, the probability of the Sun rising tomorrow is nearly 1 chance in 1. The probability of an apple containing a worm is about 1 in 1000. The probability of a tree saying 'good morning' is maybe 1 in 10^{trillion}. ❑

Estimate the probability of the following things happening.

a) throwing two heads in a row when tossing a coin ....

b) dying before the age of 50 because you smoke ....

c) having two grandchildren with blue eyes ....

d) passing all your GCSEs ....

ATTAINMENT TARGET 2

Life and living processes

Big ideas

A Plants and animals are made up of cells that are organised to carry out important life processes.

B There are variations between individuals of the same species. Variation and inheritance are the starting points for evolution.

C Populations are in balance in ecosystems. Human activity can endanger this natural balance.

D There is a flow of energy through every ecosystem. Essential nutrients are cycled through the ecosystem to keep them at a steady level.

A1 All living things are made of cells. ❑

A2 Most animal cells have the same basic parts: cell membrane, cytoplasm and nucleus.

Most plant cells have the same basic parts: cell wall, cell membrane, cytoplasm, nucleus, vacuole and chloroplasts. ❑

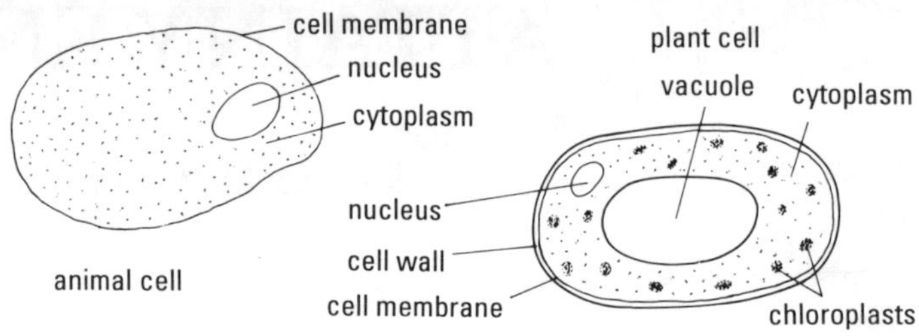

Circle the animal cells using one colour; circle the plant cells using a different colour. Complete the colour key.

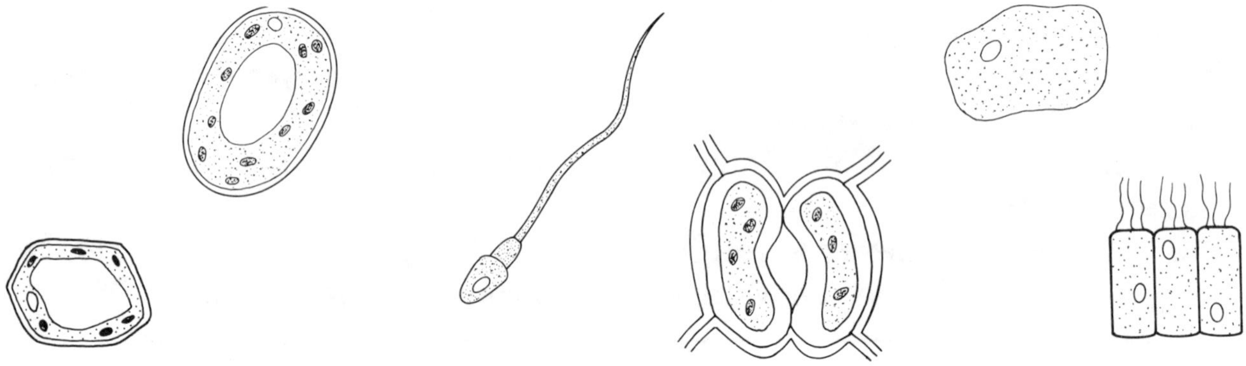

animal cells ☐ plant cells ☐

A3 Each cell part has a particular job (function). ❑

Complete the statements with the name of the correct cell part listed in A2.

In both animal and plant cells:

the .... controls what enters and leaves the cell;

chemical reactions take place in the ....;

the .... controls cell activity (for example, cell division) and carries the genes that can be passed on to the next generation.

Plant cells also contain:

.... which carry out photosynthesis;

a ....containing cell sap which gives the cell shape and provides support for the plant;

a ....which surrounds the membrane and provides support for the cell and therefore the whole plant.

A4 In multicellular organisms the cells are organised into **tissues**, **organs** and **systems** and carry out particular life processes. ❑

Draw lines to match the level of cell organisation with the correct description.

Level of cell organisation	Description
tissue	a group of organs and tissues carrying out one life process
organ	a group of cells with the same structure and function
system	a structure, made up of several different tissues, which carries out one particular function

A5 The main organs of the human body are the bones (skeleton), brain, heart, kidneys, lungs, sex organs and stomach. ❑

Draw the shape of each organ in the correct place on the body outline. Label each organ.

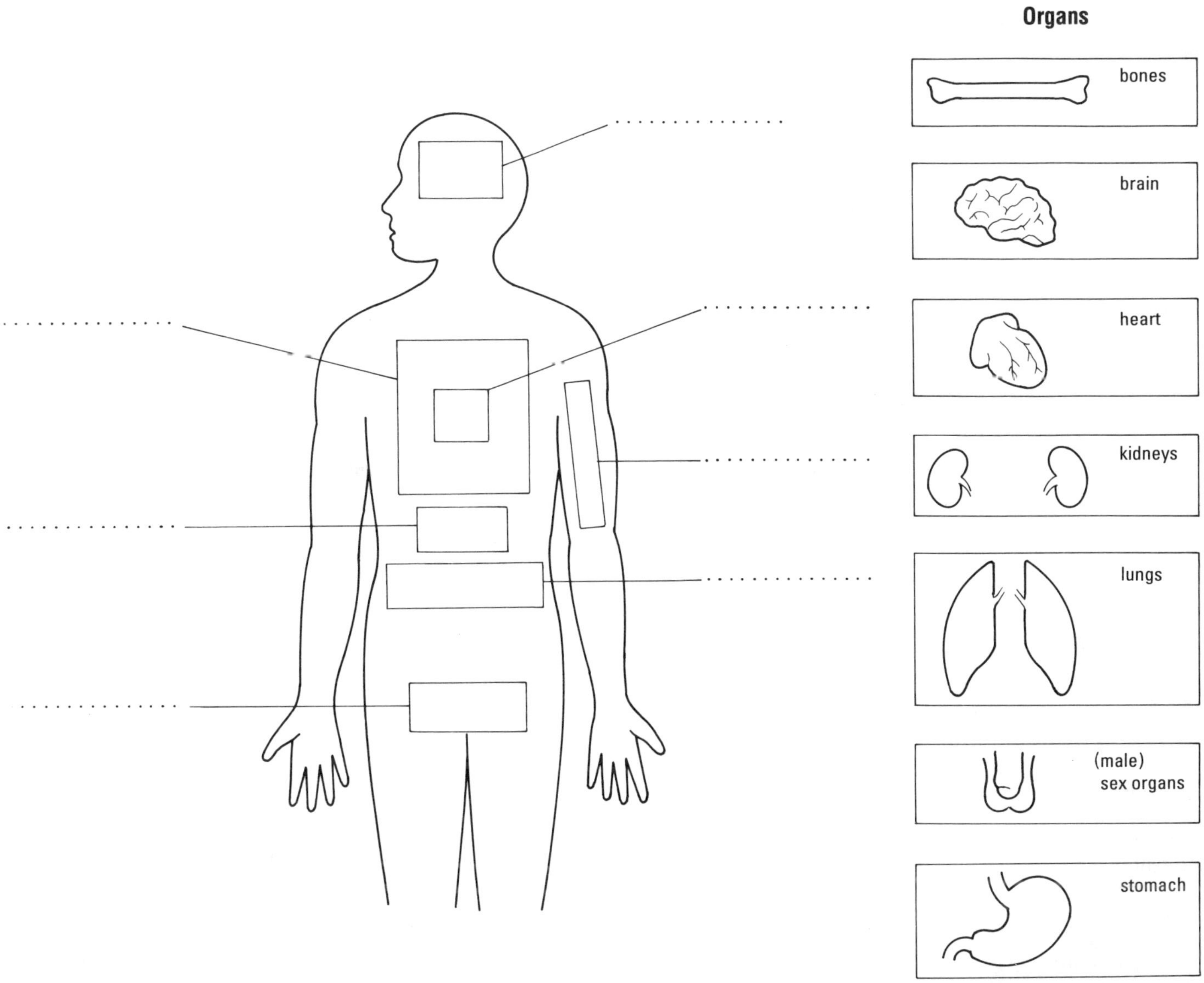

A6 Each organ or organ system has a particular life process to carry out. ❑

Draw lines to match each organ to the correct organ system. Then match each organ system to the correct life process. One has been done for you.

Organ	Organ system	Life process
brain	skeletal	breathing and gas exchange
bones	respiratory	digestion
heart	reproductive	support and movement
stomach	excretory	sensing and responding
sex organs	transport	reproduction
kidneys	nervous	excretion – removing waste
lungs	digestive	supplying organs with oxygen and food

A7 Each organ system has a particular function. ❑

Use the words from the word list to complete each statement.

arteries brain digestion heart kidneys lungs nerves ovaries
oxygen protect sperm support

1 Blood is pumped by the .... to all body organs through .... and capillaries. This provides the organs with food and oxygen. Blood transports waste from cells and returns to the heart in veins.

2 The bones of the skeleton provide.................................... and .... the organs. The muscles attached to bones allow movement to take place.

3 Large insoluble food particles are broken down in the process of .... into smaller, soluble particles by enzymes. This process takes place mainly in the stomach and small intestine, at which point the soluble food passes into the bloodstream. Undigested food passes along the large intestine and is egested at the anus.

4 Waste products in the blood are removed by the .... and stored in the bladder before being excreted.

5 The .... collects information sent to it by certain .... and enables us to respond by sending messages to the muscles.

6 Air is breathed into the ....where .... is exchanged for carbon dioxide and water vapour. Movement of the rib-cage and diaphragm causes the lungs to inflate and deflate.

7 Egg cells are produced in the .... of females and .... cells are produced in the testes of males. Fertilisation occurs when a sperm cell and egg cell meet and fuse (join up).

A8 The main organs of a flowering plant are the roots, stem, leaves and flower. Within the flower the main organs are the stamens and the ovary. ❑

Label the organs of the flower below. Draw lines to match each organ to its function.

Function

enable the plant to reproduce; stamens produce the male pollen and eggs are produced in the ovary

carry out photosynthesis

support leaves and flowers and allow materials to be transported through plant

anchor plant in soil and take up water and mineral salts from the soil

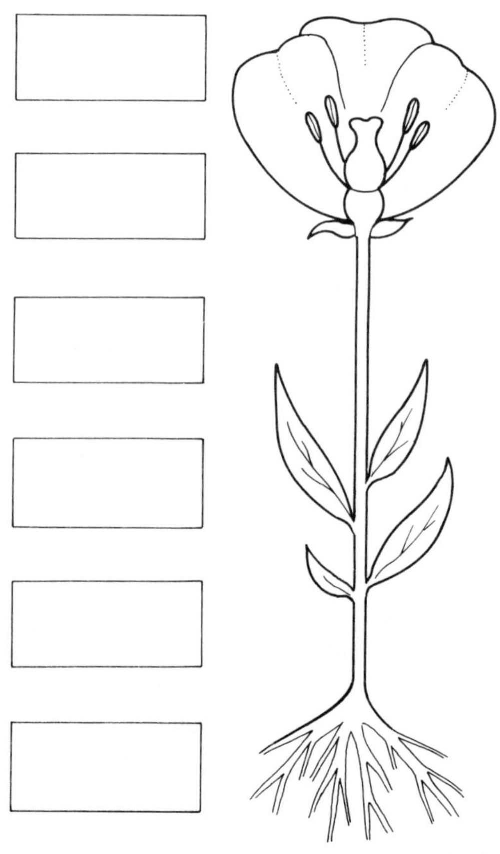

A9 In **multicellular** organisms cells develop in different ways depending on the job they will have. So, the final structure of a cell depends on its function. For example:

- cells that take in, pass out or carry substances tend to have a large surface area

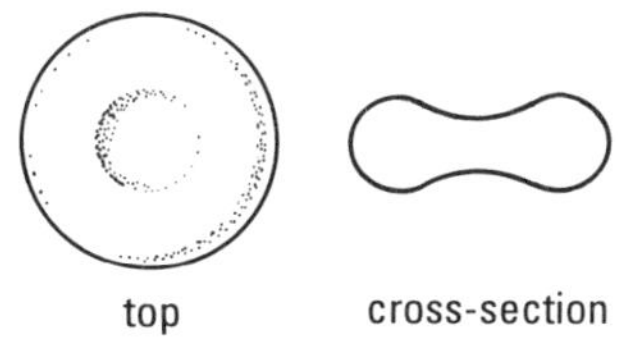

human red blood cells carry oxygen

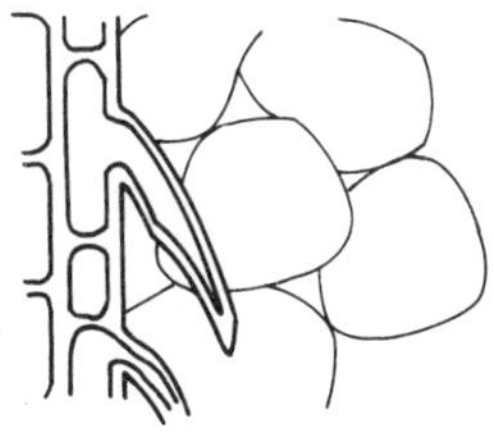

plant root hair cells absorb water from the soil

- cells that form linings or coverings tend to be long and thin. ❑

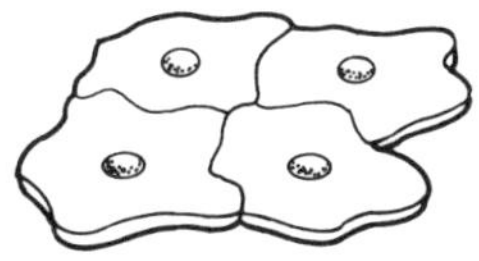

human cheek cells

leaf epidermal cells

Draw lines to match each cell below to the correct description of cell structure.

Cell		Function	Cell structure
human nerve cell (neurone)	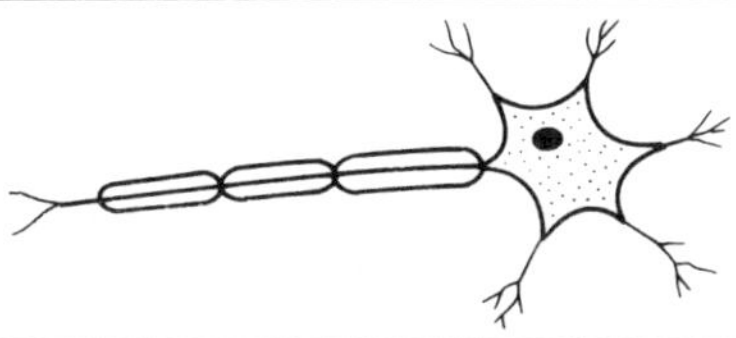	transmits nerve impulses over long distances	head part holding genetic material, tail part for movement
human sperm cell		fertilises human egg cell	long cylinder shape, lots of chloroplasts
leaf palisade cell	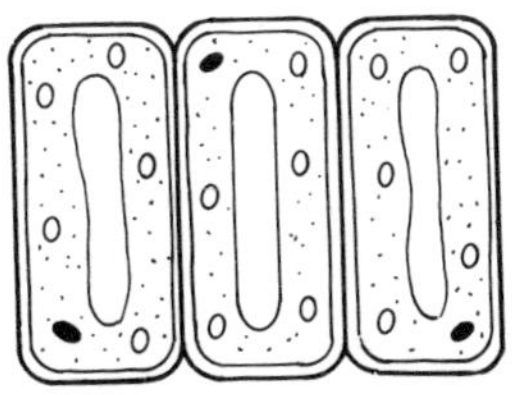	traps sunlight for photosynthesis	long thin cell covered in insulating substance

A10 Having a healthy lifestyle means avoiding damaging activities such as smoking and taking drugs. Precautions can be taken to reduce the risk of contracting sexually transmitted diseases, such as AIDS. ❑

B1 There are millions of different types or **species** of animals on Earth. Animals of the same species can breed successfully; animals from two different species usually cannot.

When different species have common features they can be grouped into sets. Grouping or classifying allows us to name them in a logical way. ❑

B2 Any animal can be put into one of two major groups:
- **invertebrate animals** – have no backbone
- **vertebrate animals** – have a backbone. ❑

Circle all vertebrates below using one colour; circle all invertebrates using a different colour. Complete the colour key.

vertebrate animals ☐ invertebrate animals ☐

B3 A biological key is used to identify and name an organism. Two common types of key are:
- branching key
- paired statement key.

Both use observable features to place animals into groups. ❑

Complete the branching key for invertebrates. Write each of the following major groups in the correct place.

arthropods coelenterates echinoderms flat worms molluscs segmented worms

invertebrates–animals with no backbone

- bodies not divided into segments
  - flat body e.g. fluke, tapeworm
  - hollow body, stinging cells e.g. jellyfish
  - hard covering with spines e.g. starfish, sea urchin
  - soft body usually with shell e.g. snail, octopus
- bodies divided into segments
  - long body with segments e.g. leech, earthworm
  - hard exoskeleton, jointed limbs e.g. crab, housefly

....

B4 The major vertebrate groups are:

mammals

birds

amphibians

reptiles

fish ❑

Complete the paired statement key with the name of each major vertebrate group. Add two examples of each group.

1	Warm-blooded animals	go to 2
	Cold-blooded animals	go to 3
2	Animals with live birth	Name ....
		Examples ....
	Egg-laying animals	Name ....
		Examples ....
3	Skin covered in scales	go to 4
	Moist skin	Name ....
		Examples ....
4	Breathe using lungs	Name ....
		Examples ....
	Breathe using gills	Name ....
		Examples ....

B5 Animals can be identified by looking at their observable features. ❑

Make a branching key or paired statement key to identify each of the following vertebrate animals using observable features.

alligator

horse

bat

mallard

buzzard

B6 Any plant can be put into one of two major groups: non-flowering plants and flowering plants. The branching key below describes the main types of non-flowering plants. ❑

Write the correct names from the list below in the boxes.

conifers ferns horsetails mosses liverworts

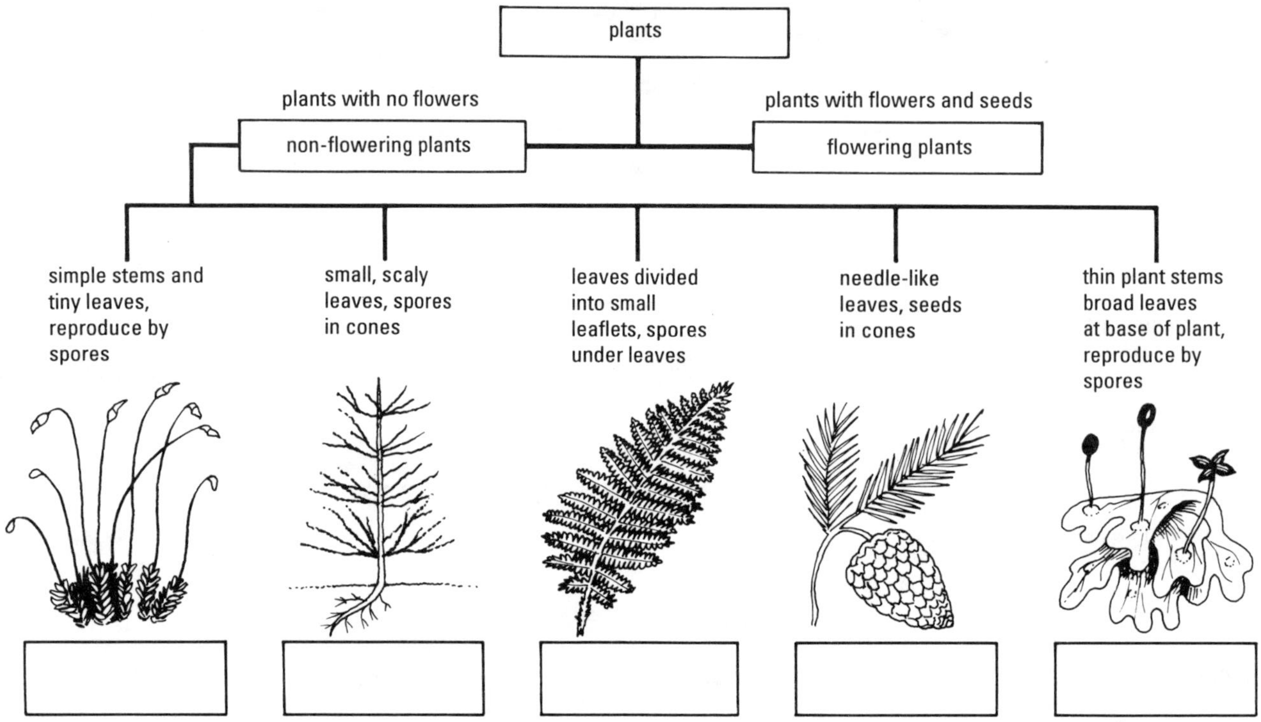

B7 Until recently botanists (plant scientists) classified fungi, such as yeast and mushrooms; and algae, such as seaweed, as plants. These are now considered as two separate kingdoms. ❑

B8 **Genetics** is the study of inherited features or characteristics. Genetic material is held in the form of genes in the nucleus of every cell. In school science we make genetics easier by looking at features that are controlled by only one gene, for example, tongue rolling in humans, coat colour in rabbits and flower colour. ❑

B9 When cells produced in the sex organs (sperm and egg in animals, pollen and egg in plants) join at **fertilisation**, genes from the male and female parents are brought together. In this way genetic information is **inherited** and passed from one generation to the next. ❑

B10 A **family tree** can indicate how a feature for example, tongue rolling in humans, is inherited. ❑

Complete the family tree to show how you expect tongue rolling to be inherited. Label the oldest and the youngest generation.

....

B11 Within a species, for example humans, there is **variation** (differences) between individuals. The variation may be caused by:

- genetics
- environmental factors
- a combination of genetics and environmental factors. ❑

For each feature below, write *genetic* or *environmental* next to each cause of variation.

	Cause of variation	
Weight of a newborn baby	both parents short	....
	mother smoked during pregnancy	....
	mother ate healthy diet while pregnant	....
Growth of pea seedlings	low light intensity	....
	acid soil	....
	parent plants tall	....

C1 All living things **compete** for resources to stay alive. Competition takes place between organisms of the same species and with other species. When resources are scarce not all the individuals in a population will survive.

Animals compete for:

- food
- water
- space
- mates.

Plants compete for:

- light
- water
- space. ❑

What scarce resource are the organisms competing for in the examples below?

plants on a woodland floor grow and flower in spring before the trees above them burst into leaf

.... for photosynthesis

gannets are seabirds that nest on very narrow ledges on cliffs

.... for reproduction

some desert cacti have very large root systems just under the surface of the sand

.... for support and photosynthesis

C2 Animals have **adaptations** that allow them to survive in their natural environment.

Terrestrial (land) animals

- waterproof surface prevents water loss
- able to breathe air
- supporting tissues to give shape and strength
- internal fertilisation for sperm to swim to egg. ❑

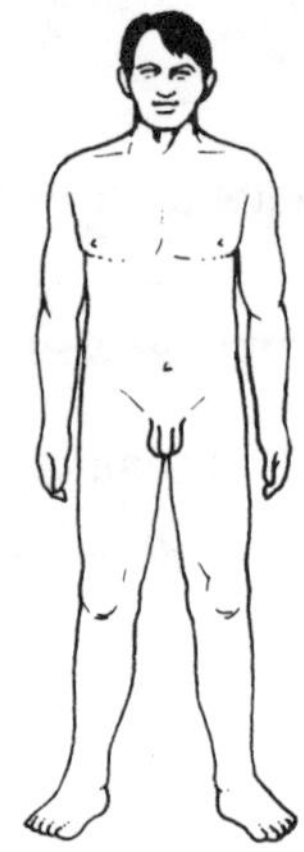

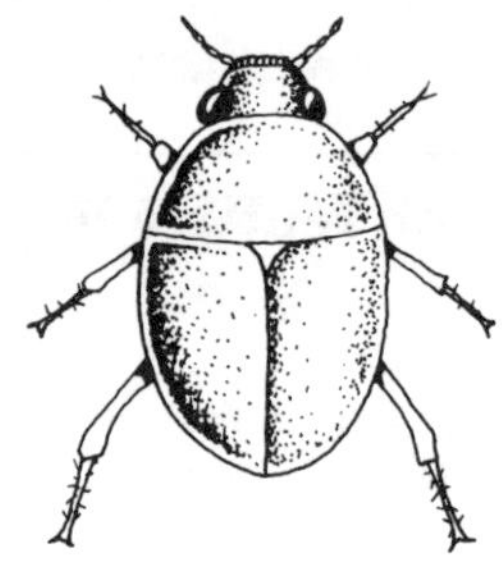

Freshwater animals – fish

Use the words below to complete the statements which describe the adaptations.

absorb external reduced streamlined water gain

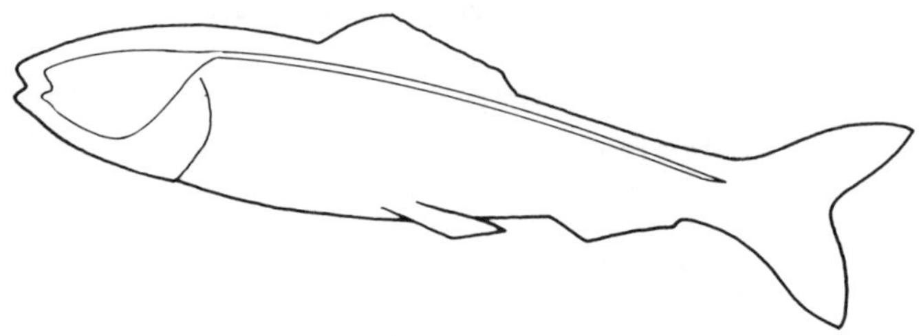

a) waterproof covering prevents ....

b) able to .... oxygen from water

c) .... fertilisation for reproduction

d) .... shape for rapid movement

e) .... skeleton for buoyancy.

C3 Plants are also adapted to survive in their natural habitats. For example, desert plants have adaptations to obtain and store as much water as possible and lose as little as possible. ❑

Complete the first three statements with the words *large* or *small*.

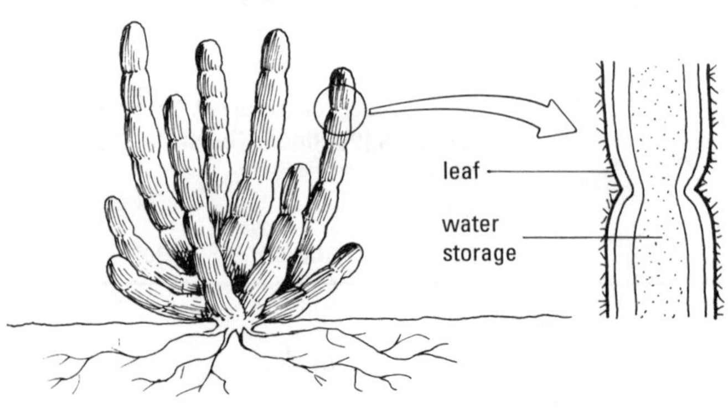

.... area of roots to absorb any available water

.... surface area of leaves to prevent water loss

.... amount of water-storing tissue

waxy covering on stem to reduce water loss

C4 Some human activity produces substances that pollute the air, water and soil. ❑

What type or types of pollution does each of these human activities cause? (Air, water or soil.)

Human activity	Type(s) of pollution	Effects of pollution
burning fuels	....	produces acid rain that damages plants and acidifies water
mining creates spoil tips	....	heavy metals in the tips poison plants and animals through the food chain
untreated sewage passes into sea	....	bacteria in sewage reduce oxygen concentration of water; nutrients encourage growth of poison-producing algae

Two more examples of human activities that cause pollution:

1 .... 2 ....

C5 The presence of certain organisms in a habitat can indicate the level of pollution. For example, the level of air pollution can be indicated by which lichens are growing in a habitat. The types of invertebrates living in a freshwater habitat give an indication of the level of pollution. ❑

D1 An **ecosystem** consists of a community of living organisms and its interactions with the physical features of its environment, such as weather, soil or water type. An ecosystem is kept in balance by the flow of energy through **food chains** and by cycling important biological materials such as carbon and nitrogen to keep them at a steady level. Anything that upsets the balance damages the ecosystem. ❑

D2 In any ecosystem there are many food chains. These indicate the flow of energy by linking each organism with what it eats. Different words are used to describe the plants and animals in a food chain, and all food chains follow the same basic pattern shown below.

Note: animals that eat both plant material and animal material are called **omnivores.** ❑

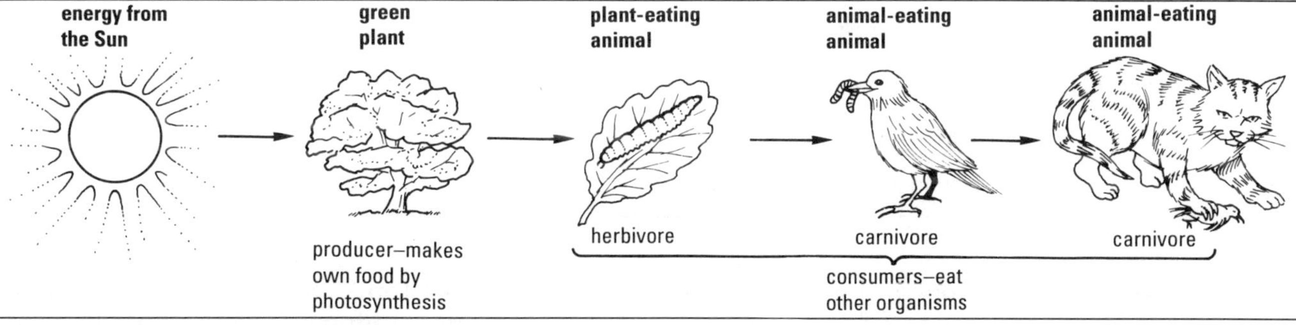

In each of the food chains below:

1 label the *producers* and *consumers*
2 circle the herbivore using one colour and the carnivores using another. Make a colour key.

colour key ☐ ☐

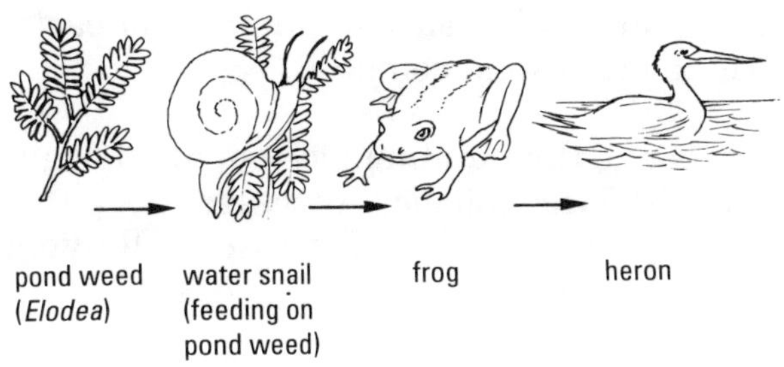

D3 Two more words are used to describe animals in a food chain: **predator** and **prey**. Predators are carnivores that eat other (live) animals – their prey. Sometimes a predator can be the prey of another, bigger predator. ❑

D4 A large change in the numbers of any organism in a food chain has a 'knock-on' effect on the other organisms in the chain.

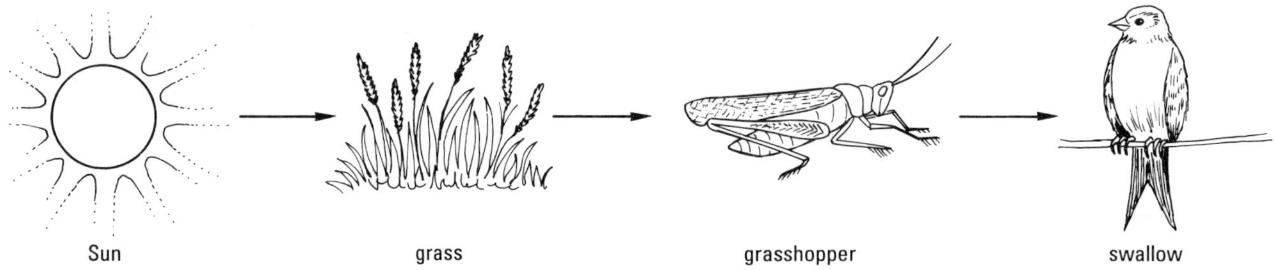

For example, in the food chain above, if many insects are killed by **insecticides** there is less food for the swallows and less damage to the green plants. ❑

Complete the sentence below the food chain with the words *increase, decrease, less* and *herbivores*. (You may use a word more than once.)

If disease killed many of the rabbits there would be ....food for the buzzards and their population would .... There would be .... damage to the plants so plant growth would .... providing more food for other ....

D5 **Decomposers** are an important group of consumers in an ecosystem. Their job is to bring about the decay of dead organisms and so to return important biological materials to the soil. They allow materials such as carbon and nitrogen to be cycled through the ecosystem.

There are three main groups of decomposers:

- bacteria
- fungi
- soil invertebrates. ❑

D6 Decay is fastest when the decomposing material is broken up or shredded and lying in a fairly tightly packed pile. The pile needs to be warm and moist. These conditions favour the growth of fungi and an increase in numbers of bacteria. Gardeners make compost heaps to decay garden waste into useful compost. ❑

D7 Carbon is the building block of all biological chemicals. It is cycled through the ecosystem as carbon dioxide. Two biological processes keep the level of carbon dioxide steady – **photosynthesis** in green plants and **respiration** in all living organisms.

Label *photosynthesis* and *respiration* in the diagrams below.

1 .... 2 ....

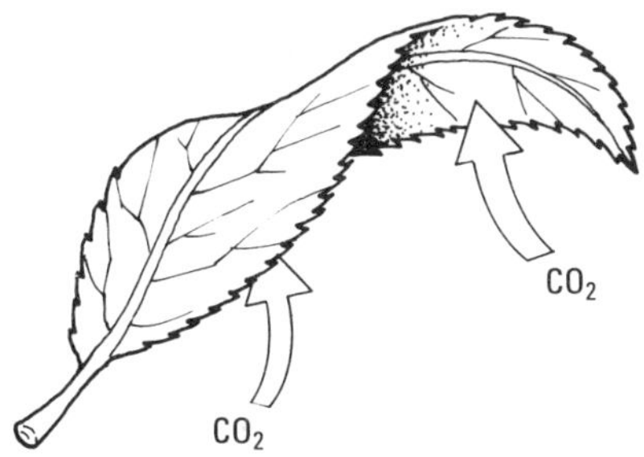

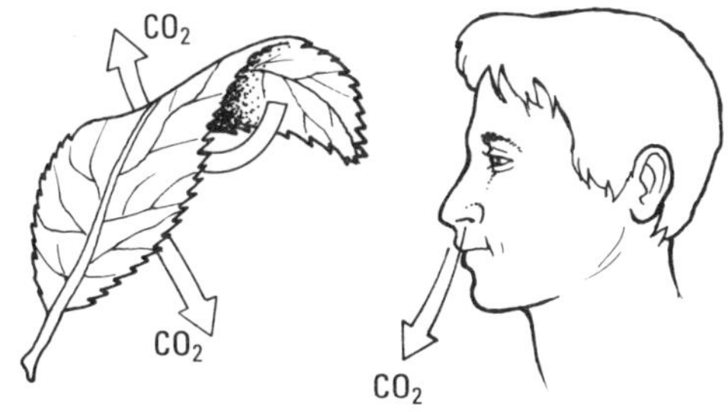

Human activities, such as burning fossil fuels, are upsetting the balance by adding carbon dioxide to the atmosphere. ❑

D8 The element nitrogen is present in many biological chemicals such as proteins and genetic material (DNA). Nitrogen from the atmosphere is passed to the soil where bacteria make it available to plants. From here it passes to animals through the food chain. The decomposition of dead plants and animals cycles nitrogen back through the soil. Some is returned to the air by the action of certain bacteria. ❑

Complete the flow chart with the words *bacteria, death and decay, food chain* and *lightning*. (You may use a word more than once.)

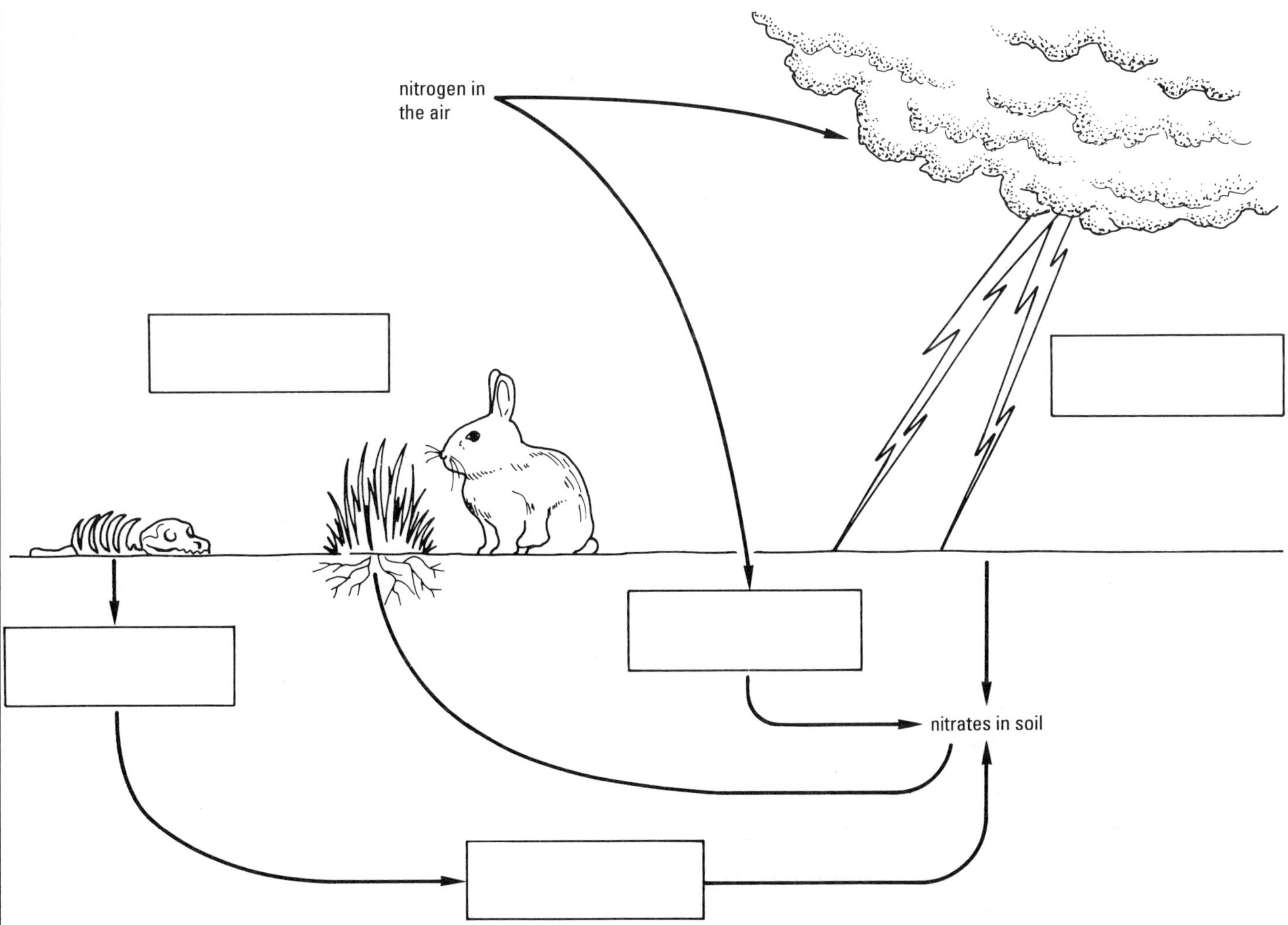

A1 The movement of water into and out of a cell across the cell membrane is called **osmosis**. Cell membranes are semi-permeable – only some substances can pass through them. Water moves by osmosis from an area where it is in relatively high concentration across a cell membrane to an area where the water concentration is lower. Water concentration depends on the amount of **solute** present. Pure water has the highest water concentration, seawater has a much lower water concentration because it contains dissolved salts.
For example:

The shape of red blood cells depends on osmosis.

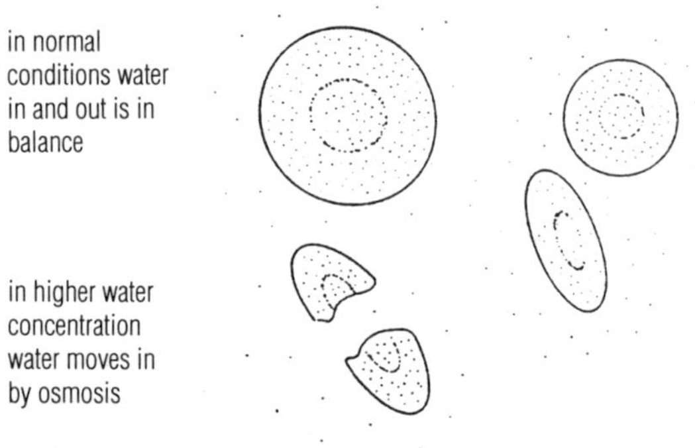

If the water concentration of the blood plasma becomes higher than the water concentration of the red blood cells, water enters the cells and they swell up. If this continues the cells eventually burst.

Water moves into root hair cells by osmosis.

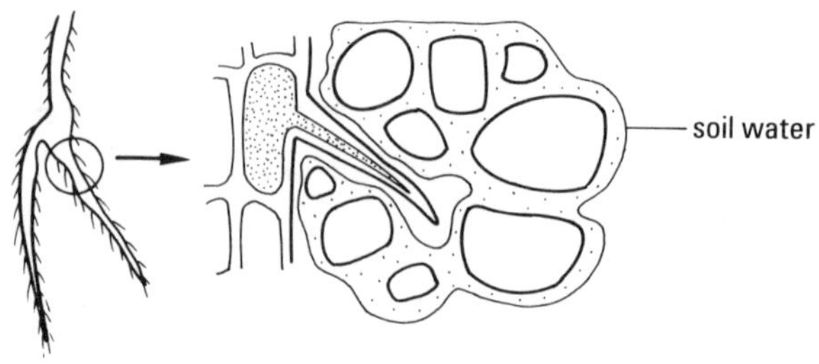

The water concentration in the cell sap of root hair cells is lower than the water concentration in the surrounding soil. Water therefore enters the root hair cells by osmosis. ❑

Complete each of the diagrams above with an arrow to show the direction of movement of water.

A2 In green plants **photosynthesis** is the process in which carbon dioxide and water are combined to produce glucose and oxygen. Light energy from the Sun is needed for this process. Light is trapped by the green pigment **chlorophyll** in the **chloroplasts** of leaf cells. Glucose can be stored as **starch** for later use, used directly as a source of energy for the plant or used to produce other materials for growth (for example, **cellulose** for cell walls). ❑

Complete the word equation for photosynthesis. Then write in the boxes what can happen to the glucose.

$$6CO_2 + 6H_2O \longrightarrow C_6H_{12}O_6 + 6O_2$$

.... + ... → glucose + oxygen

A3 The rate of photosynthesis is limited by the availability of the raw materials and by light intensity. Low light intensity, low carbon dioxide concentration and lack of water all reduce the rate of the process. ❑

A4 In plants, energy is released from glucose by the process of **respiration**. The word equation for respiration is the reverse of the equation for photosynthesis (but light and chlorophyll are *not* required). ❑

Write the word equation for respiration here.

A5 In green plants, the rate of photosynthesis is greater than the rate of respiration during the day. At night, only respiration takes place. Both processes require an exchange of gases between the cells and the atmosphere. This takes place through tiny holes called **stomata** in the stem and on the lower epidermis of leaves. (Some plants have stomata on upper and lower leaf surfaces.) ❑

Label the diagrams below using the terms *daytime gas exchange* and *night-time gas exchange.*

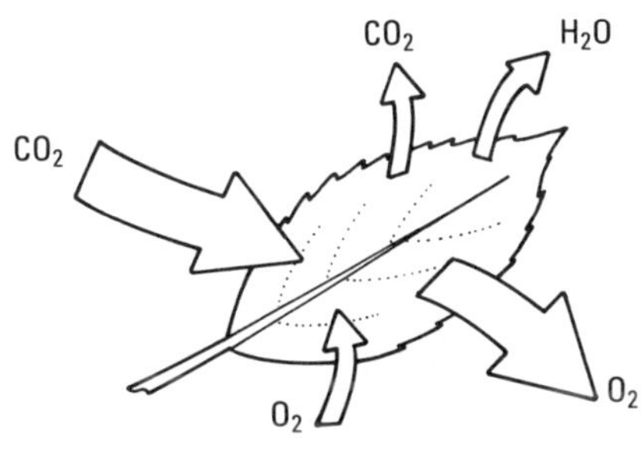

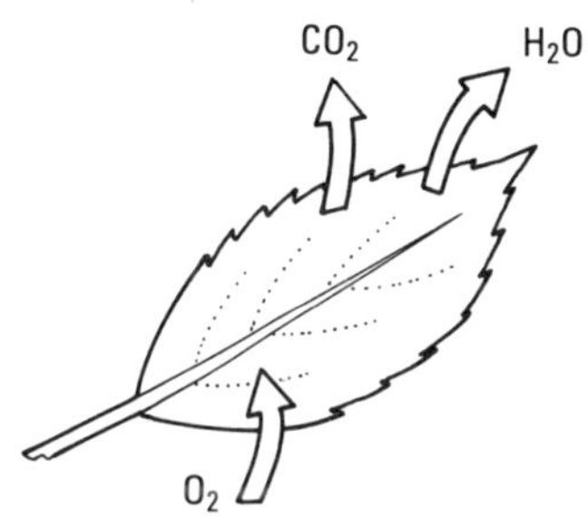

....

A6 Water vapour also escapes through the stomata. This is called **transpiration** and helps the plant in two ways:

- water evaporating from the leaf surface helps keep the plant cool
- the evaporation pulls a continuous stream of water from the roots through **xylem** vessels in the stem and leaves. This supplies all plant cells with water for support, chemical reactions in the cytoplasm and in the case of leaf cells, photosynthesis. ❑

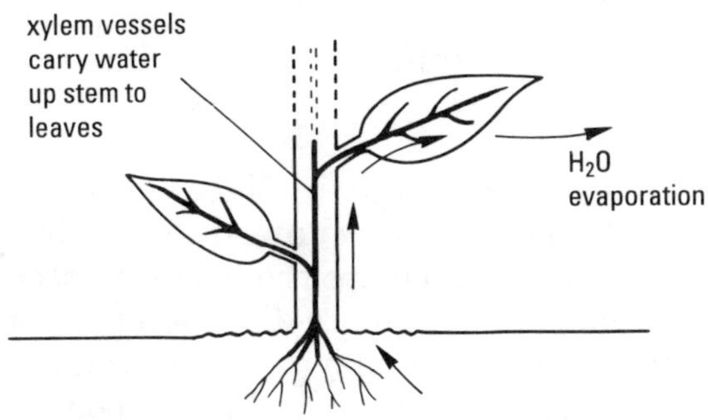

A7 Reproduction in flowering plants takes place in several stages. ❑

A8 Some plants **self-pollinate** (pollinate within the same flower) but most **cross-pollinate** (between different flowers of the same species). Cross-pollination is usually carried out by insects or by the wind. Pollen grains are adapted for wind pollination (light and large) or insect pollination (small and spiky). ❑

A9 Seeds are adapted for distribution by:

- wind – with a 'parachute' or 'wings'
- carriage on an animal – spiky
- being eaten – surrounded by a fleshy fruit.

Some seeds are distributed by exploding out of a drying fruit. ❑

Link the stages with arrows to show the direction of the cycle.

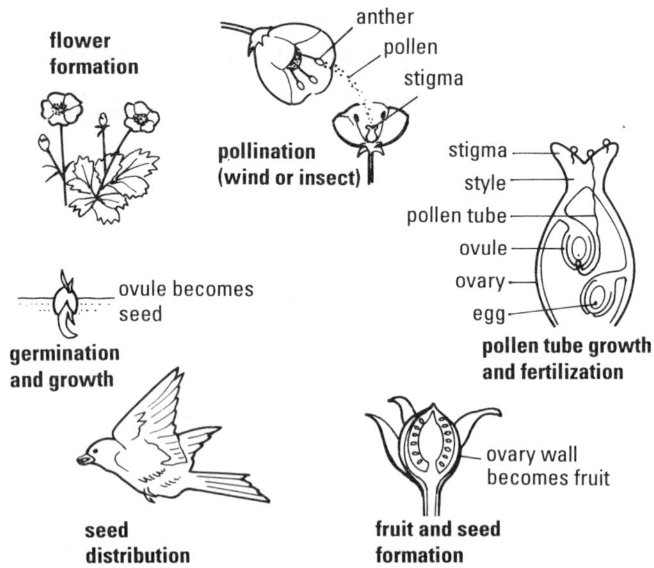

Use different colours to circle seeds distributed by *wind, carriage on an animal* or *being eaten by an animal.* Add a colour key.

colour key: ______ ______

A10 All animals must eat to stay alive. There are three stages in the nutrition of animals:

- feeding or obtaining food
- digestion
- using the food and getting rid of waste.

Vertebrate animals take food into their mouths and break it up mechanically using teeth or beaks. ❑

A11 In digestion, large, insoluble molecules are broken down chemically by the action of a group of proteins called **enzymes** into smaller, soluble molecules. In humans, some digestion takes place in the mouth before the food is passed down the gullet or oesophagus by **peristalsis** to the stomach. Here, more digestion takes place and the food is churned up. It then passes to the small intestine. Here enzymes produced in the pancreas complete the process of chemical digestion. Soluble food is absorbed into blood capillaries for transport first to the liver, then to all parts of the body. Undigested food moves through the large intestine where excess water is absorbed into the blood supply. The remaining waste is egested at the anus. ❑

Complete the flow chart of digestion by writing the words below in the correct boxes and joining them with arrows. Draw lines from the flow chart to label the parts of the human digestive system.

anus   gullet (oesophagus)   large intestine   mouth   pancreas   small intestine   stomach

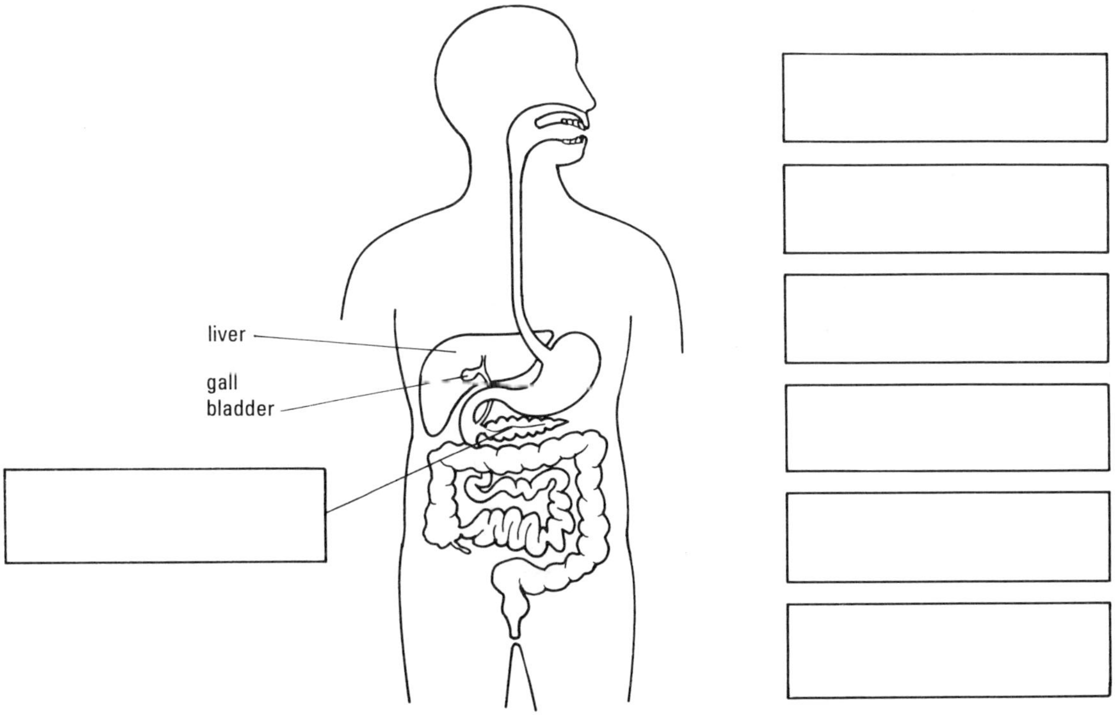

A12 Each food type is broken down by specific enzymes that work best in particular conditions. All enzyme-controlled reactions follow the same pattern:

substrate + enzyme → product + enzyme ❑

Use a different colour to highlight or circle each substrate and its *final* products of digestion.

Substrate	Where broken down	Enzymes involved	Product	Conditions required
starch	mouth	amylase	maltose	slightly alkaline
	small intestine	amylase	glucose	slightly alkaline
protein	stomach	pepsin	polypeptides	acidic
	small intestine	proteases	amino acids	slightly alkaline
fat	small intestine	lipases	fatty acids and glycerol	slightly alkaline

A13 Hydrochloric acid makes the pH of the stomach acidic. Bile salts produced in the liver and stored in the gall bladder are passed to the small intestine where they create alkaline conditions. ❑

A14 Absorption takes place through the lining of the small intestine. **Villi** increase the surface area of the lining. Only glucose, amino acids, glycerol, water and mineral salts pass into blood capillaries. Fatty acid molecules are too large and are absorbed into **lymph vessels**. ❑

Label the blood capillaries and the lymph vessel.

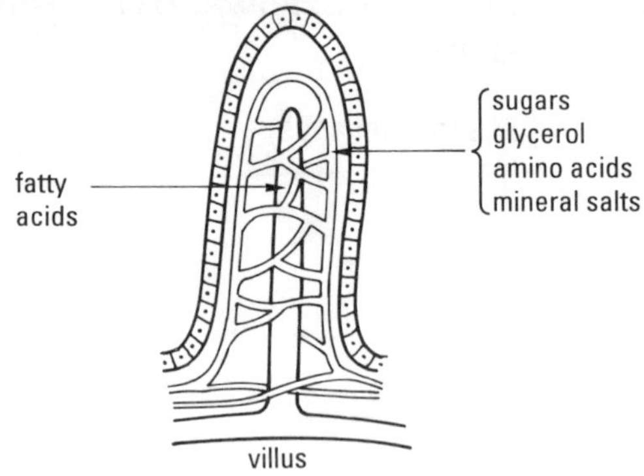

A15 Digested food is transported to the liver where excess **amino acids** are broken down. A product of these reactions is **urea**. This poison is removed from the blood by the kidneys, passed through the ureters to the bladder for storage, and then excreted.

Kidney nephrons work in two stages. First, liquid containing urea and other small molecules is forced out of a group of narrow blood capillaries called a **glomerulus** into the capsule of the kidney nephron. This liquid – the glomerular filtrate – contains substances the body cannot afford to lose, in addition to urea. In the second stage, the valuable substances such as water and mineral salts are reabsorbed into blood capillaries. In this way the kidneys ensure that the composition of the blood stays fairly constant. ❑

Describe what happens at stages 1 and 2 in the kidney nephron.

Stage 1

Stage 2

Label the kidneys, ureter and bladder in the diagram below.

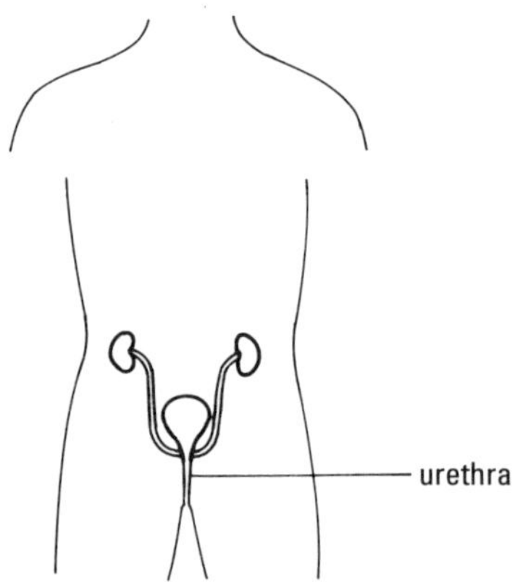

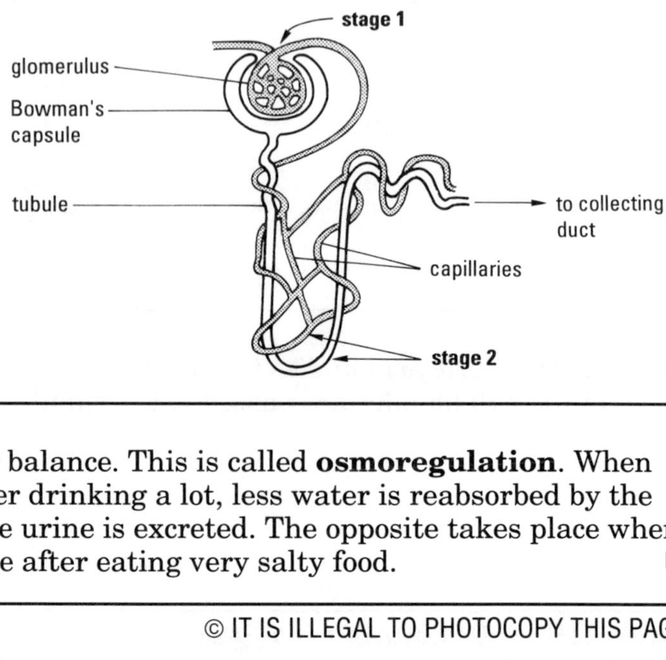

A16 In vertebrate animals the kidneys control water balance. This is called **osmoregulation**. When blood water concentration rises, for example after drinking a lot, less water is reabsorbed by the kidney nephrons and so a larger volume of dilute urine is excreted. The opposite takes place when blood water concentration decreases, for example after eating very salty food. ❑

Describe what happens in the kidneys when blood water concentration decreases. What type of urine is produced?

A17 Digested food is transported to every cell of the body where it can be used in one of several ways, including:
- as a source of energy
- for growth and repair. ❑

A18 Energy is released from food in the process of cellular respiration. In most organisms this involves oxygen and food combining to produce carbon dioxide, water and energy, which is stored in chemical form. ❑

Complete the word equation for respiration.

glucose + ... → .... + water + energy

$C_6H_{12}O_6 + 6O_2 \rightarrow 6CO_2 + 6H_2O +$ energy

A19 The process of respiration uses oxygen and produces carbon dioxide. These gases are exchanged in the lungs, which is why inhaled (breathed-in) air is different from exhaled air. Air travels through the nose, down the **trachea** and **bronchi** to the **bronchioles** of the lungs. Each bronchiole ends in an air sac made of many thin-walled **alveoli**. Here, gas exchange takes place; oxygen diffuses from the alveoli into blood capillaries, and carbon dioxide and water vapour **diffuse** in the opposite direction. ❑

Write *inhaled* and *exhaled* in the correct places in the table. Then label the main parts of the respiratory system.

Gas	....	....
nitrogen	79.00 %	79.00 %
oxygen	20.00 %	16.00 %
carbon dioxide	0.04 %	4.00 %
water vapour	low	high

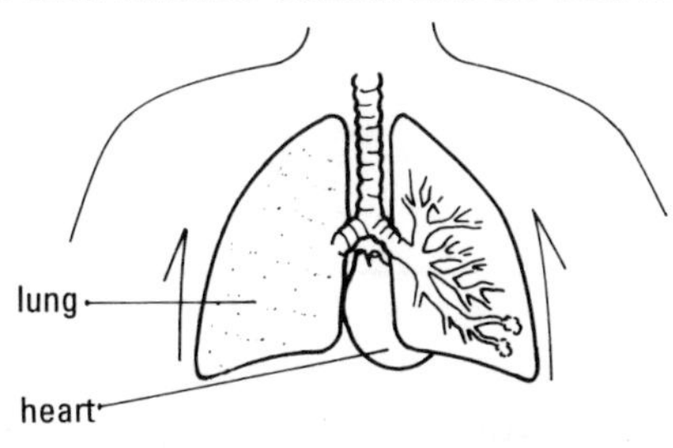

A20 The structure of the lungs aids gas exchange:
- the alveoli provide a very large surface area for gas exchange
- the alveoli have very thin walls to speed up gas exchange
- the surfaces of the alveoli are moist which aids the diffusion of gases
- there is a rich blood supply for gases to diffuse into and out of. ❑

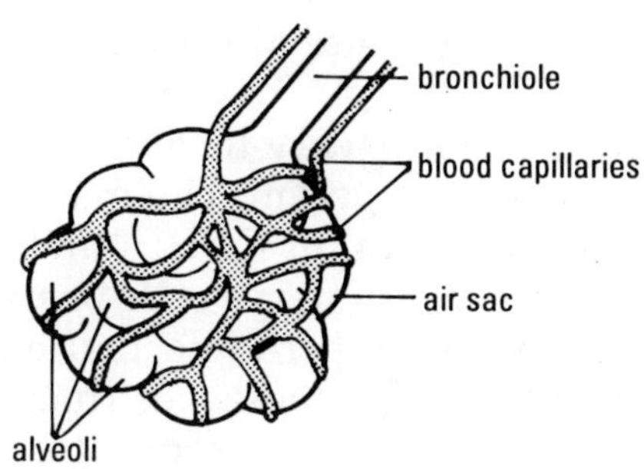

A21 The lungs inflate when we inhale and deflate when we exhale because of the action of two sets of muscles – the rib muscles (**intercostals**) and **diaphragm**. ❑

Write *inhaling* and *exhaling* above the correct descriptions. Label the *intercostal muscles* and the *diaphragm* on the diagram.

....	....
The intercostal muscles and the diaphragm relax. The rib-cage falls. The diaphragm pushes up reducing the volume of the thorax. Pressure increases and air passes out of the lungs.	Both muscle sets contract. The rib-cage rises. The diaphragm pulls down increasing the volume of the thorax. Pressure in the lungs decreases and air is drawn into the lungs.

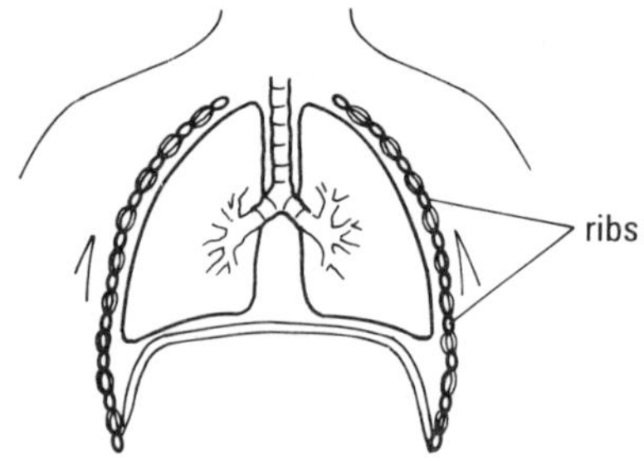

A22 The reproductive system is similar in most vertebrates. In females, eggs are produced in the **ovaries** and released at **ovulation**. One or more eggs pass down an **oviduct** (**Fallopian tube**) to the **womb** (**uterus**). Sperm from the male are passed into the female's body through the **vagina**, which is the passage leading from the uterus to the outside.

Adult males produce sperm cells continuously in the **testes**. In mammals these are held in a sac called the **scrotum**. During sexual intercourse sperm pass from the testes along a sperm tube to the **urethra** in the penis. When the **penis** is placed in the **vagina**, sperm are released and swim from the vagina, through the uterus to the Fallopian tubes. If an egg is present, a single sperm cell may enter it. The male and female nuclei fuse. This is called **fertilisation**. The fertilised egg becomes embedded in the uterus where it grows into a **fetus**. ❑

Label the main parts of the male and female reproductive systems. On the diagram of the female system label the location of *release of sperm*, *fertilisation*, *development of the fetus*, *ovulation*.

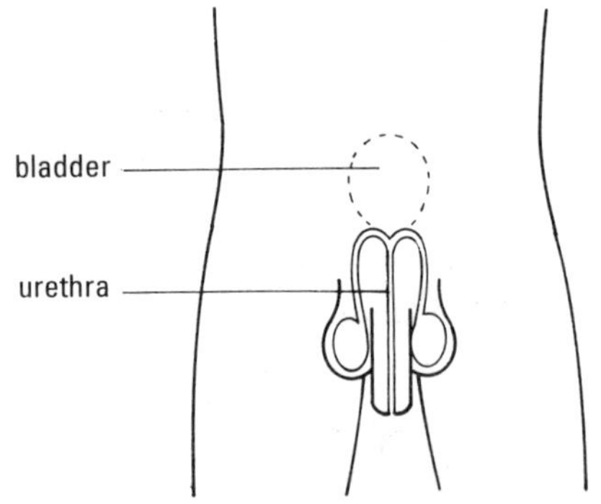

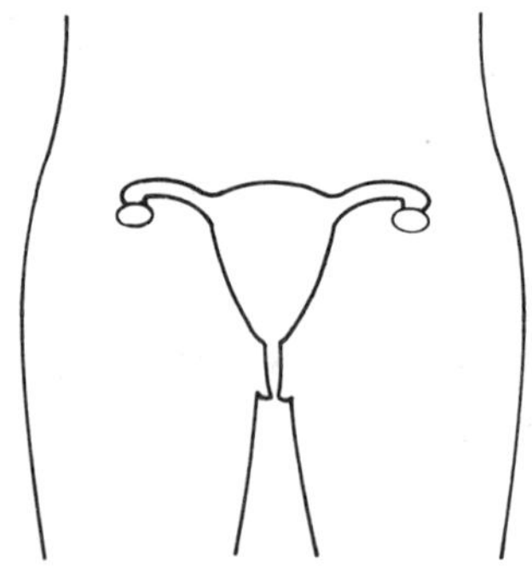

A23 Growth takes place in three stages. First, the number of cells increases by cell division or **mitosis**. Then the cells enlarge, and finally the cells change or **differentiate** to take on particular functions. In humans, growth in the uterus depends on the developing baby receiving food and oxygen from the mother through the **umbilical cord** and across the **placenta**. Waste materials pass in the opposite direction. This maintains the internal environment of the embryo. ❑

A24 Animals are sensitive to, and respond to, changes in their surroundings. Sensitivity is controlled by the nervous system. The main parts are the brain and spinal cord – called the **central nervous system** (or **CNS**) – and the nerves joining these structures to the rest of the body. There are three types of nerve cells or **neurones**. Sensory neurones are attached to the sense organs (receptors) and return information from them to the brain. Motor neurones allow the body to respond by taking messages from the brain back to the effector muscles. These two types of neurones are linked by connector neurones in the brain or spinal cord.

Most behaviours follow a similar pattern. For example, when you walk into a brightly lit place:

pattern:	stimulus	→	receptor	→	co-ordinator	→	effector	→	response	
example:	light in eye		retina		brain		iris muscles		pupil contracts	❑

Copying the pattern above, think of another behaviour, for example, moving your leg away from the warmth of a fire.

A25 Movement in vertebrate animals depends on muscles, bones (the skeleton) and nerves. ❑

Draw lines to match each tissue to its correct description.

Tissue	
bones	act in opposing or antagonistic pairs – when one contracts the other relaxes
muscles	bring nerve impulses from the central nervous system to stimulate muscle contraction
nerves	muscles are attached to these. Contraction of muscles results in movement at a joint

A26 Bones are joined together by elastic **ligaments**. Muscles are attached to bones by inelastic **tendons**. ❑

A27 There are several different types of **joint**, each allowing a different amount of movement. The structure of all joints allows smooth movement or articulation of the bones. ❑

Label the *ligaments* and *tendons*.

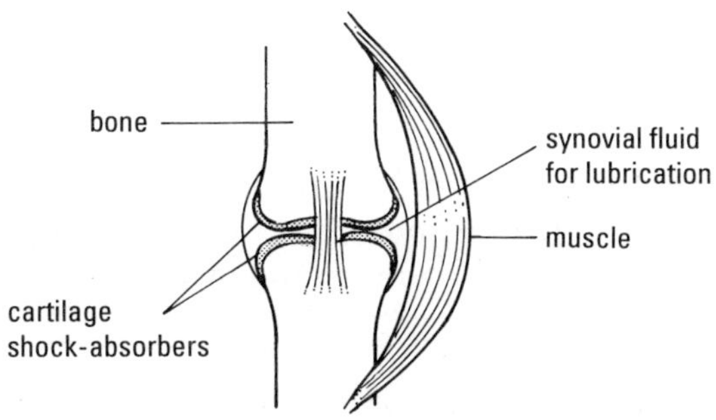

Label the *contracting muscle* and the *relaxing muscle*.

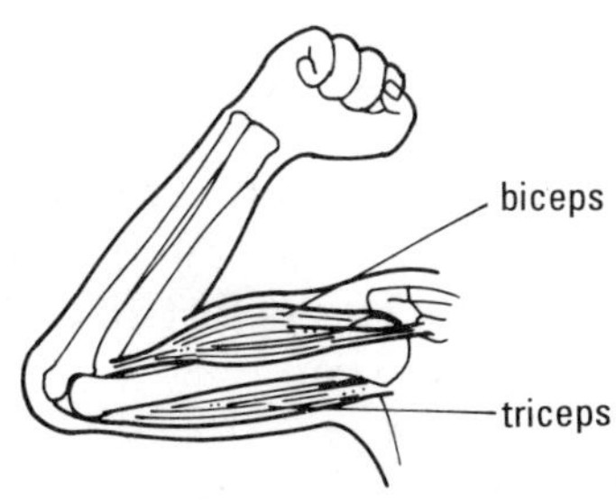

A28 Humans have several defences against infection:
- skin which is a barrier to bacteria and viruses
- blood clotting which seals a wound
- white blood cells which destroy bacteria
- antibodies made by white cells which help to destroy bacteria and viruses. ❑

B1 Genetic information is held on structures called **chromosomes** in the nucleus of the cell. Human body cells have 46 chromosomes, cabbage cells have 18. Chromosomes are involved in the process of cell division. During division, they are visible through a microscope. When cells are not dividing the chromosomes become very long and thin and cannot be seen easily. ❑

B2 There are two types of cell division:
- **mitosis**, which increases the number of cells for growth and tissue repair
- **meiosis**, which produces sex cells for reproduction. ❑

Complete the first row of the table below comparing mitosis and meiosis.

	Mitosis	Meiosis
Function		
Location	growing points of plants and animals	sex organs of plants and animals
Product	2 cells with identical genetic information	4 sex cells which may have different genetic information
Chromosome number	full number of chromosomes	half the full number of chromosomes

B3 Just before mitosis starts, the chromosomes produce a copy of themselves. They then line up across the middle of the cell. The chromosome copies separate, each set going to a new cell (daughter cell). Each daughter cell inherits identical genetic information. Division is complete after the cytoplasm divides and, in plants, when a new cell wall has formed. ❑

Draw arrows between the dividing cells to show the correct sequence. Number the sequence 1 to 5.

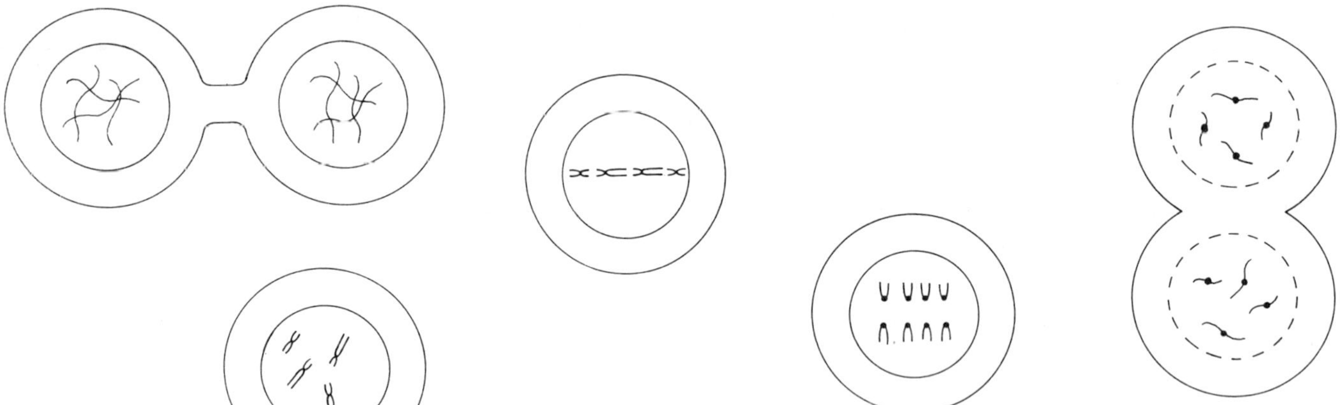

B4 In humans, sex is determined by two sex chromosomes. Females have two X chromosomes; males have one X and one Y chromosome. Egg cells always carry one X chromosome, so the sex of a baby depends on whether the egg is fertilised by a sperm cell carrying an X chromosome or by a sperm cell carrying a Y chromosome. ❑

B5 In organisms produced as the result of sexual reproduction, one half of the chromosomes in each cell is inherited from the female parent, and the other half from the male parent. So 23 chromosomes are inherited from each parent in humans, and 9 from each parent in cabbages. ❑

B6 There are two cycles of division in meiosis. In the first division the chromosomes inherited from the female parent pair up with those inherited from the male parent. The chromosome pairs then separate. This results in two cells each with half the original number of chromosomes. The second division of meiosis is just like mitosis – the chromosomes divide, producing four new sex cells each with half the original number of chromosomes. Fertilisation, when sperm and egg fuse, results in a cell with the full chromosome number. ❑

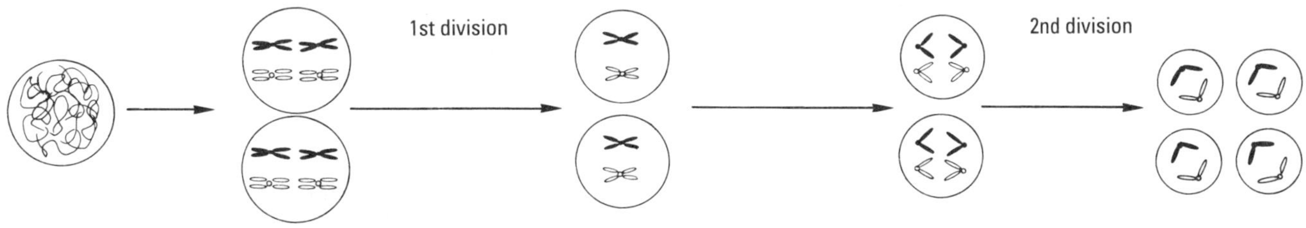

B7 The study of genetics allows us to predict the pattern of inheritance of a characteristic, for example tongue rolling in humans. There are four basic rules:

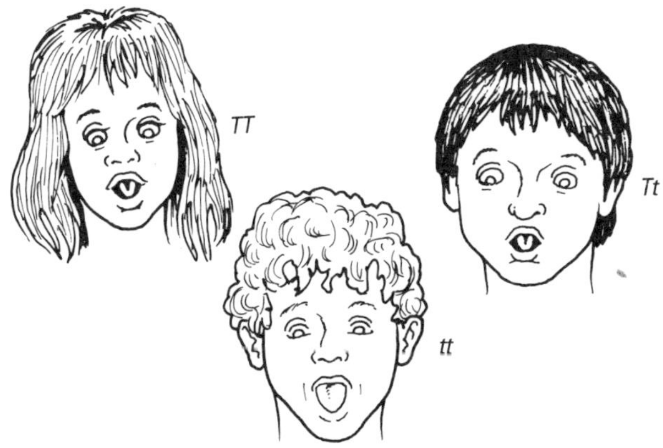

1 We inherit one gene from each parent for this characteristic. A pair of genes for the same characteristic are called **alleles**.

2 All body cells carry two alleles for tongue rolling, but sex cells (as a result of meiosis) carry only one allele for tongue rolling.

3 There can be two forms of an allele – a **dominant** allele or a **recessive** allele. Alleles are normally shown as letters – a capital letter for dominant (*T* for tongue rolling) and a small letter for recessive (*t* for non-tongue rolling).

4 Any individual can have one of three combinations of alleles:

- 2 dominant alleles (*TT*) – a tongue roller
- 1 dominant and 1 recessive allele (*Tt*) – a tongue roller
- 2 recessive alleles (*tt*) – a non-tongue roller. ❑

B8 The results of a cross (or mating) can be shown using letters to describe the alleles, for example, in these crosses between fruit flies (*Drosophila*): ❑

1 A fly with straight wings **phenotype** (physical appearance) and *SS* **genotype** (2 dominant alleles) is crossed with a fly with curly wings phenotype (*ss* genotype).

	male parent	×	**female parent**
genotype of parents	*SS*		*ss*
genotype of sex cells	all *S*		all *s*
genotype of offspring		all *Ss*	
phenotype of offspring		all with straight wings	

2	**male parent**	×	**female parent**
genotype of parents	*Ss*		*Ss*
genotype of sex cells	*S* or *s*		*S* or *s*
genotype of offspring		*SS* *Ss* *Ss* *ss*	
phenotypic ratio		3 straight wings : 1 curly wings	
genotypic ratio	1	2	1
	homozygous dominant :	heterozygous :	homozygous recessive

Show the results of the cross below. Give both the phenotypic and genotypic ratios in the offspring.

male *Ss* × *ss* female

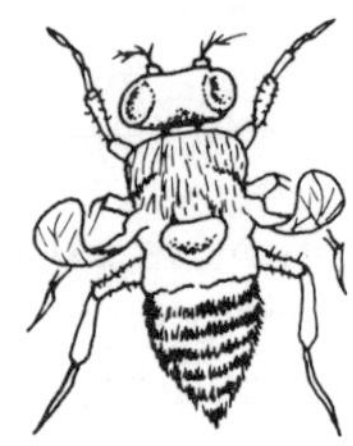

curly winged fruit fly (*ss*)

B9 Genetics has been used in the **selective breeding** of varieties of plants and animals that have desirable characteristics. For example, wild forms of wheat have been crossed with cultivated wheat to produce new varieties which give a bigger yield and have better resistance to disease. ❑

Describe two other examples of selective breeding.

C1 A population grows in size when the birth rate is greater than the death rate. Population decline can be caused by:

- environmental resources such as oxygen and food becoming limited
- disease
- the activity of predators.

For example, the number of bacteria in a sealed culture vessel will increase rapidly at first when lots of food and oxygen are available. When these resources become more limited the numbers increase more slowly. Finally, the numbers fall as the resources are used up and as waste within the culture builds up. ❑

Draw a graph showing the change in the number of bacteria in a sealed culture vessel against time.

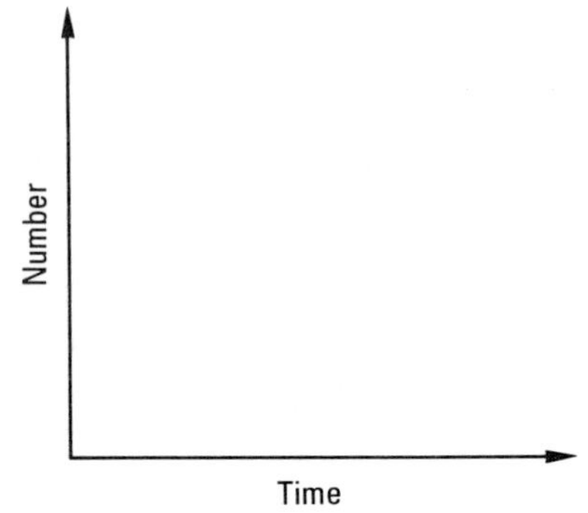

C2 Human activity can damage the environment. The scale of the damage depends on:
- the size of the population
- the type of activity. ❑

C3 Environmental damage can be caused by the build-up of human waste, by industrial processes and by over-exploitation as a result of economic factors such as the demand for food and fossil fuels. ❑

Draw lines to match each human activity with two consequences.

Human activity	Consequences
obtaining and burning fossil fuels	over-use of fertilisers causing water pollution
producing food	formation of spoil tips causing land pollution
	release of greenhouse gases and creation of acid rain
	destruction of habitats for farmland

D1 Energy flow in a food chain can be estimated in two ways:
- by counting the number of organisms at each point in the chain
- by measuring the mass of organisms (the biomass) at each point in the chain.

These measurements can be shown in diagrams called **pyramids of number** and **biomass**. For example, look at the following food chain:

Sun → grass seeds → mouse → owl

The number of organisms at each point gets smaller.

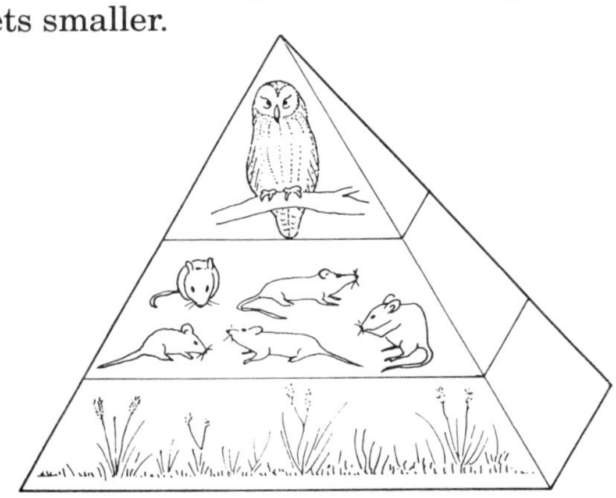

The total biomass of organisms gets smaller (but individuals may get bigger). ❑

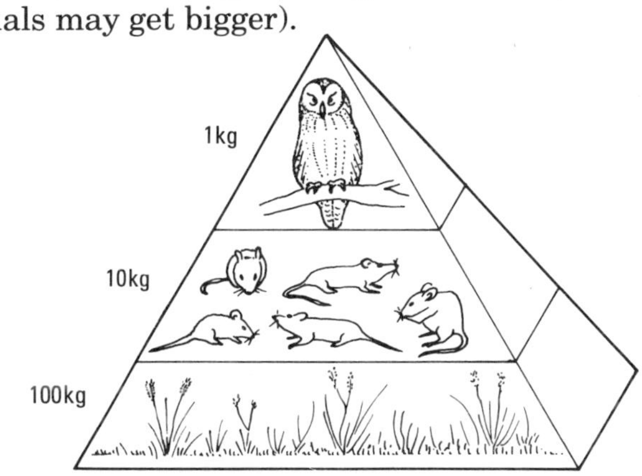

D2 Certain microbes can decompose biological material. Microbes are used to help purify water in sewage works. One group of microbes digests solid material in the settle tanks and a second group digests any remaining biological (organic) material as water passes through the filter beds. ❑

Label the *settle tank* and *filter bed* in the diagram.

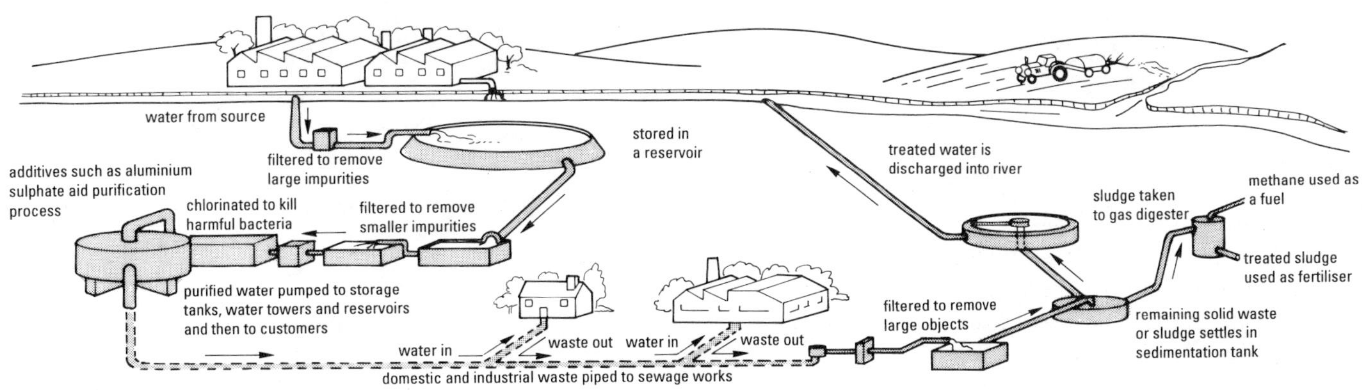

D3 In the nitrogen cycle, there are two groups of bacteria that help make nitrogen in the soil available to plants in the form of soluble nitrates:

- **nitrogen-fixing bacteria** in the soil change atmospheric nitrogen directly into nitrates. The roots of some plants (for example, peas, beans and lupins) contain nitrogen-fixing bacteria
- microbes produce nitrogen-containing ammonia from the decomposition of dead plant and animal material. Ammonia is changed to nitrites then nitrates by **nitrifying bacteria.**

The soil may also contain **de-nitrifying** bacteria that deplete the soil of nitrates and return nitrogen to the air.

Label the *nitrogen-fixing bacteria, nitrifying bacteria* and *de-nitrifying bacteria* in the diagram below.

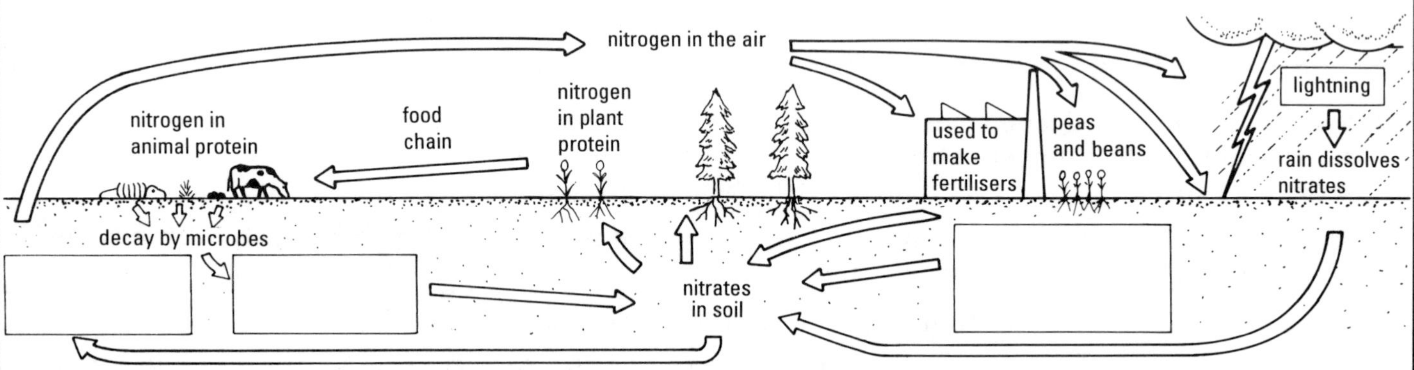

A1 Co-ordination and control in mammals depends on two systems:
- the nervous system which uses electrical impulses for rapid co-ordination and control of movement
- the **endocrine system** which uses chemicals called **hormones** to co-ordinate and control long-term changes in the body such as growth and sexual development. ❑

A2 The brain and spinal cord (CNS) is the co-ordinating centre of the nervous system. ❑

Label the three main parts of the brain.

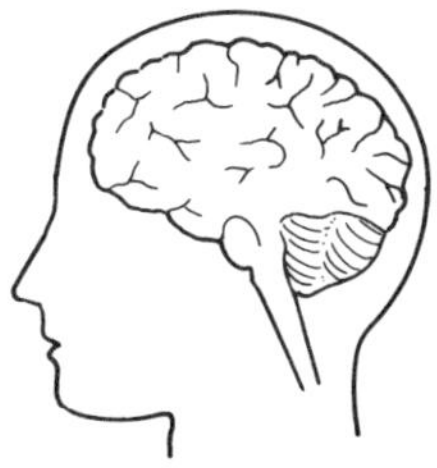

1 **medulla oblongata** – controls involuntary actions, for example, heart rate, breathing, blinking

2 **cerebellum** – co-ordination of movement and balance

3 **cerebrum or cerebral hemispheres** – control movement and sensations; responsible for memory, thought, feelings

A3 Each human endocrine gland produces different hormones, each with their own function. Hormones are produced in tiny amounts and travel in the bloodstream to specific target organs where they bring about a particular response. ❑

Label the location of each endocrine gland.

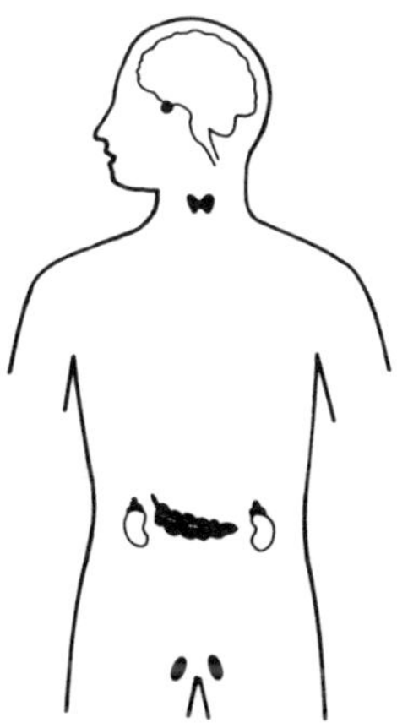

Gland	Hormone	Function
1 **sex organs**	sex hormones	control sexual development
2 **pancreas**	insulin	controls blood sugar level
3 **thyroid**	thyroxine	controls metabolic rate
4 **adrenal**	adrenaline	prepares body for response/ action
5 **pituitary**	growth hormone	controls growth and development

A4 **Adrenaline** can bring about a rapid response to danger. The nervous system co-operates by co-ordinating movement. ❑

Explain how the action of adrenaline prepares the body for action.

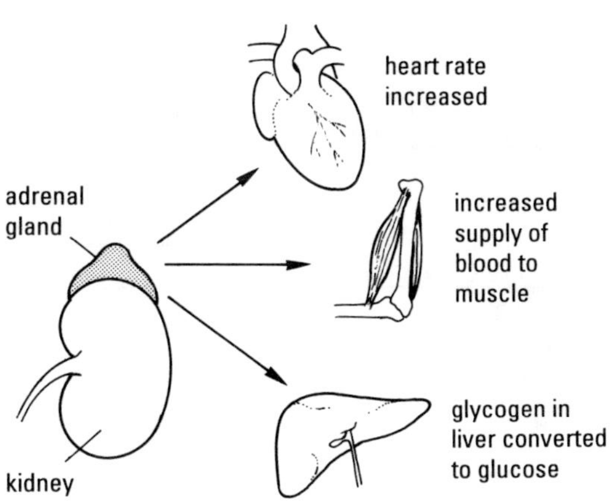

A5 Few organisms can tolerate variation in their internal environment. For example, humans must maintain a constant:

- water balance
- body temperature
- blood pH
- blood sugar level.

Keeping conditions constant is called **homeostasis**. ❑

A6 Homeostasis depends on feedback loops to maintain a steady state. They all follow a similar pattern. ❑

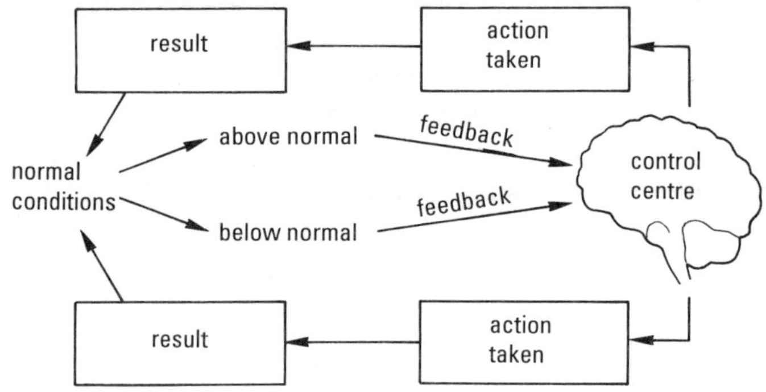

A7 Water balance or **osmoregulation** is controlled by the action of a hormone (produced by the pituitary gland) on the kidney. When blood water concentration falls, more hormone is produced. This causes additional water to be reabsorbed from the kidney nephrons. ❑

Complete the feedback diagram for control of water balance.

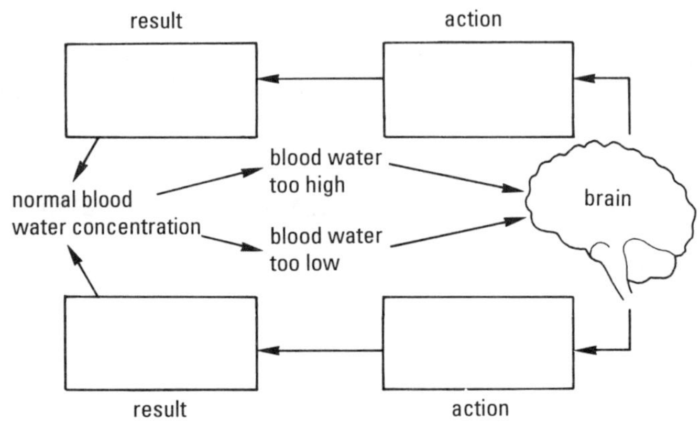

A8 Blood sugar level is controlled by the hormone **insulin**. When blood glucose rises above normal more insulin is produced. This acts on the liver, where excess glucose is removed from the blood and converted to glycogen. If blood glucose falls below normal, insulin production falls and glycogen in the liver is changed back to glucose. ❑

Complete the feedback diagram for control of blood glucose level.

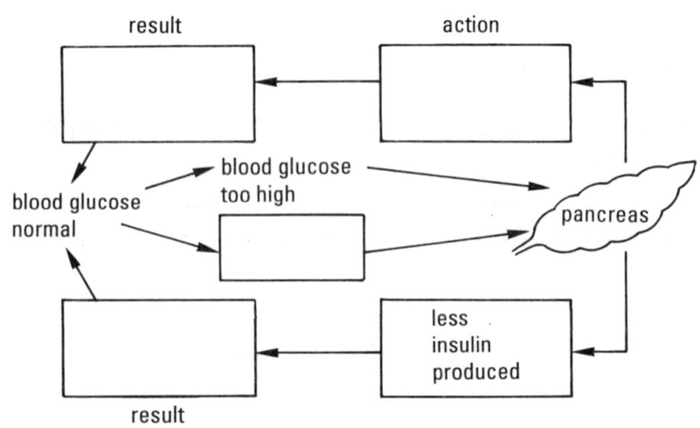

A9 The maintenance of body temperature in mammals depends on **metabolism** (the body's chemistry) to generate heat. Most heat is generated from respiration in the muscles and liver. Special cells in the brain detect changes in blood temperature and the brain responds to these changes in a number of ways. The responses to an increase in blood temperature are the opposite to the responses to a decrease in blood temperature.

When it is too cold:

- thyroid is stimulated to increase metabolic rate of cells
- shivering begins
- blood is diverted away from skin surface
- body hairs are raised by contraction of hair muscles
- sweating stops. ❑

What happens when it is too hot?

A10 Blood pH depends on the amount of dissolved CO_2 from respiration. CO_2 is an acidic gas. The brain detects any alteration in CO_2 concentration and responds by stimulating the intercostal muscles and diaphragm to alter the breathing rate. ❑

> **Complete the sentences with the words *increases* and *decreases*.**
>
> When blood pH falls the breathing rate ....
>
> When blood pH rises the breathing rate ....

B1 Genetic variation can arise in a number of ways:

- sexual reproduction, which produces offspring with a combination of genes from both parents
- meiosis, which shuffles genes into new combinations, resulting in variation between sex cells
- mutations, which alter the genetic material. ❑

B2 In meiosis, variation results from the way in which the paired chromosomes line up at the first division. ❑

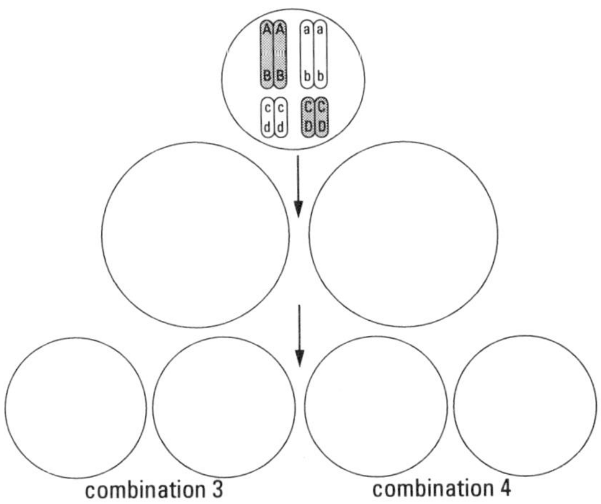

> **Complete the diagram by showing two more possible chromosome combinations.**

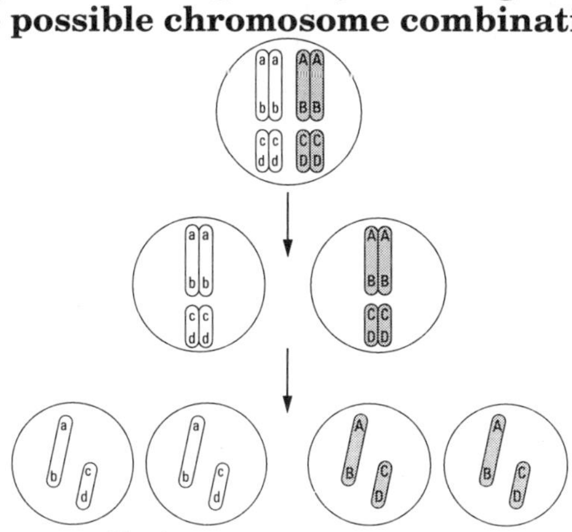

B3 Mutations can be caused by radiation or certain chemicals, and also occur naturally. Mutations are random and are only passed on to the next generation if they affect the sex cells. Mutations can affect a whole chromosome or a small part of a single gene. For example, the condition Down's syndrome in humans is caused by a mutation which produces one extra chromosome. Sickle-cell anaemia, however, results from a small mutation within the gene for haemoglobin – the red pigment responsible for carrying oxygen in red blood cells. This can reduce the efficiency of oxygen transport. Sickle-cell anaemia is an example of an inherited disease. ❑

B4 Variation between individuals of the same species is the starting point of **evolution**. In any population some individuals are better adapted to their environment than others. **Natural selection** ensures that the fittest survive and reproduce. In this way the species survives even if environmental conditions change. The peppered moth is a good example. Natural selection works in favour of moths that are well camouflaged against the bark of trees. Before the industrial revolution peppered moths with a speckled colouring had the best chance of avoiding predators because they couldn't be seen on lichen-covered tree trunks. Then tree trunks in industrial areas became blackened by factory smoke. In these areas, darker coloured moths were, and still are, selected for. ❑

Use the words below to complete the flow chart.

against darker for

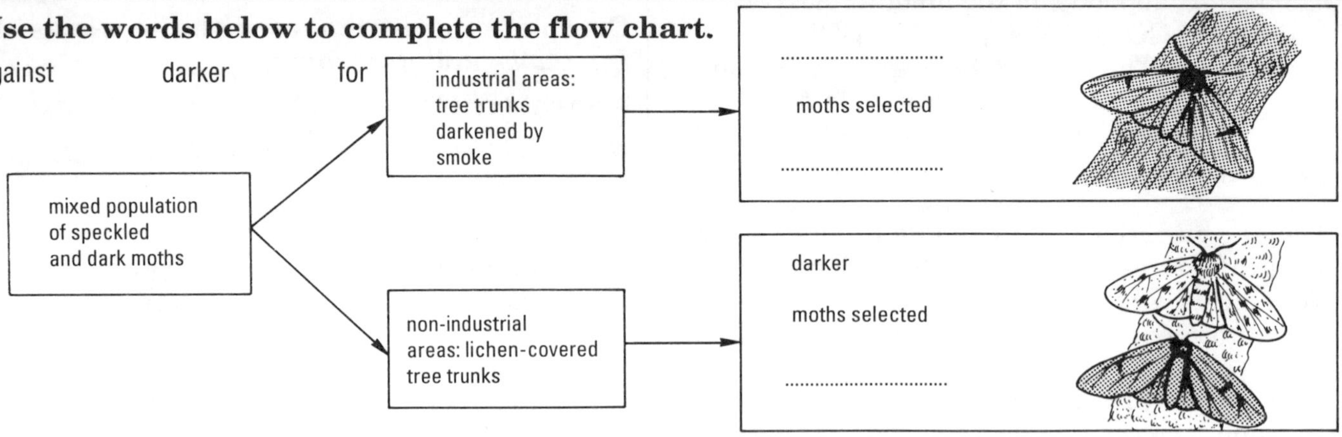

B5 Evolution ensures that each species is well adapted to its particular place in the environment, or fits its **ecological niche**. New species arise by evolution. Good examples, showing the stages involved, are the Galapagos finches. The evolution of different finch species each adapted to feed on different food was described by Charles Darwin. ❑

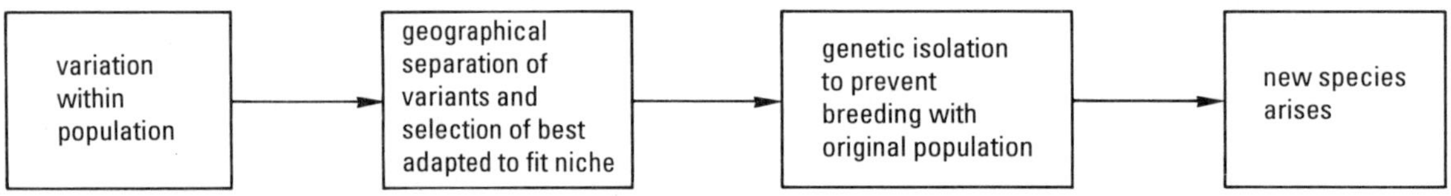

B6 Evolution depends on the inheritance of genes. These are made of the chemical **DNA**, **d**eoxyribo**n**ucleic **a**cid. The DNA molecule is a double helix (double spiral). ❑

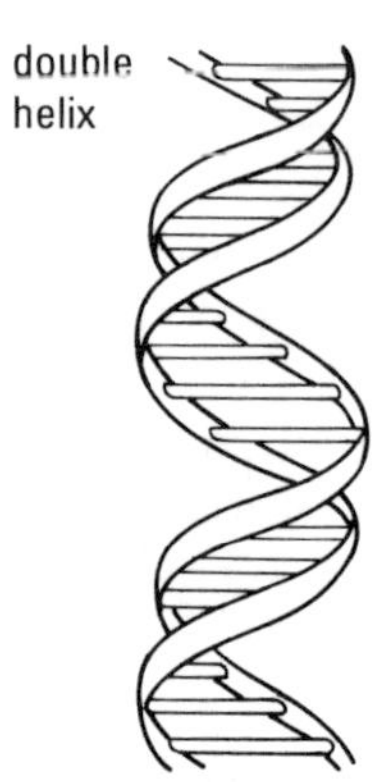

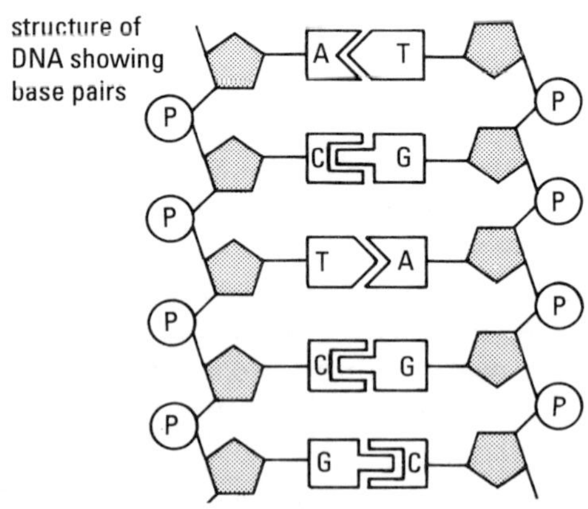

B7 There are four bases in the DNA molecule and these can only pair in two ways to make the cross-links. They are usually shown by using their first letters. **C** always pairs with **G**, and **T** always pairs with **A**. ❑

B8 Most cells in an organism contain all the chromosomes. For example, all human cells contain 46 chromosomes except the sex cells which contain half this number. When a cell divides the DNA must be copied (replicated) to ensure that the daughter cells contain the complete set of chromosomes. ❑

Complete the diagram by writing the letters of the correct bases in the empty spaces.

Stages of DNA replication
1 DNA double helix unwinds
2 Bonds between bases break
3 Matching bases joined to sugar and phosphate molecules build a new parallel strand
4 Two identical DNA molecules are formed

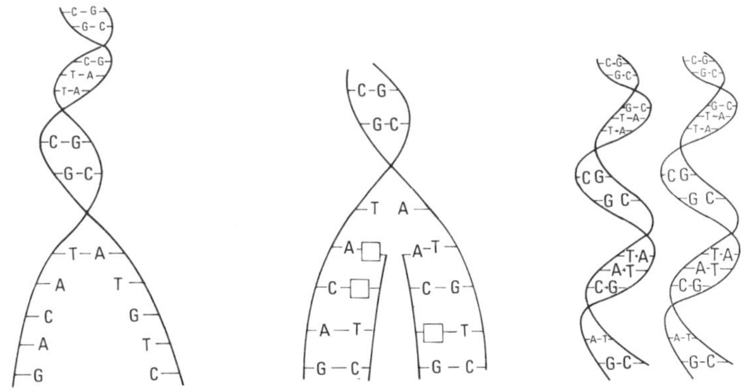

B9 A gene is a section of DNA and has a unique sequence of bases. The bases are a code for the production of a particular protein. This protein allows the inherited characteristic to develop. For example:

gene →	production of protein →	development of characteristic →	characteristic
brown eye colour	particular enzyme produced in iris cells	enzyme controls formation of brown pigment in iris cells	brown eyes

❑

B10 DNA is in the nucleus of the cell but protein synthesis (production) takes place in the cytoplasm. A messenger molecule takes the genetic code from the nucleus to the cytoplasm. The messenger code is read in groups of three bases called **triplets**. Each triplet attracts a particular amino acid. The protein is built up amino acid by amino acid, and the order depends on the order of triplets on the DNA. When the complete message has been read (translated) the protein is complete and can carry out its function. ❑

Label the following on the diagram: *DNA, protein, messenger molecule, amino acid.*

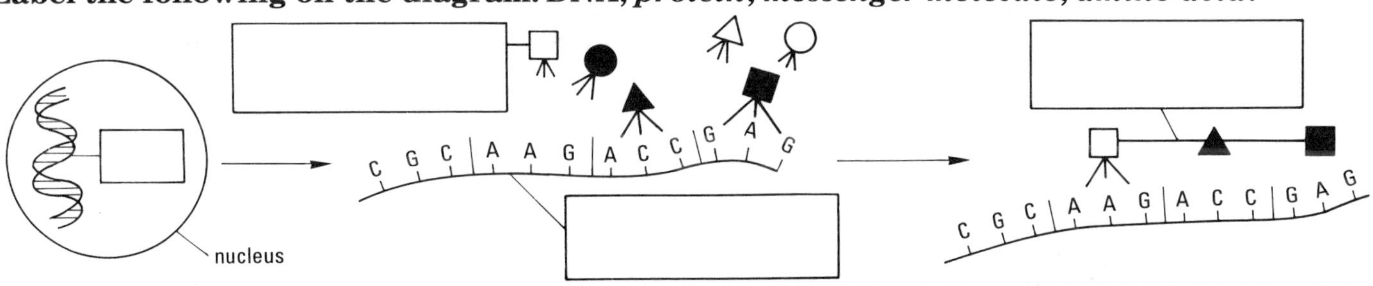

B11 Understanding genetics allows humans to carry out selective breeding – breeding for specific desirable characteristics. This is also called artificial selection. The results can be seen in the variety of dogs and cats kept as pets, and commercially in plant and animal varieties that give bigger yields and have better resistance to disease. ❑

B12 It can be an advantage to produce **clones** – individuals that are genetically identical. Many fruit plants are clones grown from cuttings, and the grower can rely on obtaining the desired product from every tree. Cloning avoids sexual reproduction which would introduce variation into the offspring. So far, animals are not cloned on a commercial scale. ❑

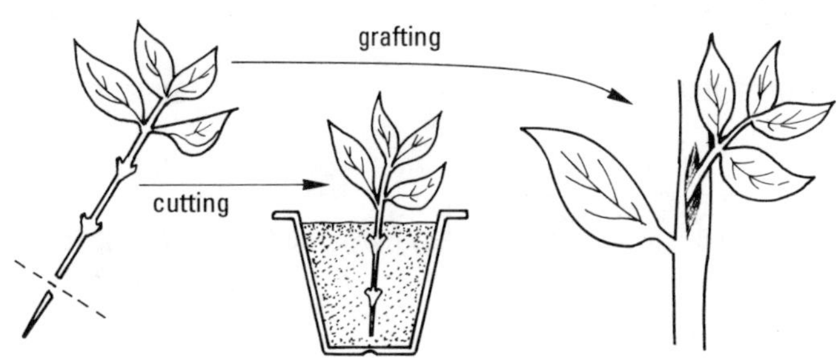

B13 Understanding genetics at the molecular level has led to the development of genetic engineering – a form of **biotechnology**. Genetic engineering involves inserting a fragment of DNA containing one or more genes from one organism into the DNA of another organism, usually a bacterium. When the bacterium divides the altered DNA is passed to both daughter cells, and each individual makes the protein coded for by the inserted gene. The bacteria soon produce a very large population of clones from which the protein can be collected and purified. Human insulin is now produced in this way. ❑

Label the following on the diagram: *bacterial DNA, clones, extraction and purification, human insulin gene.*

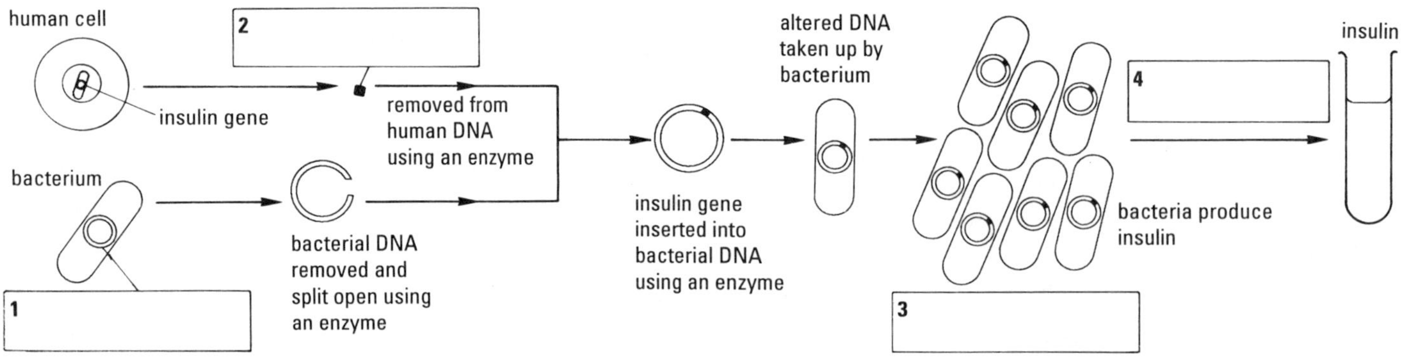

B14 In the future, it may be possible to alter the genes in a fertilised egg by introducing those which would produce more desirable characteristics or by replacing undesirable disease-causing genes. This has serious social and ethical implications. Genetic engineers work to a very strict code of practice. ❑

C1 The **biosphere** is made up of the Earth's crust and surrounding atmosphere along with all the living organisms present. The main parts of the biosphere are interdependent. Human activity can have a harmful effect on the biosphere. ❑

For each human activity, draw lines to match each effect with the correct part of the biosphere affected.

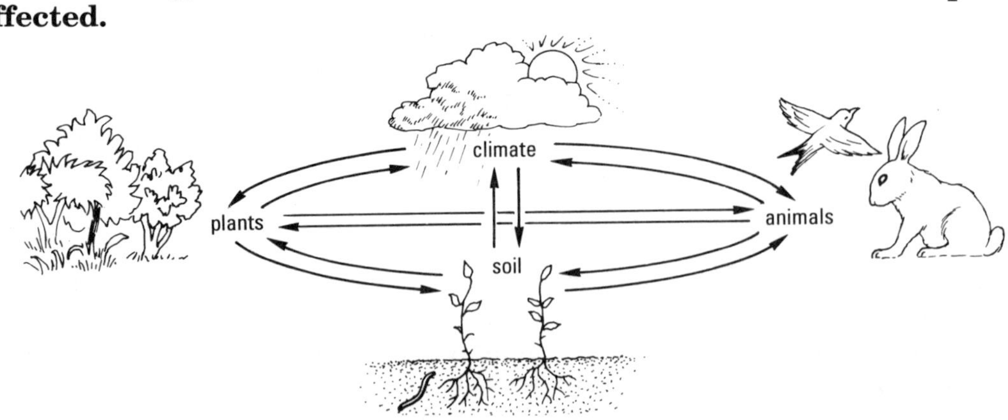

Human activity	Part of biosphere affected	Effects
deforestation	atmosphere soil organisms	• global warming • organisms must adapt to environmental changes • soil erosion
greenhouse gases from burning fossil fuels	atmosphere organisms	• habitats destroyed • less photosynthesis so more CO_2, less O_2
release of CFC gases	atmosphere organisms	• UV rays damage skin, for example cancers • ozone layer damaged

C2 Economic demands can lead to the poor management of ecosystems. For example, the need to produce more food can lead to **desertification**. ❑

grass ecosystem → overgrazed → soil erosion → less water held by soil → nutrients washed (leached) from soil → desert forms

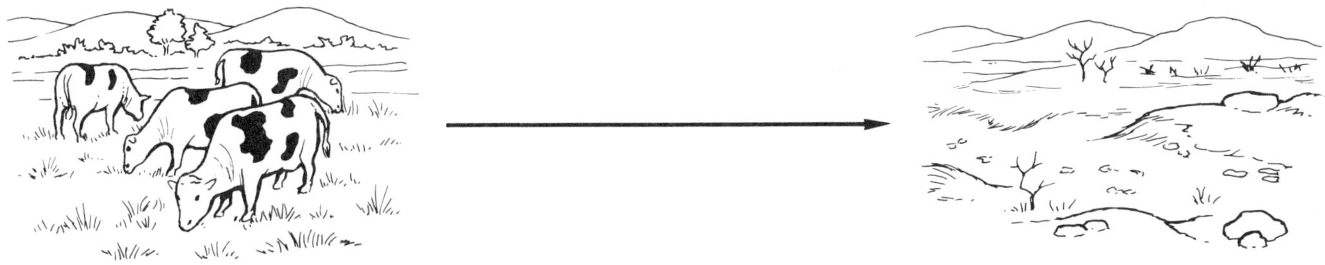

D1 Materials for growth and energy are transferred through ecosystems by food chains and webs and by recycling which involves decomposers. Energy transfer is not very efficient and minerals and other nutrients can be lost by **leaching** (being washed from the soil by rain). ❑

D2 Energy is lost at every link in a food chain, and very little ends up as growth of the next organism in the chain. Energy is lost as heat from respiration and movement. Uneaten and excreted material can be lost if it is not recycled by decomposers. Within a food web there are various levels of energy. ❑

Label the highest and the lowest energy levels in the food web.

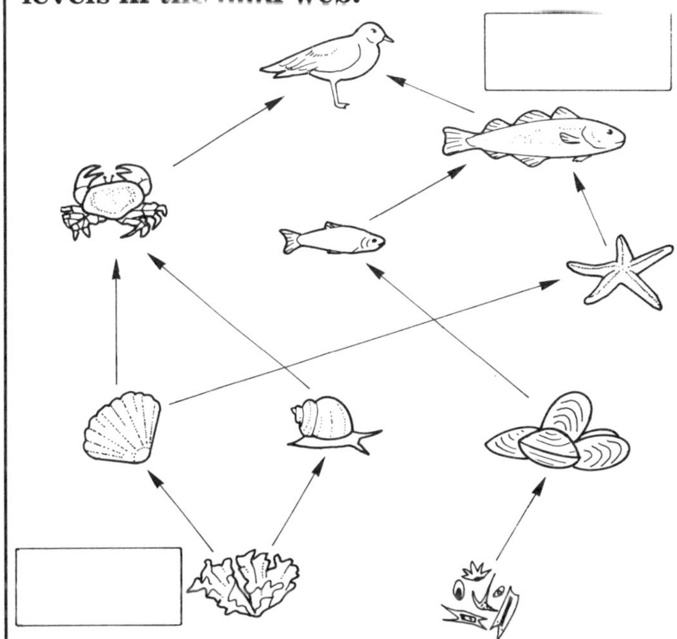

D3 The nitrogen and carbon cycles maintain the balance of these elements in an ecosystem. Other elements such as phosphorus (required for the genetic material DNA and for energy-storing chemicals) are also cycled. ❑

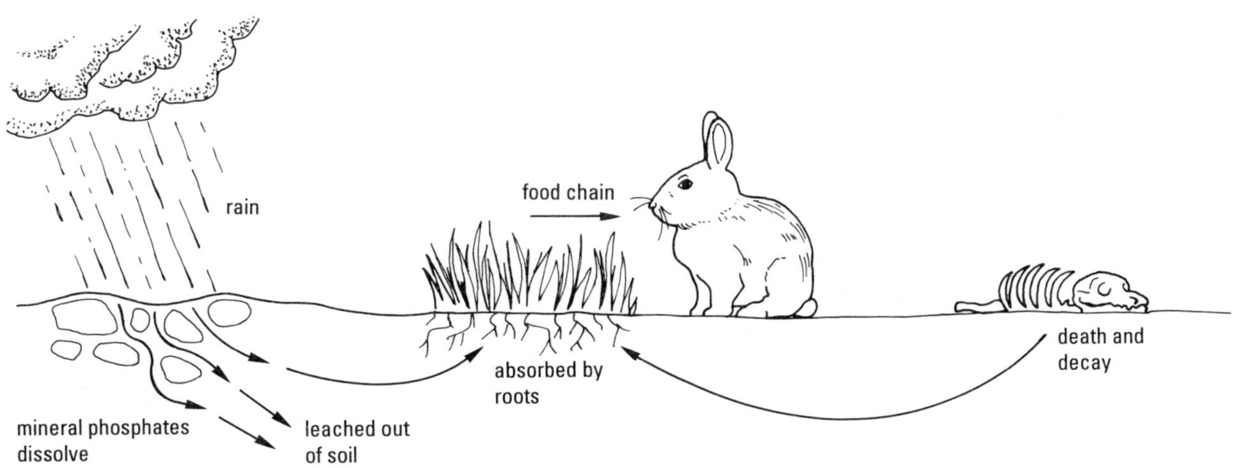

D4 As the human population grows, more and more food is required. Ecosystems must be managed carefully to reduce energy losses and maximise yields. Management must be sensitive so that ecosystems are not damaged. ❑

Draw lines to match each danger to the correct agricultural process for maximising yield.

Crop yield maximised by	Dangers to be avoided
removing hedges to increase area of fields, making ploughing and harvesting easier	rapid spread of disease or pests
adding fertilisers to the soil	destruction of habitats
using insecticides to kill pests	fertilisers leached from soil into waterways causing pollution
growing same plants in huge areas (monoculture)	poisons pass into food chains and are concentrated along chain

ATTAINMENT TARGET 3

Materials and their properties

Big ideas

A There are different types of materials. They come from different sources. The uses of a material depend on its properties.

B The properties can be explained by thinking about the material's structure.

C Chemical reactions change materials.

D The materials that make up the Earth are affected by natural processes.

A1 A **material** is a substance that is **useful** to people. It can be used to make
- an object
- another substance. ❑

Complete this table with six examples of your own.

Name of material used to make objects	Name of material used to make other substances

A2 Materials can be grouped (classified) into **solids, liquids** and **gases**. Different types of materials have different **properties**. ❑

Solids
- stay where they are put
- stay the same shape

Liquids
- flow over the surface
- change shape, form puddles

Gases
- flow everywhere
- change shape, fill space

Three examples are:	**Three examples are:**	**Three examples are:**
● metal	● petrol	● air
●	●	● ....
●	●	● ....

A3 Materials can be mixed. Complete mixtures occur when a solid or a gas dissolves into a liquid to form a **solution**, or when a liquid is **miscible** with another liquid. Incomplete mixtures occur too, for example when liquids mix without dissolving to form an **emulsion**. ❑

Foams are incomplete mixtures of ....with liquid; **gels** are incomplete mixtures of ....with ....

A4 The substances in a mixture do not join together and so they can be separated quite easily.

The mixture called **air** can be separated by **fractional distillation** (liquefying then boiling off the gases separately) to give pure gases, for example, **oxygen** and **nitrogen**. ❑

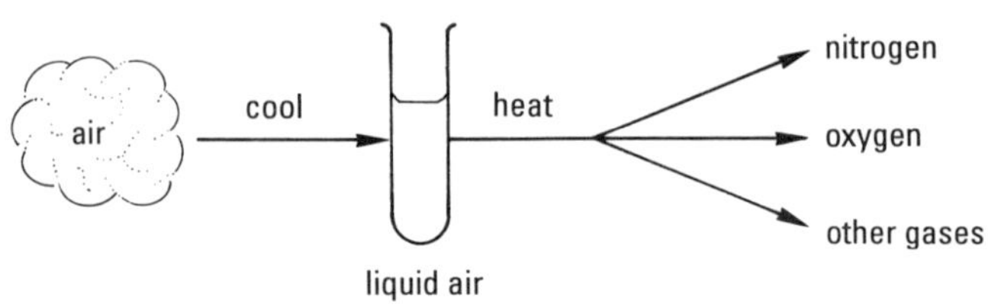

The mixture called **crude oil** can be separated by fractional distillation to give pure liquids, for example ....and ....

The mixture called **sea water** can be separated by crystallization to give pure ....and pure solids like ....

A5 Mixtures can be **separated** by:

- **using water**
  - a) dissolving
  - b) crystallizing
  - c) decanting
  - d) filtering
- **changing the temperature**
  - e) evaporating
  - f) condensing
  - g) freezing
  - h) distilling.

❑

Use the letters above to identify the separation method that is being used in each diagram.

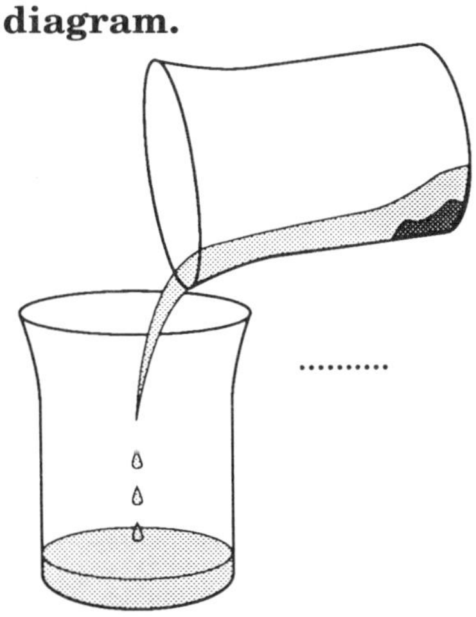

....

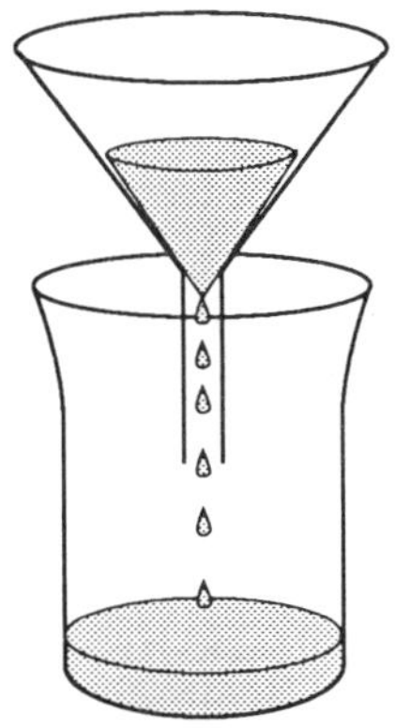

....

....

....

A6 Different methods can be used to separate mixtures. ❑

Which method of separation above would you use to make:

pure salt from seawater? ....

pure oxygen from air? ....

pure petrol from crude oil? ....

A7 All materials are built from **elements**, which are substances that cannot be broken down into simpler substances. The periodic table of elements has **metals** on the left-hand side and **non-metals** on the right. ❑

On the periodic table below, draw a dividing line between metals and non-metals. Then, colour all the elements that are gases at room temperature. Use a different colour to identify the two elements that are liquid at room temperature (bromine and mercury). Use two more colours to identify the most common non-metal and most common metal in the Earth's crust. Add a colour key.

Colour key: [ ] [ ]

							H										He
Li	Be											B	C	N	O	F	Ne
Na	Mg											Al	Si	P	S	Cl	Ar
K	Ca	Sc	Ti	V	Cr	Mu	Fe	Co	Ni	Cu	Zn	Ga	Ge	As	Se	Br	Kr
Rb	Sr	Y	Zr	Nb	Mo	Tc	Ru	Rh	Pd	Ag	Cd	In	Sn	Sb	Te	I	Xe
Cs	Ba	La	Hf	Ta	W	Re	Os	Ir	Pt	Au	Hg	Tl	Pb	Bi	Po	At	Rn
Fr	Ra	Ac	Ku	Ha													

A8 Metals are shiny and easy to reshape. They are often hard, strong and quite dense. They **conduct** electricity and also heat. ❑

Use the periodic table to predict the results of the experiment below.

Element	Does the bulb light?
copper	
magnesium	
sulphur	
Ag	
Ar	
Al	

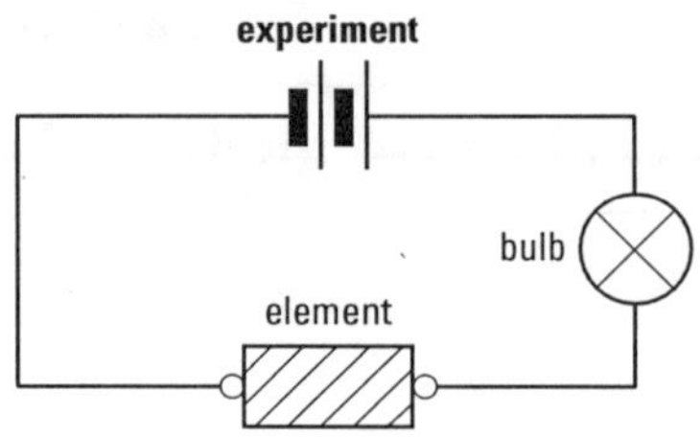

A9 Elements join together to form **compounds**. The name of the compound indicates which elements are present in it. Copper nitr**ide** is made from copper and nitrogen **only**. Copper nitr**ate** is made from copper, nitrogen **and** oxygen. Carbon **di**oxide is made from carbon and **two** oxygens. Sulphur **tri**oxide is made from sulphur and **three** oxygens. ❑

Carbon tetrachloride is made from .... and .... chlorines.

Sodium chlorate is made from .... and .... and ....

.... is made from copper, sulphur and oxygen.

A10 Compounds that are made from metal joined to non-metal are **ionic**. Compounds that are made from non-metal and non-metal are **covalent**. ❑

Use one colour to underline all the ionic compounds in A9 above. Use another colour to underline all the covalent compounds. Add a colour key.

A11 Ionic compounds have high melting points and are therefore solids at room temperature. They conduct electricity when molten or dissolved in water. ❑

Covalent compounds have .... melting points and are therefore often liquids or gases at room temperature. With electricity, they .... These properties can be used to separate compounds of different types.

A12 The **state** of a material changes with temperature. ❑

solid gold →	liquid gold →	gaseous gold
at 20 °C	at 1064 °C	at 2807 °C

solid water →	liquid water →	gaseous water
at - 5°C	at ....°C	at ....°C

A13 A material's properties change when its state changes. The **water cycle** is a good example of this. ❑

Draw a diagram to show how water can move from sea to clouds to snow to river, and to sea again. Add these labels to your diagram:

heating evaporation condensation wind freezing melting flowing river

B1 The **particles** are arranged differently in a solid, a liquid and a gas. ❑

Use particle drawings to illustrate the different properties of ice, water and water vapour.

Ice has a fixed shape because the particles are held together strongly.	Water changes shape because the particles are held more loosely and can move about.	Water vapour spreads because the particles are separate and move quickly.

C1 **Chemical reactions** can change one material into another one. ❑

Milk is changed by an enzyme in bacteria to make ....

Wood is decomposed by heat to form ....

An ore containing copper compounds is smelted by heat to make .... metal.

An ore containing aluminium compounds is melted and electrolysed to make .... metal.

Sugar is fermented by yeast to make .... and carbon dioxide.

C2 Some chemical reactions are **exothermic** – they give out heat. Others are **endothermic** – they take in heat. ❑

Label the following reactions as *exothermic* or *endothermic*.

ice pack
liquids reacting

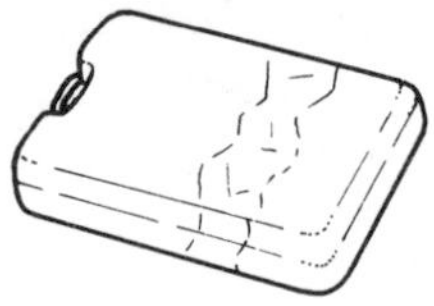

....

coal fire
combustion

....

acid
neutralisation

....

animal
respiration

....

C3 The amount of energy released in a reaction can indicate the relative **reactivity** of a metal. A reactive metal like sodium gives out a lot of energy when it reacts with oxygen. ❑

Complete the table of relative reactivity, using the oxygen column to guide you. Also try to work out why the strange sentence is written down the left-hand side.

	Metal symbol	Name	Reaction with water	Reaction with oxygen	Reaction with acid
Please	K	....		↑	
Send	Na	....			
Lord	Li	....			
Charles	Ca	....			
McLean	Mg	....			
A	Al	....		More energy released	
Zebra	Zn	....			
If	Fe	....			
The	Sn	....			
Lame	Pb	....			
Horse	H	....			
Cannot	Cu	....			
Munch	Hg	....			
Sweet	Ag	....			
Grass	Au	....			

C4 A metal can **displace** (push out) from solution any other metal that is below it in the reactivity series. ❑

When nickel is added to a solution of copper chloride, brown copper metal is formed. Nothing happens when copper is added to nickel chloride solution. However, nickel is formed when iron is added to the nickel chloride solution.

Write the three metals in order of increasing reactivity.

....

C5 One important exothermic reaction is **combustion**. A fuel burns during combustion and makes energy and waste gases. Common fuels include coal, oil, kerosine, wood, petrol and candle wax.

petrol + oxygen ⟶ water + carbon dioxide (and heat energy)

wax + oxygen ⟶ water + carbon dioxide (and heat energy) ❑

According to the equations on the previous page, petrol and wax burn to produce .... energy and a waste gas called .... Water is also produced.

C6 During combustion, the particles join with oxygen to form compounds called **oxides**.

hydrogen + oxygen → hydrogen oxide (water)

$$2H_2 + O_2 \rightarrow 2H_2O$$

carbon + oxygen → carbon dioxide

$$C + O_2 \rightarrow CO_2$$ ❑

C7 **Rusting**, like burning, is an **oxidation** reaction.

- Burning: fuel + oxygen → oxides (like carbon dioxide)
- Rusting: iron + oxygen → iron oxide (rust). ❑

Complete the following word equations:

copper + oxygen →.............................

.... + oxygen → sulphur dioxide

.... + ... → calcium oxide

methane + oxygen → .... + ...
(CH_4)

ethanol + ... → water + ...
(C_2H_6O)

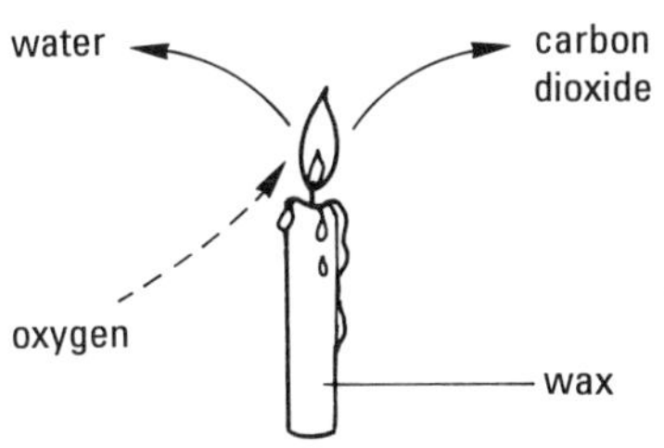

burning

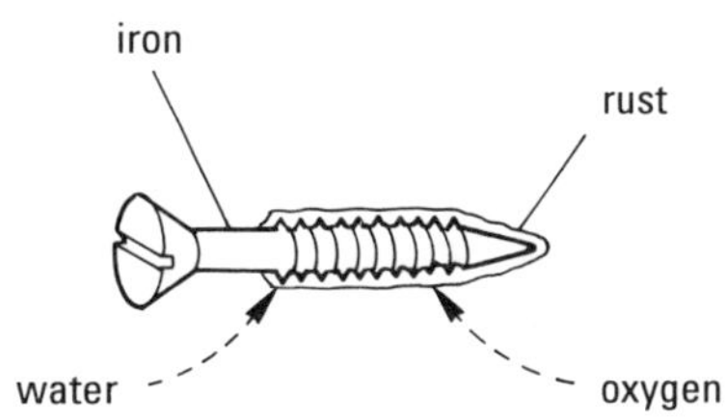

rusting

Rusting involves the corrosion of iron by reaction with .... and ....

C8 The rusting reaction needs water as well as oxygen. It can be slowed down by using electricity, coating with a more active metal or by **reducing** the amount of water and oxygen available to the metal. For example, the iron can be covered with paint or oil.

The burning reaction needs oxygen. It can be slowed down by reducing the amount of oxygen available. ❑

Give three ways of slowing down the burning reaction.

1 .... 2 .... 3 ....

C9 A solution forms when a substance dissolves in a liquid. The substance is called the **solute** and the liquid is called the **solvent**. Many **dilute aqueous** solutions are used in everyday life. ❑

Two everyday examples of dilute aqueous solutions are:

1 .... 2 ....

C10 Aqueous solutions can be acidic, neutral or alkaline. This property is tested by using an **indicator**. ❑

An indicator changes .... in solutions of different pH.

C11 Universal indicator has a range of colours, each one indicating a particular pH.

Add the correct colour of universal indicator to each of the panels on the diagram. Now show the positions of the following substances: *pure water, lemon juice, bleach, tea, vinegar.* Orange juice (a weak acid) has been done for you.

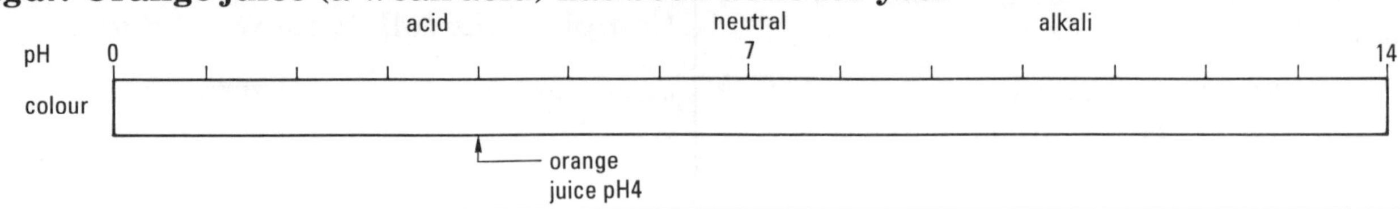

C12 An acid will be 'cancelled out' by a **base**. The solution then becomes **neutral**. For example: ❑

acid + alkali → salt + water

The type of reaction described above is known as ....

C13 An ionic solution conducts electricity. The passage of electricity through an ionic solution produces elements at the electrodes. This is called **electrolysis** (breaking up by using electricity). A covalent compound does not usually dissolve in water. If it does, it has no free ions and cannot conduct electricity. ❑

Identify the elements that are being produced in these two experiments.

Electrolysis of copper sulphate

....

....

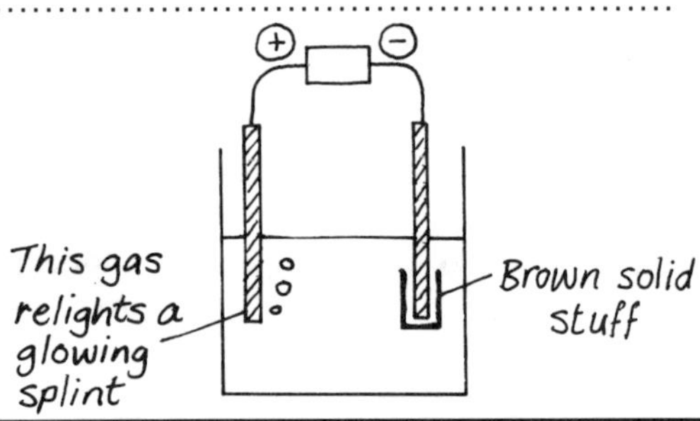

Electrolysis of acidified water

....

....

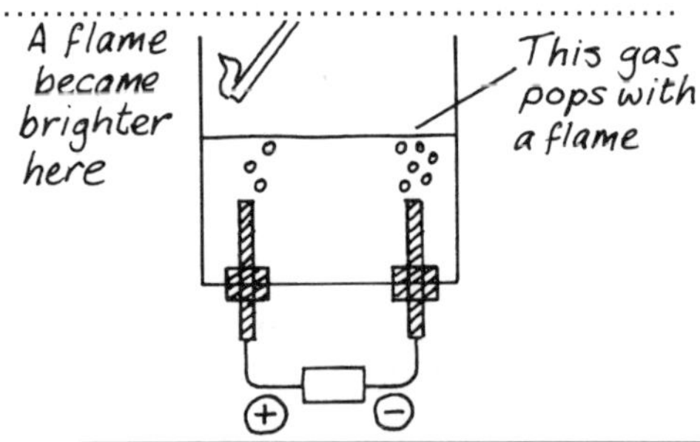

D1 The weather can be described by measurements of variables like temperature, rainfall, windspeed and wind direction. Weather maps predict what these measurements will be, using symbols like these: ❑

Draw symbols to show the weather on two different days:

Day 1 10th June
sunny; temperature of 22 °C; south wind of 10 mph

Day 2 10th December
rain and then snow; temperature of 6 °C; north wind of 25 mph

D2 The weather can be predicted by
- using scientific knowledge about how the **atmosphere** behaves
- finding patterns in weather measurements and observations that have been made over a long period. ❑

Write one example of a) *using scientific knowledge* and b) *using long-term observation or measurement* in weather forecasting.

a) .... b) ....

D3 Our knowledge of how the air behaves is important in weather prediction. ❑

Complete the following sentences about *airflow:*

When air is heated it expands and becomes .... dense, therefore it .... As it rises it cools, gets denser and begins to fall. This movement is called a ....current.

As air rises and falls it also spins because the whole Earth is spinning. It spins more .... than the Earth.

Cold air and hot air do not mix very well. At the boundary of cold and hot air, very fast winds are formed. These are called .... and they circle the Earth at a height of about 10 km.

D4 A **low** is an area of low air pressure. Wind moves around a low anticlockwise. A **high** is an area of high air pressure. Wind moves out of a high in a clockwise direction. ❑

Label a *low* and a *high* on the diagram below.

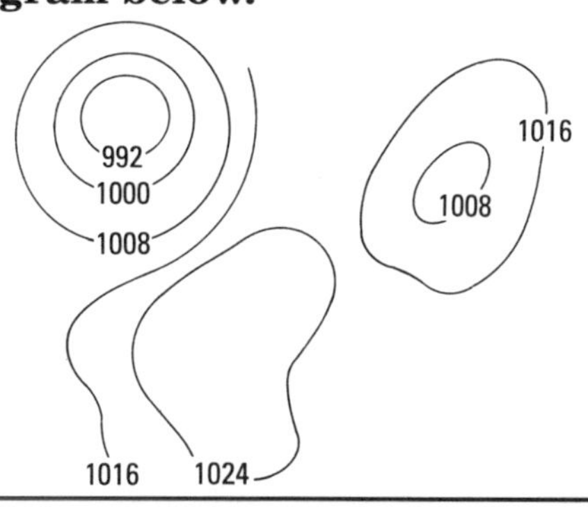

D5 Draw lines to match each description of air pressure with a weather prediction.

middle of a low	clear day; sunny; frost at night
deep low, moving away to the east	warm, cloudless day; hot
middle of a high in summer	'close' day; no rain; no wind; cloudy
middle of a high in winter	heavy rain; gale force winds

D6 Rain, snow, ice and wind all affect the materials on the Earth. **Weathering** of rock causes **erosion** of the land. Mountains are eventually worn away by water and by changing temperature. The process of weathering and erosion occurs as follows:

a) heat from the Sun causes cracks to develop
b) water gets into the cracks
c) water freezes and cracks widen
d) rock breaks
e) bits of rock are washed away by rainwater
f) rock fragments are transported away to form sediments and soils. ❑

This diagram of weathering and erosion is not complete. Read the sequence in D6 on page 55 and then complete the diagram by drawing in the missing parts.

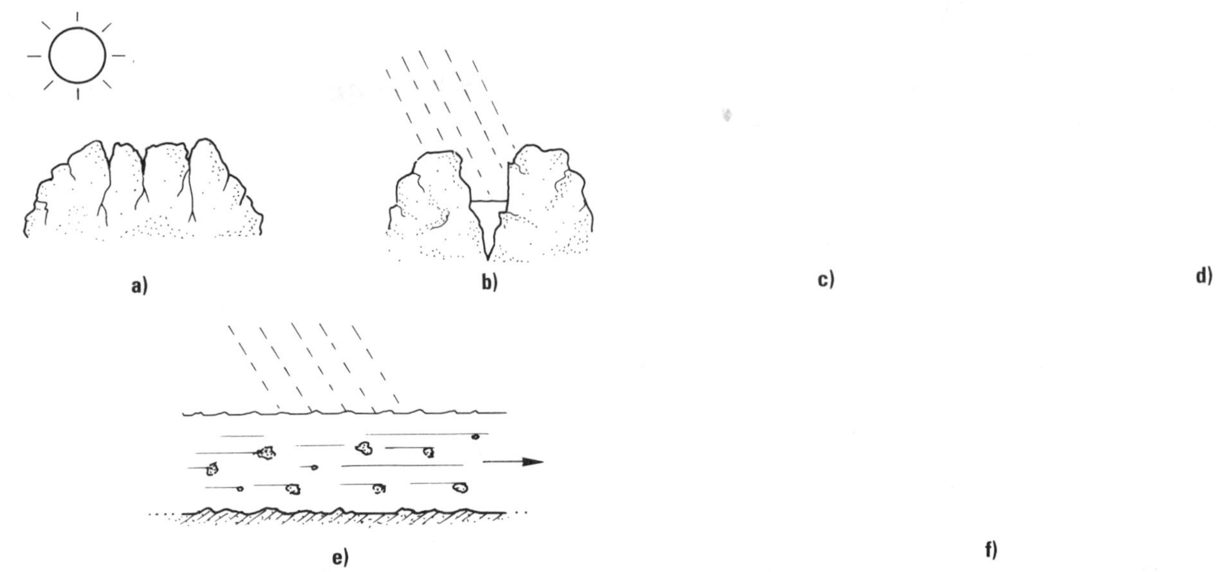

D7 Rocks have been formed over many millions of years.

- **Igneous** rocks are formed when molten rock cools. They are crystalline.
- **Sedimentary** rocks are formed from pieces of other rocks and the remains of living things.
- **Metamorphic** rocks are formed when existing rocks are changed into new forms by great heat and pressure.

Give two examples of each rock type below:

Igneous	Sedimentary	Metamorphic
....	....	....
....	....	....

The diagram below shows part of the rock cycle. Add the following labels.

volcanic eruption weathering and erosion magma igneous rock sedimentary rock metamorphic rock

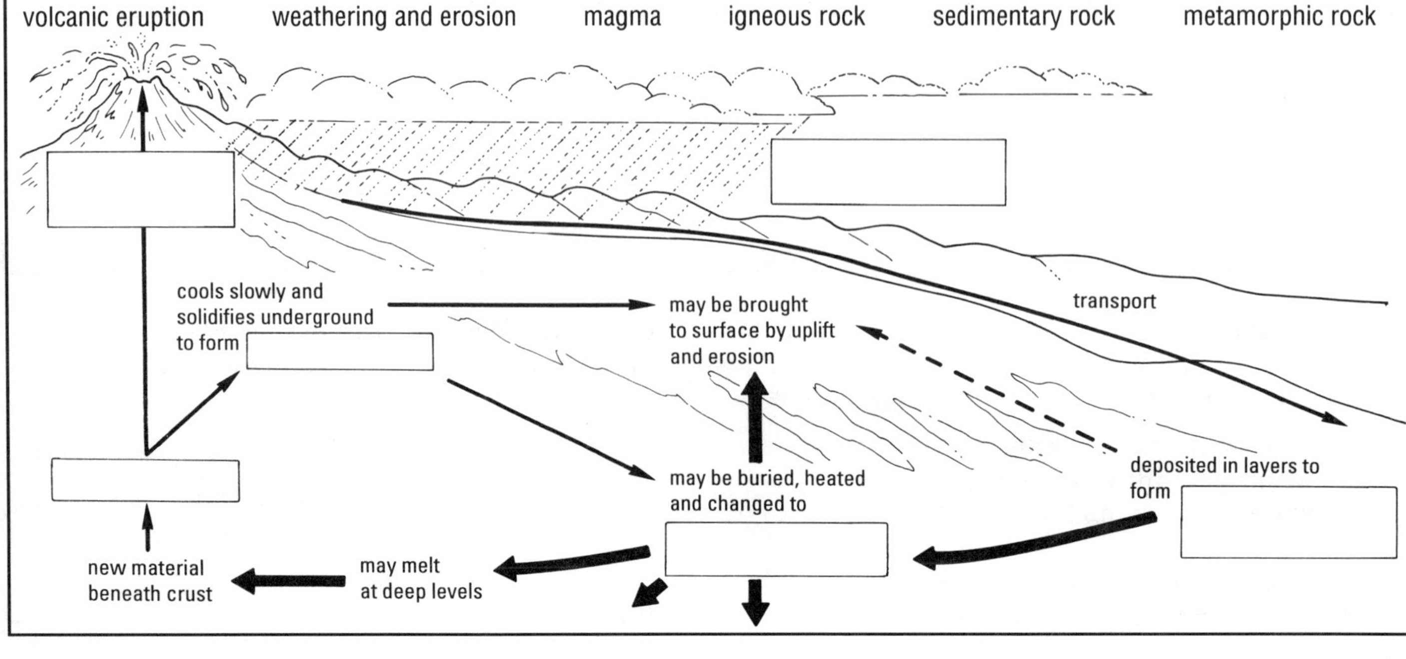

D8 Explain how each of the following three rock types was formed, using some of the words below to help you.

limestone containing many tiny fossilised shells | granite with unusually large crystals | marble containing limestone minerals but not shells

metamorphic sedimentary igneous molten cooled quickly slowly creatures heated

D9 Most of the valuable materials on Earth are present as part of a thin layer of rock on the surface of the Earth. The five most abundant elements are O (47 %), Si (28 %), Al (8 %), Fe (5 %), Ca (4 %). ❏

Draw a bar chart to show this data.

D10 The Earth has a magnetic field. Although it is weak, it still causes magnetised iron to point to the North. It can also be used to work out how the rocks have changed over millions of years. ❏

A1 Something with mass is called **matter**. A **material** is a type of matter that can be changed into a useful object. The object is **manufactured** from **raw materials** (found in the Earth, sea, air and living things). This process costs time, energy and money. It may also have an environmental cost.

These ideas are shown in the spider diagram below. ❑

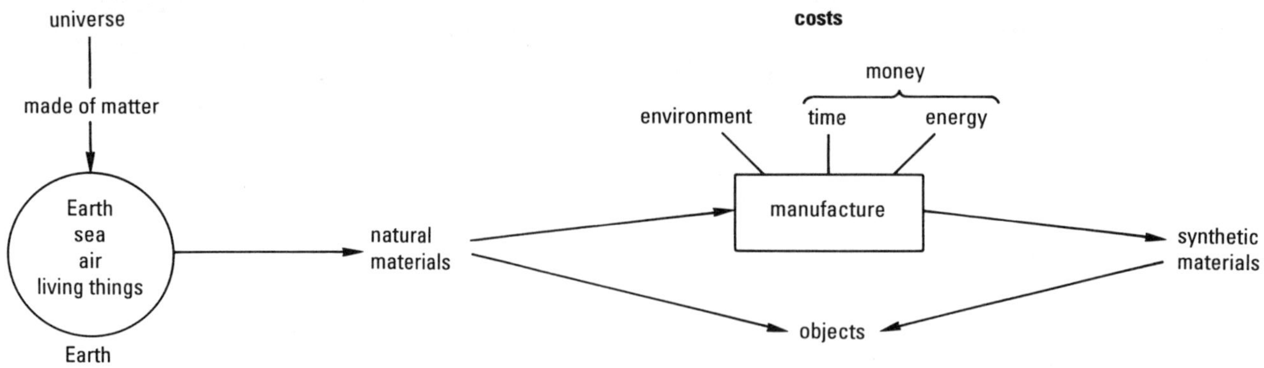

A2 The choice of raw material depends on its properties and the intended use of the object. A raw material has **physical properties** (for example, melting point and hardness) and **chemical properties** (for example, how well it reacts with oxygen or acid). ❑

The properties of polyethene, a plastic, are given below. Write *P* beside each physical property and *C* beside each chemical property. Look up the meaning of any property that you do not understand.

a) floats in water ....
b) low melting point ....
c) burns with a smoky flame ....
d) low density ....
e) low porosity ....
f) no change in acid ....
g) good elasticity ....
h) low thermal conductivity ....

A3 Materials can be **classified** in various ways, for example natural/synthetic or cheap/expensive. If they are divided according to properties then five main groups emerge:

- metals
- plastics
- fibres
- glasses
- ceramics. ❑

Complete the table below by adding two examples of each group.

Group	Source	Main properties	Your two examples
metals	ores in the ground	conduct well; easily shaped; strong	
glasses	made from rocks (sand, limestone)	transparent; brittle; unreactive	
plastics	made from oil	insulators; easily shaped; long-lasting	
ceramics	made from clay	hard; high melting points; unreactive	
fibres	natural (synthetic from oil)	form long, thin strands; flexible; strong	

A4 The five main groups of material (ceramic, metal, plastic, glass and fibre) have been used to manufacture this house. Draw lines to match each of the useful properties to at least one material.

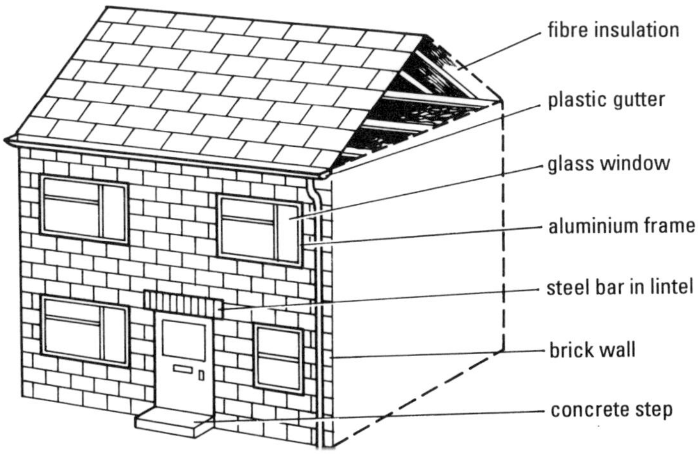

Properties
high tensile strength
high compressive strength
low porosity
low thermal conductivity
high thermal stability
low cost

A5 The 92 natural elements are placed in different **Groups** in the periodic table. The elements in each Group are chemically similar, though there is a gradual change from top to bottom of the Group. For example Group 1, the alkali metals, are all very reactive metals but Li is less reactive than Na, which is less reactive than K. Group 8, the rare gases, are all very unreactive non-metal gases at room temperature, though the density of the gases increases down the Group. ❑

On the outline of the periodic table below, label the following:

all Groups, 1–8 the reactive metals the transition metals the noble gases the halogens a Period

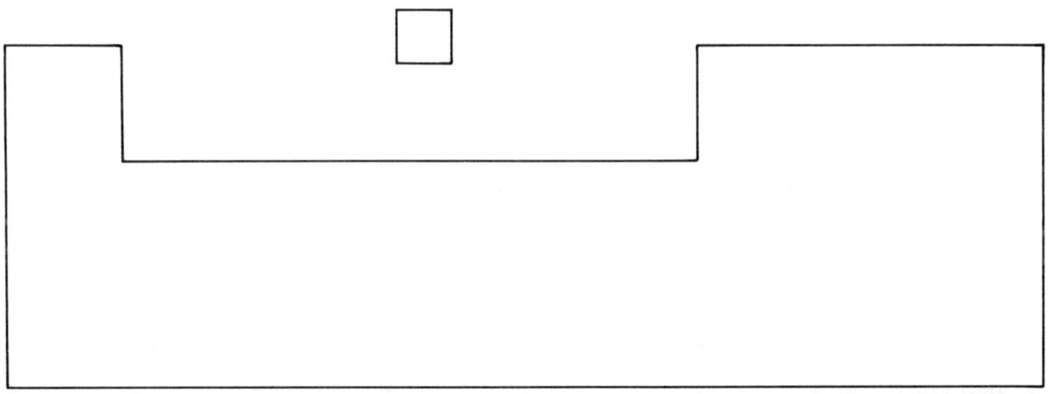

A6 There are **trends** within the Groups of the periodic table. In Group 1, the melting points decrease as we descend the Group. The metals become softer and the reactions become more energetic. The chemical behaviour of the elements remains similar however, because they contain similar atoms. ❑

A7 There are also trends in physical and chemical properties across each Period of the table. This is called **periodicity**. For example, the size of the atoms decreases from Li to F and from Na to Cl. ❑

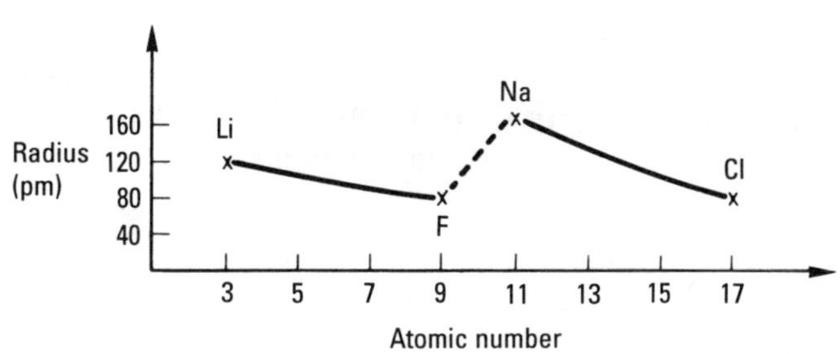

A8 Most metal elements have various physical properties in common. ❑

Complete the diagram to show the periodic change in melting point of the elements from Na to Cl.

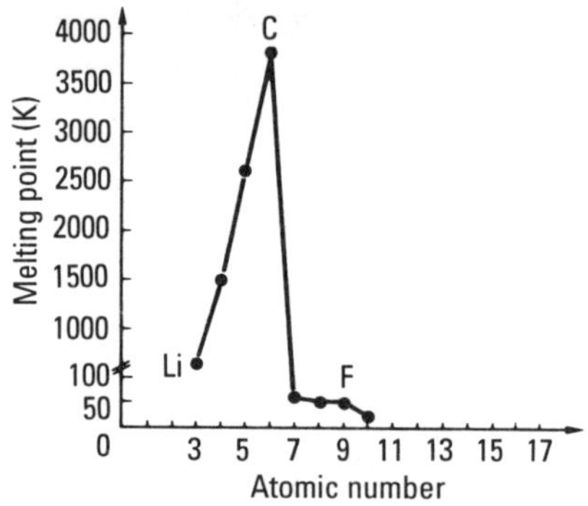

Use a dictionary to find the meanings of these typical metal properties.

malleable ....

....

....

ductile ....

....

....

high tensile strength ....

....

....

B1 An element contains one kind of atom. Each atom is made from three types of particle. ❑

Draw arrows from the labels to the correct part of the drawing.

nucleus

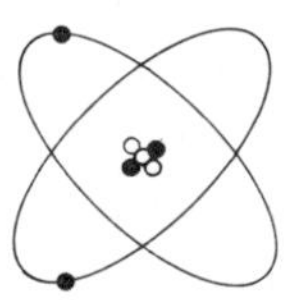

proton (mass 1, charge +)

neutron (mass 1, charge 0)

electron (mass very small, charge -)

B2 The nucleus contains protons.

atomic number (Z) = number of protons

In a **neutral** atom, number of protons = number of electrons. ❑

Calculate the numbers of protons and electrons in each example.

$_3$Li	$_6$C	$_{11}$Na	$_{12}$Mg	$_{17}$Cl
3 protons (+ + +)	...... protons	...... protons	...... protons	...... protons
3 electrons (– – –)	...... electrons	...... electrons	...... electrons	...... electrons

B3 The nucleus also contains neutrons.

mass number (A) = protons + neutrons

For example, this atom has:
- 3 protons (atomic number)
- 3 electrons (neutral atom)
- 4 neutrons (mass number minus atomic number). ❑

mass number —— 7

$^7_3$Li —— symbol

atomic number —— 3

Use the symbols to complete the table.

Symbol	Number of protons	Number of electrons	Number of neutrons
$^{27}_{13}$Al			
$^{19}_{9}$F			
$^{197}_{79}$Au			

B4 **Isotopes** are atoms of the same element (*same atomic number*) which have different numbers of neutrons (*different mass number*). For example, ^{35}Cl and ^{37}Cl have 17 protons each. Therefore the first isotope has (35 –17) neutrons; the second has (37 –17) neutrons. ❑

Work out the numbers of protons, neutrons and electrons in these two isotopes of carbon.

^{12}C p = ... n = ... e = ...

^{14}C p = ... n = ... e = ...

B5 Some atoms are **radioactive**. They have an unstable nucleus which can become more stable by breaking up and emitting energy in the form of alpha particles, beta particles or gamma radiation. This is called **radioactive decay** and it is a random process. Alpha (α) and beta (β) radiation can be detected by using a Geiger-Müller tube to count the particles or by causing the particles to leave tracks in a cloud chamber. ❑

Label the different types of radiation in the diagram *alpha, beta* or *gamma*.

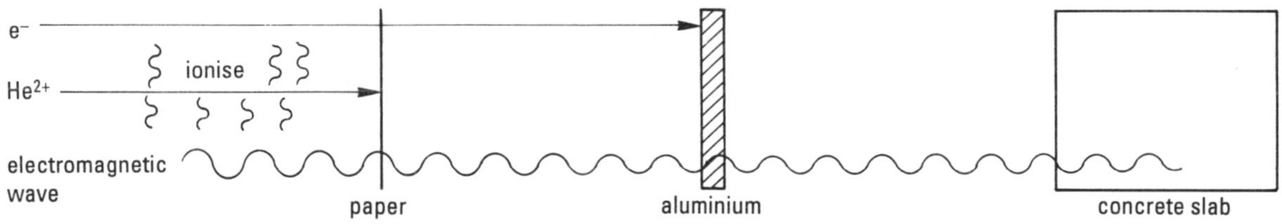

B6 Radioisotopes are useful. The radiation can be used directly in various ways, for example to trace something that is difficult to see, to kill cancer cells, to measure very small distances, to show up hidden cracks in metal, to date ancient objects, etc. It can also be used indirectly to make electrical energy. ❑

Rearrange the steps by writing the letters in the correct boxes below to show how fission is used to generate electrical power.

a) A chain reaction begins and a lot of heat energy is released. This reaction is controlled.
b) The hot substance transfers heat to water in a steam generator.
c) A radioisotope (like U^{238}) is split by slow-moving neutrons. It releases energy and more neutrons.
d) The steam is used to move the turbine which then makes electricity.
e) The heat energy is used to heat up water or another substance like carbon dioxide.
f) These neutrons split more nuclei and release even more energy and yet more neutrons.

B7 Radioisotopes can also be dangerous. The **radiation** can cause harm to living things by breaking chemical bonds and by ionising molecules in the body. Such change can induce cancer or damage sex cells and cause mutations. This is why nuclear waste, which is radioactive and toxic, must be transported and stored with great care. ❑

B8 An atom can lose or gain electrons and become a charged **ion**. For example, the Li atom has 3 electrons; the Li^{+} ion has only 2 electrons: + + + (3 positive protons), – – (cancelled by only 2 negative electrons). ❑

Work out how many electrons each ion has.

$_{11}Na^{+}$	$_{12}Mg^{2+}$	$_{9}F^{-}$	$_{8}O^{2-}$
......	......	......	......

B9 The electrons are arranged around the nucleus in energy levels, called **electron shells**. The first level holds only 2 electrons, the second 8, the third 8, and so on. ❑

B10 From the table opposite, it is evident that the number of electrons in the **outer shell** is the same as the Group number in the periodic table. The outer shell is important for determining chemical properties because it is the first part of an atom to collide with another atom. This is why elements in the same Group of the periodic table have similar chemical properties. ❑

Complete the table below.

Atom	Number of electrons	Arrangement of electrons
$_{3}Li$	3	2, 1
$_{11}Na$	11	2,8,1
$_{19}K$	19	2,8,8,1
$_{4}Be$		
$_{12}Mg$		
$_{20}Ca$		

B11 Metal atoms have only a few electrons in the outer shell. They react with non-metals to form ionic compounds. Non-metals have a lot of electrons in the outer shell. They react with non-metals to form covalent compounds. (Metal atoms join with other metals to form **alloys**). ❑

B12 An ionic compound has a giant structure called an **ionic lattice**. In the lattice, the positive and negative ions are attracted to each other. The lattice is very strong, which is why ionic compounds have high melting and boiling points. However, it does break up when it is melted or dissolved in water. The charged ions are then free to move and electricity can be conducted. ❑

Label each drawing as fully as you can using one or more of the following words:

atom molecule ion element(s) compound(s) mixture ionic covalent

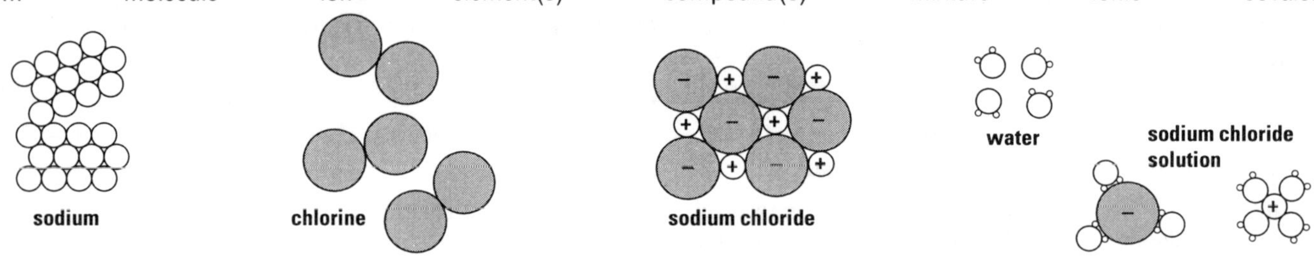

B13 Covalent molecules are held together by strong covalent bonds. However, the attractions between the separate molecules are often weak. Many covalent substances therefore have low melting and boiling points, and are often gases or liquids at room temperature. They have no ions and so cannot conduct electricity. ❑

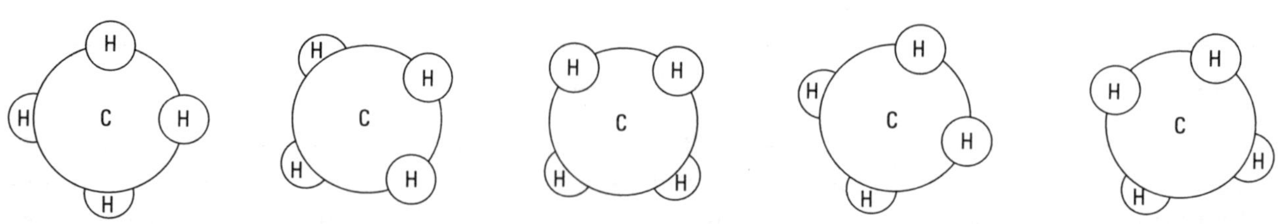

a covalent molecular structure

B14 A few covalent substances like quartz and diamond have high melting points. This suggests that they have giant **network** structures containing many bonds. ❑

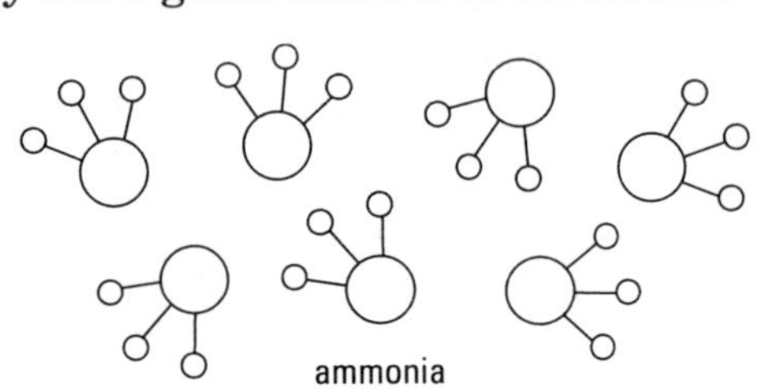

molecular = few bonds, low melting point

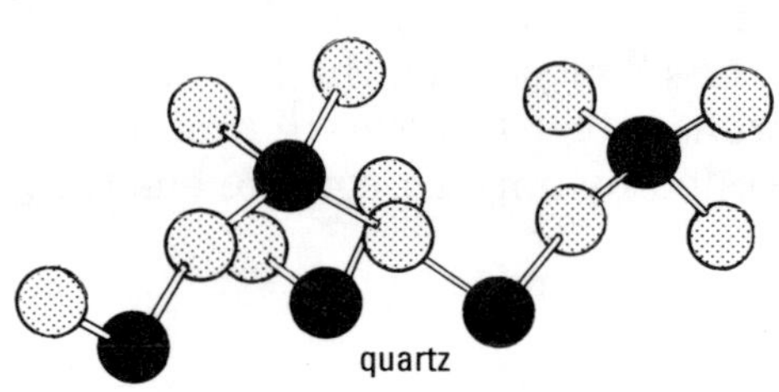

network = many bonds, high melting point

B15 Elements and compounds have many different types of structures, ranging from single atoms, through **diatomic** molecules and **polyatomic** molecules to giant networks. Some examples are described below. ❑

Use the descriptions to sketch the structures in the spaces provided.

Copper Metallic lattice with positive metal atoms attracted in all directions to a sea of negative electrons

Sodium chloride Ionic lattice with positive sodium ions attracted in all directions by six negative chloride ions

Glucose Covalent molecules held together by fairly weak attractions of slight electrostatic charges on the molecules

Diamond Covalent 3D network of atoms tetrahedrally joined in four directions by strong covalent bonds

Graphite Covalent 2D network with atoms joined together in three directions to form plates. Weak bonds between the plates

Polyethene Polymer of small covalent molecules linked together in a chain by strong covalent bonds

B16 All particles of matter have kinetic energy, including single atoms, molecules and networks. Particles move about which is why you can smell perfume in all parts of a room. The particles **diffuse** through the air to your nose, moving from an area of high concentration to one of low concentration. Brownian motion provides indirect evidence for this. ❑

B17 When a substance is heated, its particles move about more. The spaces between them increase and the substance **expands** (gets bigger). Eventually it **changes state**; a solid melts and finally the liquid vaporises. These steps all require energy, and are shown in the diagram below, going from left to right. ❑

Write one word to describe each step in the reverse process, going from right to left.

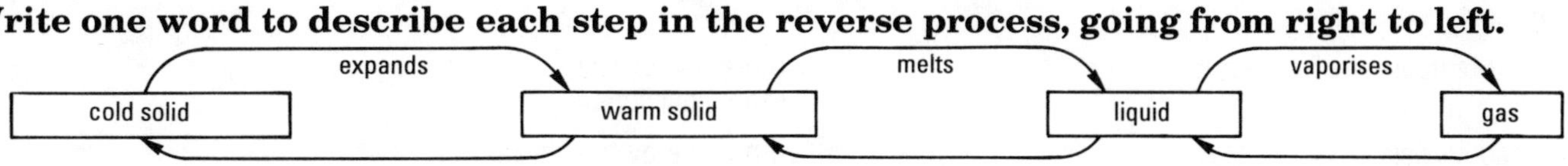

....

B18 Particles move faster as the temperature increases. The heat energy is changed into kinetic energy. In the diagrams on the next page, the gas particles are in a box with movable sides. When it becomes hotter (increased temperature), they move about faster and collide more forcefully with the walls of the box (increased pressure). The walls are pushed out so that the gas particles take up more space (increased volume). The relationship between these three variables is shown by the **gas equation**:

$$\frac{\text{pressure} \times \text{volume}}{\text{temperature}} = \text{constant value}$$ ❑

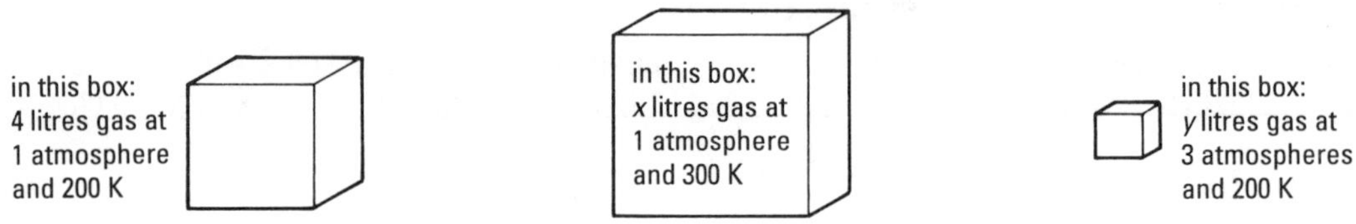

To calculate *x*:

$$\frac{P_1 V_1}{T_1} = \frac{P_2 V_2}{T_2}$$

$$\frac{1 \times 4}{200} = \frac{1 \times x}{300}$$

$$x = \frac{300 \times 4}{200}$$

$$= 6 \text{ litres}$$

Now you calculate *y*:

C1 A **chemical reaction** involves

- energy changes
- formation of new substances. ❑

C2 The **rate** of a chemical reaction is increased by

- increasing the concentration of the reactants
- increasing the temperature
- increasing the surface area of the reactants (by breaking them into smaller pieces)
- adding a catalyst. ❑

The first diagram below shows a reaction in progress. Look at the other diagrams and write down whether the reaction rate will *increase* or *decrease*.

....

C3 In a reaction, the reactant particles must **collide**. The rate of reaction depends on the number of **successful collisions**. ❑

Draw lines to match each factor with the correct description of how it changes the reaction rate.

increased temperature	more particles so more collisions
decreased particle size of reactants	more energy to activate more successful collisions
catalyst present	more particles touching so more collisions
increased concentration of reactants	particles better positioned so more successful collisions

C4 We use these ideas (from C3) about rates of reaction every day. For example, washing powders contain **enzymes** to dissolve biological stains. Enzymes are biological catalysts. ❑

Give an example from your own everyday experience of increasing a rate of reaction by:

using heat ....

breaking into smaller pieces ....

adding a catalyst ....

increasing the concentration of one of the reactants ....

C5 In industry it is common to find the rate of reaction being increased by
a) using heat (for example, in a blast furnace)
b) using a catalyst (for example, in the Haber process)
c) breaking into smaller pieces (for example, in cement manufacture)
d) using a highly concentrated reactant (for example, in an oxyacetylene torch). ❑

Read the notes below about the blast furnace (process a) above) and then write similar notes for the other three processes.

a) Blast furnace: Iron ore reduced to Fe. Reaction with CO using heat.

b) ....

c) ....

d) ....

C6 There are chemical patterns that enable us to predict the form of reaction and its associated energy changes. The table below shows the pattern of reactivity of the common metals with water, acid and chlorine. ❑

C7 Reactive metals give out a lot of energy when they react and they form **stable** compounds. Unreactive metals form unstable compounds which break up easily needing only a little energy to do so. ❑

C8 Our supply of metals is **finite**, which means it will not last forever. Used metal should therefore by **recycled**. ❑

C9 Although their reactivity varies, metals have many similar chemical properties. For example, they react with non-metals to form positive ions, they mix with other metals to form alloys and they corrode in the presence of oxygen and water. ❑

C10 Metals are extracted from metal compounds called **ores**. The more reactive the metal, the more stable its ore. For example, copper can be **extracted** from its ore simply by heating whereas iron ore needs to be heated with carbon to extract iron. To make aluminium, the aluminium ore (bauxite) must be melted and then electrolysed. ❑

Use a colour to highlight the blocks of reactions that are highly exothermic and a different colour for those that are not.

<table>
<tr><th></th><th>with water</th><th>with acid</th><th>with chlorine</th></tr>
<tr><td>K</td><td rowspan="4">displace hydrogen gas from cold water</td><td rowspan="3">violent explosive reaction</td><td rowspan="8">combine very energetically with chlorine to form stable ionic chloride salts</td></tr>
<tr><td>Na</td></tr>
<tr><td>Li</td></tr>
<tr><td>Ca</td><td rowspan="7">displace hydrogen from acid</td></tr>
<tr><td>Mg</td><td>↓ ↑</td></tr>
<tr><td>Al</td><td rowspan="4">only displace hydrogen from steam</td></tr>
<tr><td>Zn</td></tr>
<tr><td>Fe</td></tr>
<tr><td>Sn</td><td rowspan="4">combine quickly to form stable salts</td></tr>
<tr><td>Pb</td><td rowspan="6">do not displace hydrogen from water or steam</td></tr>
<tr><td>Cu</td><td rowspan="5">do not displace hydrogen from acid</td></tr>
<tr><td>Hg</td></tr>
<tr><td>Ag</td><td rowspan="3">combine slowly to form unstable salts</td></tr>
<tr><td>Au</td></tr>
<tr><td>Pt</td></tr>
</table>

colour key

highly exothermic ☐ not highly exothermic ☐

Use the facts given in C10 to help you complete the summary of how metals are extracted.

Metals	Extracted from ore by
K, Na, Li, Ca, Mg, Al	
Zn, Fe, Sn, Pb	
Cu, Hg	
Ag, Pt, Au	

C11 Metals react with oxygen to form **basic oxides**. These are alkaline if they dissolve (like Group 1 metal oxides) and neutral if they do not (like the transition metal oxides). Non-metal oxides are acidic. ❏

Label the main blocks of oxides in the table as *alkaline, neutral* or *acidic*.

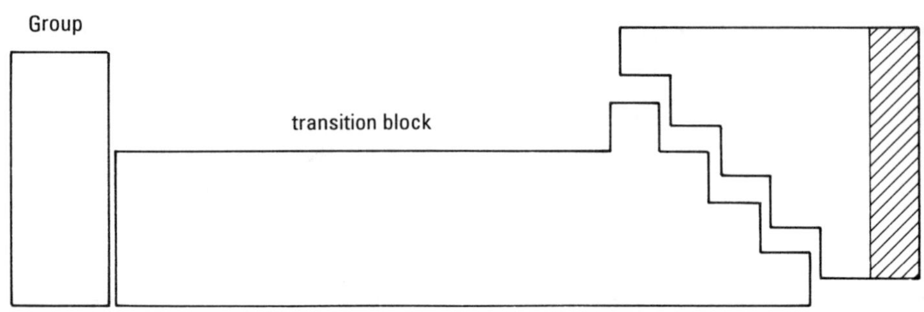

C12 **Acids** are compounds that contain **H^+ ions**. They are ionic. Some acids produce more H^+ ions per formula unit than others. Common laboratory acids are hydrochloric (H^+Cl^-), nitric ($H^+NO_3^-$) and sulphuric ($2H^+SO_4^{2-}$). ❏

C13 Acids can be **neutralised** ('cancelled out') by bases (**antacids**). When an acid is neutralised the H^+ ions become either H_2 gas ($H^+ + H^+ \rightarrow H_2$) or part of an H_2O molecule ($H^+ + OH^- \rightarrow H_2O$). ❏

Which of the acids named in C12 would need more base than the other two to cancel out the same number of acid molecules? ....

C14 During neutralisation, the metal part of the base and the negative ion in the acid remain as ions. These ions (which together make up the **salt**) are usually dissolved in the solution. ❏

Nitric acid gives nitrate salts.

Hydrochloric acid gives .... salts. Sulphuric acid gives .... salts.

C15 There are four major types of base, which are shown in the general word equations below. ❏

Underline the bases and learn the equations below.

reactive metal + acid → salt + hydrogen

metal oxide + acid → salt + water

metal hydroxide (alkali) + acid → salt + water

metal carbonate + acid → salt + water + carbon dioxide

C16 Hydrocarbons are covalent compounds. Crude oil is a mixture of hydrocarbons. It is changed into useful products by the following processes:

- The mixture of hydrocarbons is **distilled**. Smaller hydrocarbons boil at lower temperatures than larger hydrocarbons. Fractions with small molecules burn well and are in great demand as fuels. Those with larger molecules are not as useful.
- There is too much of some of the heavy fractions. Their molecules are **cracked** (using heat and a catalyst) to make smaller molecules. Some of these are unsaturated.
- The unsaturated molecules are **polymerised** to make big molecules.
- Some molecules are **reformed** to change their structures. ❑

The processes described above are shown in the diagram. Add the following names to it:

distillation cracking polymerisation reforming

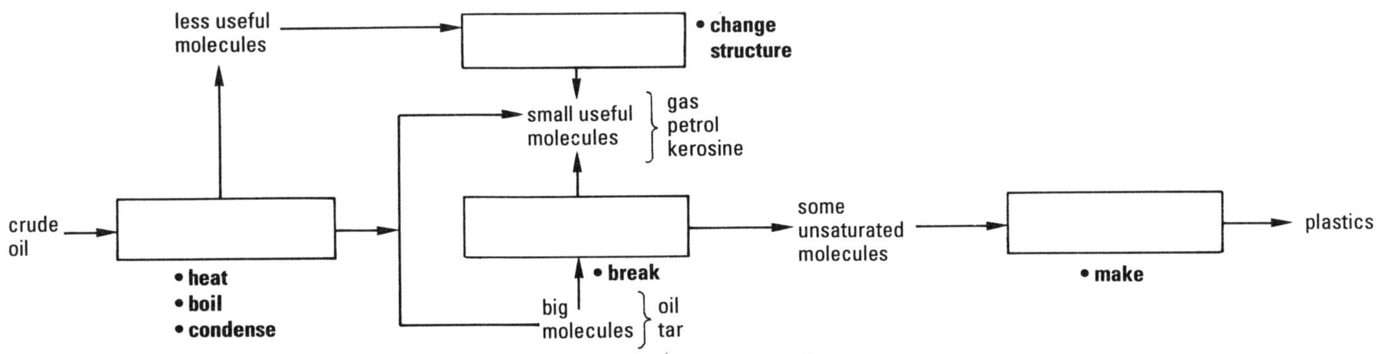

C17 Hydrocarbons are molecules containing hydrogen and carbon only. Two important families (homologous series) of hydrocarbons are **alkanes** and **alkenes**. ❑

Some data are given below for the alkanes; write the corresponding data for the alkenes.

	Alkanes	Alkenes
First in series	methane	
Molecular formula	CH_4	
Structural formula	H | H – C – H | H	
General formula for the series	C_nH_{2n+2}	
Trend in physical properties	boiling point and viscosity increase as molecules get bigger	
Chemical properties	small ones burn well; decolorise bromine water slowly; single C–C bonds so fairly unreactive	

C18 Hydrocarbons are used as **fuels**. When they burn completely, they produce water and carbon dioxide:

$$CH_4 + 2O_2 \rightarrow 2H_2O + CO_2$$

Larger hydrocarbon molecules cannot get enough oxygen to burn completely and therefore they often produce carbon (soot) and/or carbon monoxide (CO). ❑

C19 The combustion of hydrocarbons, for example petrol in car engines, is a major source of air pollution. ❑

Draw lines to match the pollutants formed in a car engine with possible effects on the environment.

Pollutant	Possible effect
CO_2	acid rain
CO	brain damage
NO_2	greenhouse gas
lead compounds	poisonous

C20 Atoms join together to achieve a stable, full outer electron shell. Sodium has to lose 1 electron to do so and its combining power (or **valency**) is therefore 1. Carbon has to share 4 electrons and its valency is therefore 4. Valency is related to Group number. ❑

Complete the gaps in this summary table.

Group	1	2				6	7	8
Valency	1	2	3	4	3	2		

C21 The valency of **transition elements** is variable. In a compound, the valency of the metal atom is given as a Roman numeral after its name, for example, copper(II) chloride and copper(I) chloride. ❑

C22 Some ionic compounds contain **groups** of atoms that act like a single unit. The formulae and valencies of the most common groups are given below. ❑

Valency	1	2	3
	ammonium, NH_4	sulphate, SO_4	phosphate, PO_4
Group	hydroxide, OH	carbonate, CO_3	
	nitrate, NO_3		

C23 Chemical formulae are a short-hand way of describing substances. To work out a **chemical formula**, follow these rules.

1 write down the name of the substance
2 look up the symbols for the elements/groups
3 write the valency of each atom/group
4 if they don't balance, swop the valancies. ❑

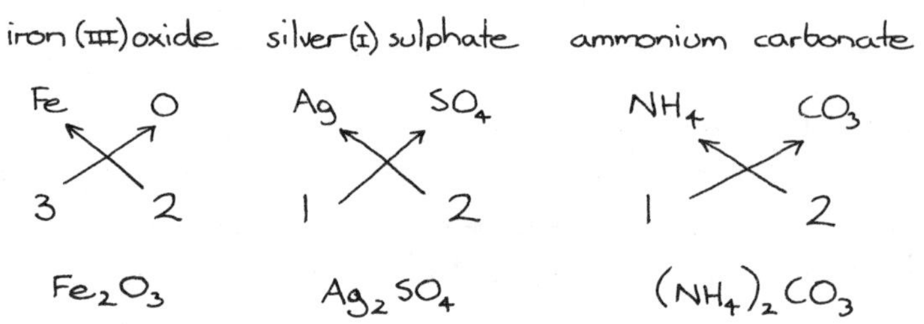

Write the formulae for the following substances, laying out your working in the same way as shown above.

sodium oxide   hydrogen fluoride   magnesium chloride   silver(I) sulphide   iron(II) chloride   lithium nitrate
aluminium phosphate   calcium hydroxide   ammonium carbonate

C24 Covalent compounds often have names that describe their formula: carbon **di**oxide is CO_2 and carbon **mon**oxide is CO; sulphur **di**oxide is SO_2 and sulphur **tri**oxide is SO_3. ❑

C25 A **chemical equation** is a precise description of a chemical reaction. It can be built up in steps.

1 write the equation in words
2 put it into symbols, using the correct formulae
3 add arithmetic symbols and balance by multiplying the formulae
4 include the state symbols.

Remember:
- never change the correct formula to balance the equation
- the state symbols are (s) = solid, (l) = liquid, (g) = gas, (aq) = aqueous solution. ❑

1, iron + chlorine ⟶ iron (III) chloride

2, Fe Cl_2 $FeCl_3$

3, $2Fe + 3Cl_2 \longrightarrow 2FeCl_3$

4, $2Fe_{(s)} + 3Cl_{2(g)} \longrightarrow 2FeCl_{3(s)}$

Use the rules above to write equations for:

the **neutralisation** of hydrochloric acid by calcium carbonate

the extraction of copper from copper oxide by **reduction** with carbon

the **combustion** of methane

C26 **Half-equations** are used to describe what happens to particular ions within a reaction. For example, solid zinc displaces copper ions from solution:

zinc + copper ions → copper + zinc ions

The more active zinc atoms pass electrons to the ions of the less active copper. The two half-equations are therefore:

$Zn(s) \rightarrow Zn^{2+}(aq) + 2e^-$ (change in zinc atoms)

and $Cu^{2+}(aq) + 2e^- \rightarrow Cu(s)$ (change in copper ions) ❑

C27 Similar ion–electron half-equations are used to describe electrolysis. ❑

When copper(II) chloride is electrolysed, copper forms at the negative electrode and chlorine forms at the positive electrode. Translate the two half-equations into words.

At the negative electrode: $Cu^{2+}_{(aq)} + 2e^- \rightarrow Cu_{(s)}$

At the positive electrode: $2Cl^-_{(aq)} \rightarrow Cl_{2(g)} + 2e^-$

D1 The weather is caused by the movement of air blocks due to pressure and temperature changes. When a cold block is followed by a warm one the boundary between them is called a **warm front**. Warm followed by cold gives a **cold front**. ❑

D2 Weather phenomena can be explained by thinking about how blocks of warm and cold air move in order to **transfer energy**. Energy can be transferred by movement (winds), electrical potential (lightning) or latent heat (evaporation and condensation). ❑

Mark the warm and cold fronts on this diagram of a low that is moving from left to right (west to east) over the house.

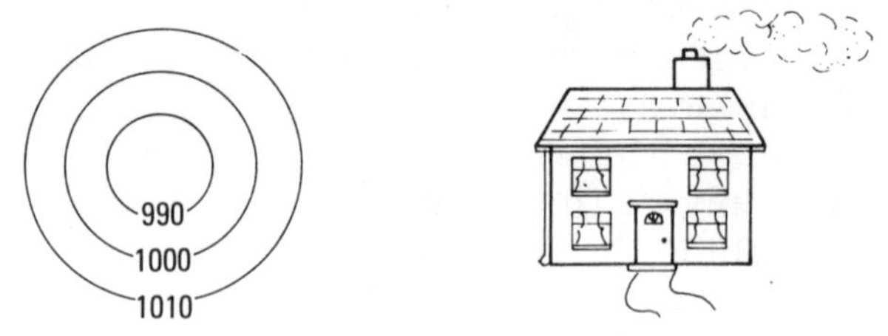

Draw lines to match each weather condition with its correct explanation.

Condition	Explanation
mist and fog	there is a large pressure difference between a deep low and the surrounding area
thunder and lightning	without clouds to retain the heat, the land becomes very cold at night and water condenses and then freezes
frost	the ground is cool. It cools the still warm air above and water droplets condense
summer heat-waves	there is damp, warm air near the ground and cold air above it. The warm air rises and the cool air falls, producing ions as they flow past each other
gales	the jet-stream moves north and allows warm tropical air to become established

D3 The air contains about 78.0 % nitrogen, 21.0 % oxygen, 0.9 % argon, 0.03 % carbon dioxide and small amounts of other, noble, gases. ❑

Show the information given above on a bar graph or pie chart.

D4 The Earth is over 4 billion years old and for most of that time there has been no oxygen in the atmosphere. Present oxygen levels have been built up gradually over the last 2000 million years as a result of photosynthesis by green plants. The levels of gases in the atmosphere are kept fairly constant by balanced, natural processes. ❑

Name the gas which each pair of processes keeps in a steady state.

photosynthesis/respiration	fixing/decay	evaporation/condensation
....	....	....

D5 A **mineral** is a single substance. A rock is usually a mixture of different minerals. The minerals in a rock can be identified by using chemical tests and by measuring physical properties like hardness and density. ❑

Underline the minerals in this list:

calcite marble rock salt basalt fluorite iron pyrites

D6 The structure of a rock indicates how it was formed.

- **Igneous** rocks contain crystals that have formed as the molten rock cooled. The crystals may be small, as in basalt, or, if the molten rock cooled more slowly, they may be large, as in granite. Pumice and similar rocks even contain bubbles left by escaping gas.
- **Sedimentary** rocks are often layered because the fragments of mineral which make up the rock settled out from moving water. Shale contains very small fragments, sandstone is made of bigger ones and conglomerate has fragments as big as stones in it.
- **Metamorphic** rocks are usually hard and may contain unusual minerals.

Rocks are often hundreds of millions of years old: a piece of sandstone, for example, might have been formed 185 000 000 years ago. ❑

D7 Convection currents inside the Earth cause the **plates** in the Earth's crust to move. Forces are exerted on the crust and this may cause layers of rock to break (causing **faults**) or bend (causing **folds**). ❑

Add these labels to the diagram below:

folding faulting anticline force applied suddenly force applied slowly

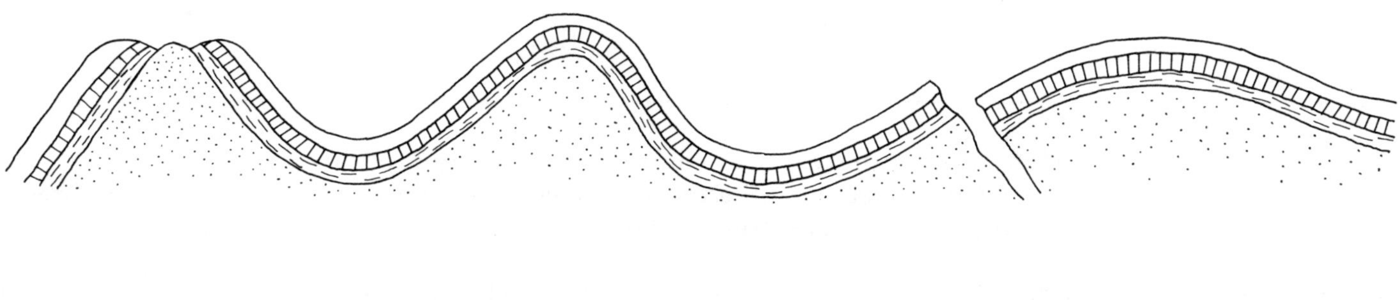

A1 Any object can be made from a range of materials. The manufacturer needs to judge which one is best, taking into account the material's properties. For example, a material used to make the body of a car seat needs to be strong, easily shaped, thermally stable, inexpensive, etc. From a range of possibilities, the manufacturer makes an **optimal** choice.

A2 Many modern materials contain **polymers**. A polymer is made by joining small **monomers** together.

Addition polymers

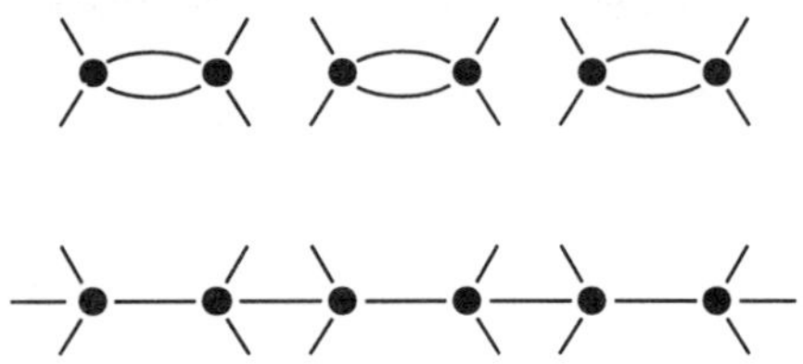

ethene

polyethene

add across a double bond

Condensation polymers

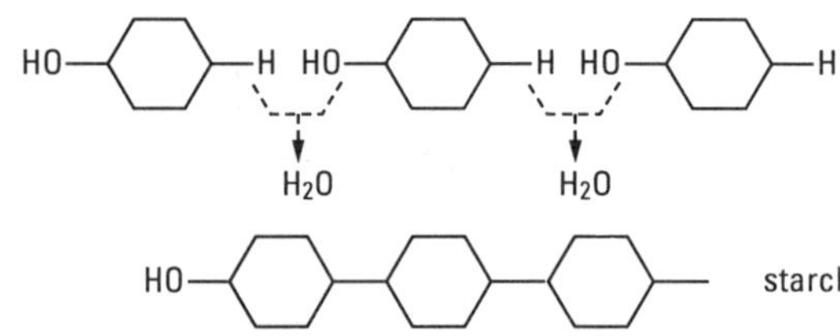

glucose

starch

add by losing a small molecule

Underline the *addition* polymers in the list of polymers below.

polypropylene   nylon   urea-formaldehyde   starch   polyvinylchloride   polyethene   protein

A3 Polymers have many useful properties:
- many are strong
- can be made into fibres
- easy to mould
- cheap to make.

It is now possible to design a polymer to do a particular job.

Complete this specification for a new polymer that is to be used as part of an engine housing in a new passenger aircraft.

Property	Specification
tensile strength	very high
thermal stability	
thermal conductivity	
melting point	above 1500 °C
boiling point	
solubility in water	
compression strength	
thermoplasticity	
biodegradability	

A4 Building materials are often **composite** – they contain two or more separate materials whose properties are combined in the new material. Examples of composite materials are glass-reinforced plastic, concrete, steel-reinforced concrete, bone and brick.

B1 The properties of a material depend on its internal structure. The structure can be altered deliberately to change the properties.

B2 Metals have a regular **crystalline** structure. The metallic lattice is **close-packed** – many atoms are present in a small space and the metal is therefore dense. The diagram opposite shows how the metallic structure enables the metal to be pulled into a wire. ❏

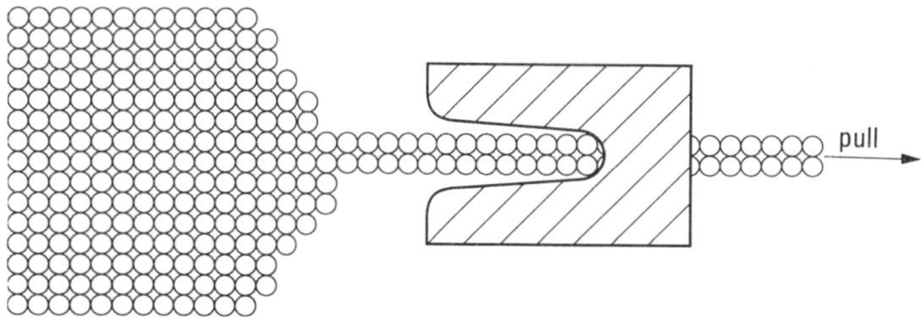

Draw a diagram similar to the one above to show the effect of alloying.

B3 Ceramics and glasses have a **network** structure. This makes them hard and gives them high melting points and boiling points. However, the atoms are locked together in the structure and it will break if enough force is exerted on it. This makes it brittle. ❏

This diagram shows the structure of quartz (ground-down quartz is a major constituent of glass). Work out the repeating unit in the structure and then write down the formula for quartz.

Formula:

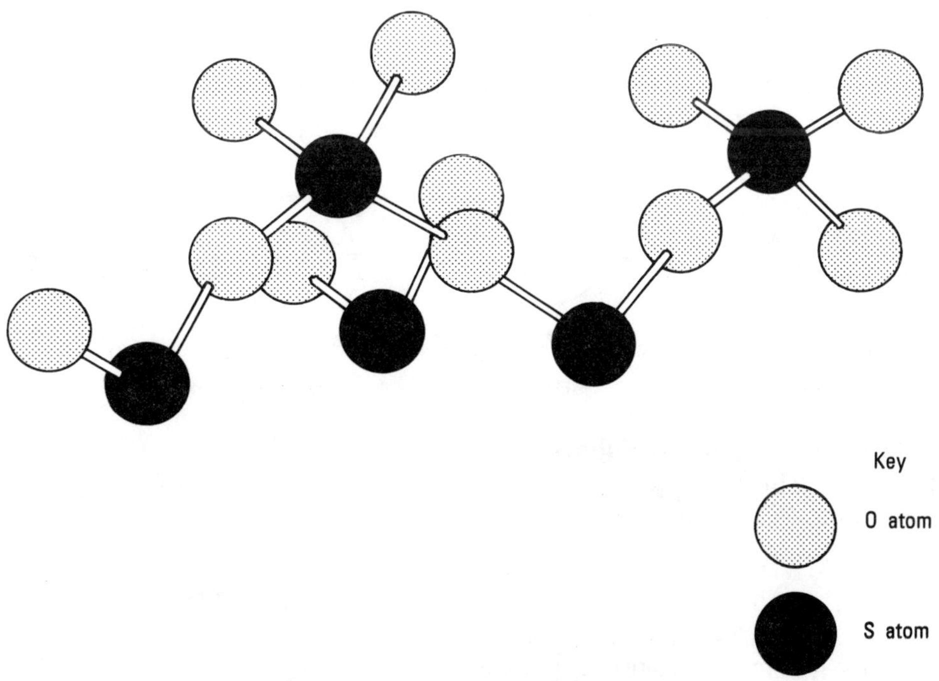

B4 Plastics and fibres are polymers. They have a thread-like structure, which is sometimes **cross-linked**. The amount of cross-linking affects the properties of the material. ❑

Predict the properties of the materials below, and list them underneath each diagram.

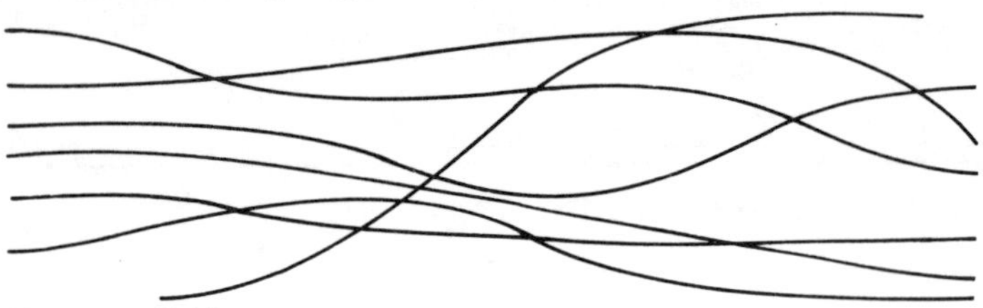

No cross-linking

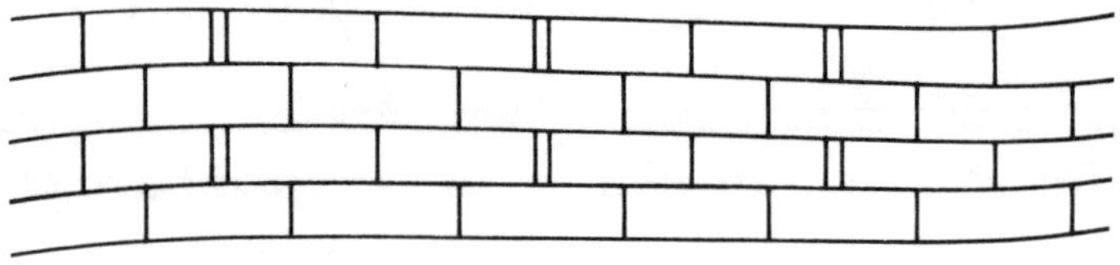

Lots of cross-linking

B5 Different materials have different **inter**molecular forces (forces between molecules). The **intra**molecular bonds within a molecule also vary. ❑

Label the *intermolecular forces* and *intramolecular* bonds in the diagrams below.

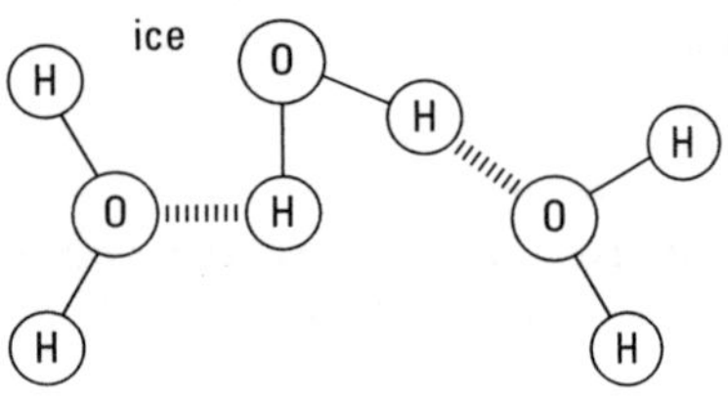

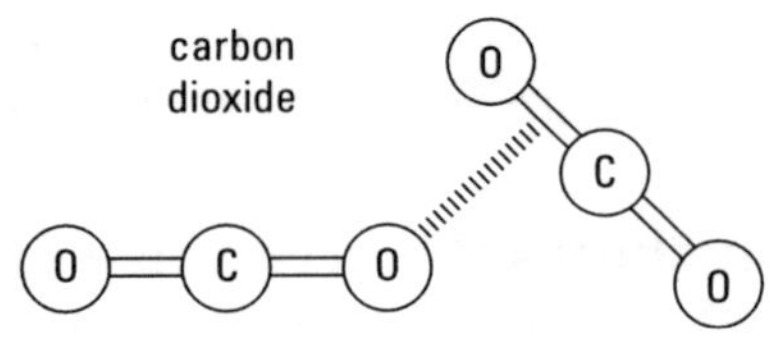

B6 A full outer shell of electrons is very stable. For example, Group 8 elements all have full outer shells; these gases are also very unreactive. ❑

B7 Atoms can become stable by reacting to form compounds. In a reaction, the atom is rearranged to have a full outer shell of electrons. ❑

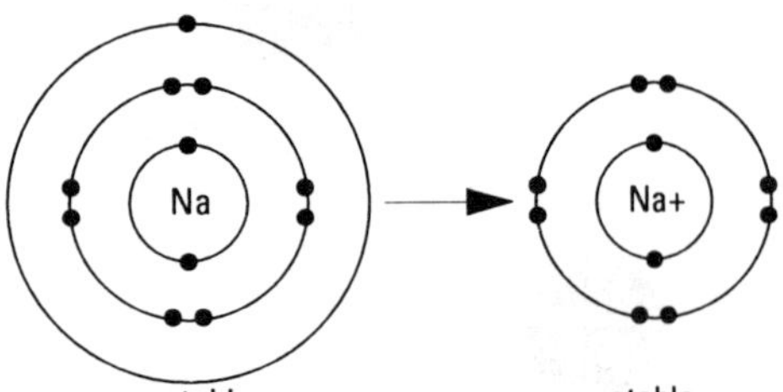

unstable stable

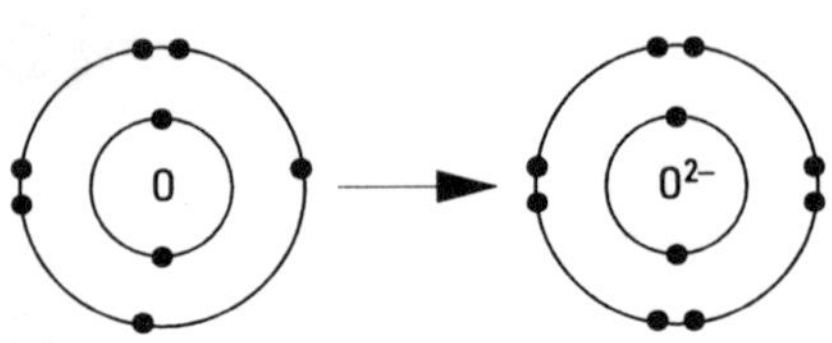

unstable stable

B8 In a covalent compound, the atoms share electrons to become stable, and a covalent bond is formed. ❑

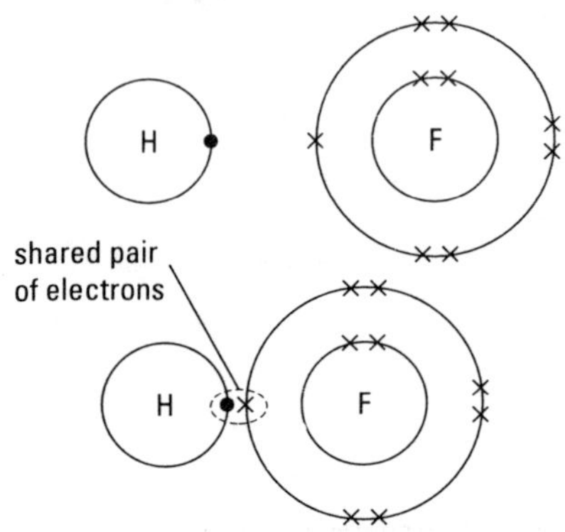

This diagram shows the outer shell electrons in a molecule of hydrogen fluoride. The H atom has a share of 2 electrons; the F atom has a share of 8 electrons. In this way, both atoms end up with a full outer shell. The shared pair of electrons is called a covalent bond. Note how the electrons are in pairs.

Draw diagrams similar to those on page 74 to show how the atoms in a molecule of water (H_2O) and a molecule of ammonia (NH_3) have become stable.

B9 In covalent compounds, the valency number of the constituents is the same as the number of electrons that were originally unpaired. ❑

Draw the outer electron shell of the following atoms and write the valency number of the atom underneath. The first one has been done for you.

carbon

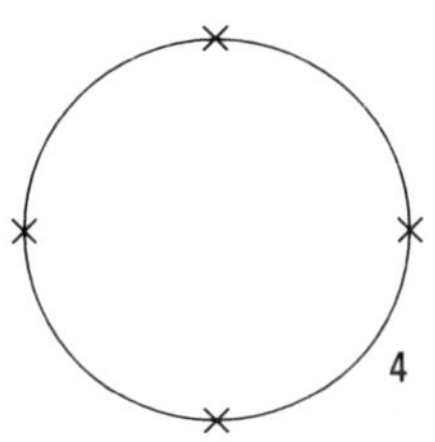

nitrogen

oxygen

fluorine

silicon

phosphorus

sulphur

chlorine

B10 In an ionic compound, electrons are transferred from the metal to the non-metal atom(s). The metal atom loses electrons and becomes a positively charged ion. The non-metal gains electrons and becomes a negatively charged ion. Ions of opposite charge attract and join to make a huge ionic lattice. ❑

Number the diagrams to show the correct sequence of events in the formation of the ionic lattice of sodium chloride.

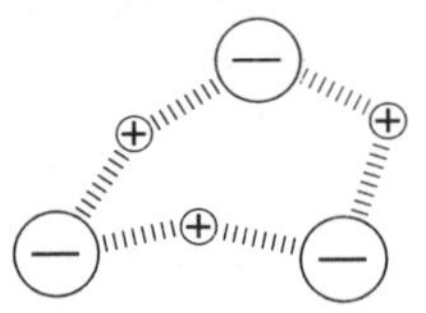

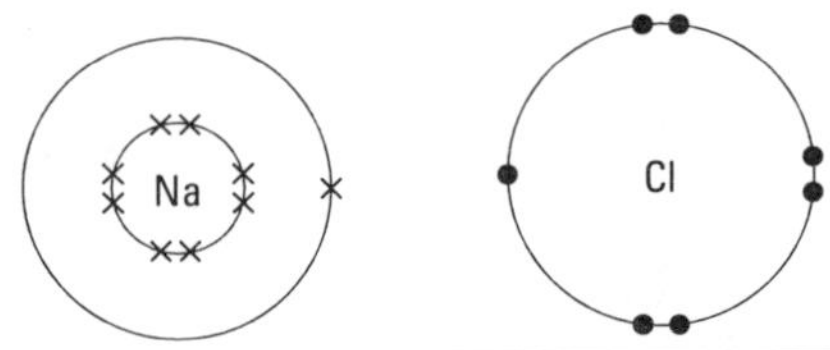

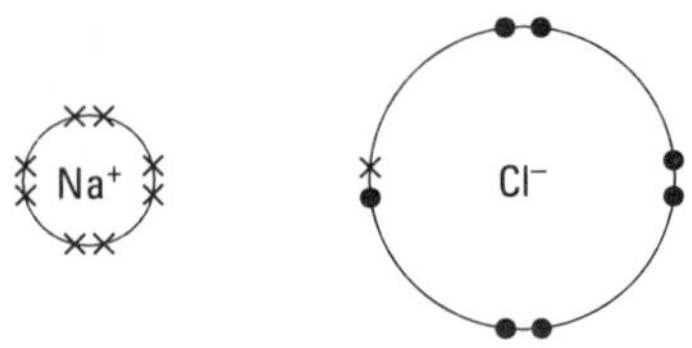

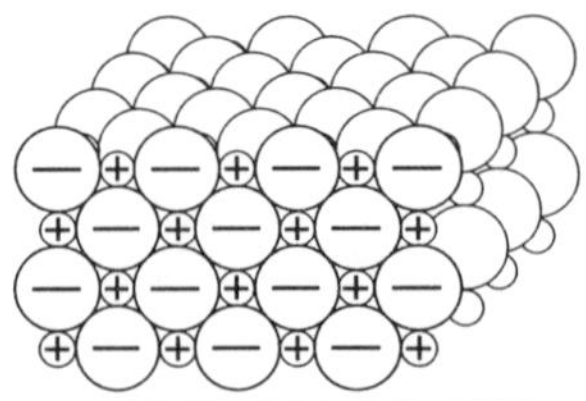

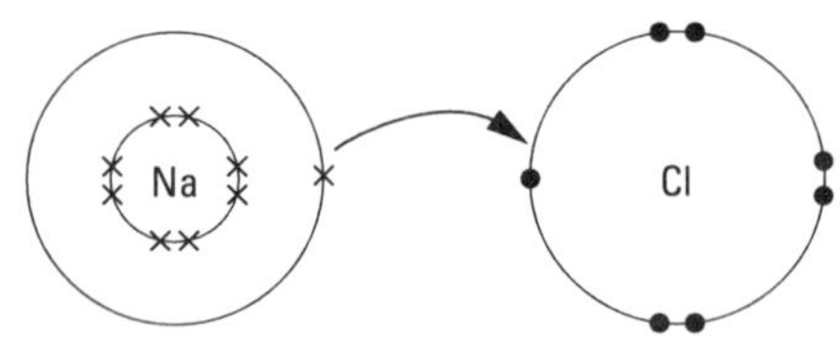

B11 The valency number of the constituents of an ionic compound is the same as the charge on the ion. ❑

Complete the table below.

	Metal				Non-metal		
Group	1	2	3	4	5	6	7
Electrons in outer shell	1				5		
To become stable		lose			gain		
	1				3		
Ion formed	+				3–		
Example	Na^+				N^{3-}		

B12 The outer electron shell of an atom therefore indicates
- whether the atom is a metal or a non-metal
- whether it forms ionic or covalent compounds
- the group and valency (and thus chemical properties) of the element. ❑

B13 The position of an element within a Group also indicates its chemical properties. ❑

The halogens are all poisonous non-metals in Group 7. Use this information (and that in B12) to describe what the halogens have in common.

B14 There are also some gradual changes in the properties of the elements as you descend Group 7. ❑

Complete the profiles below to show some of the differences in the Group 7 elements.

Element	Colour	Density	Reactivity	Displacement	Uses
F					water, toothpaste
Cl					bleach, pesticides
Br					film, petrol additive
I					antiseptic, film

B15 Many large atoms are radioactive. A radioactive sample becomes less active (**decays**) with time. **Half-life** is the time taken for half of the nuclei to decay. ❑

Complete this graph to show how the count-rate of the radioisotope ^{14}C changes with time. (The half-life of ^{14}C is 5600 years.)
Initial count rate = 100 cpm

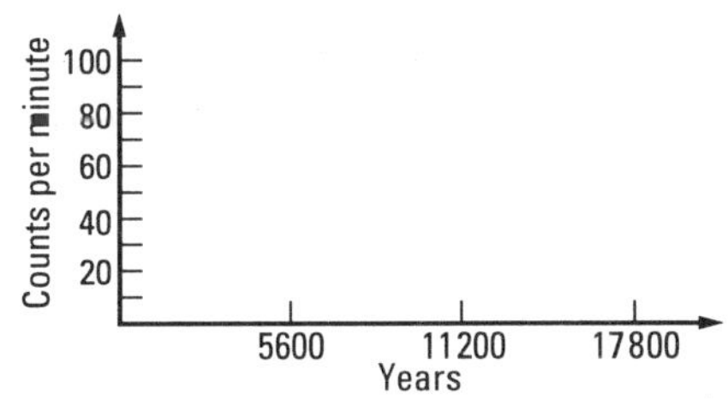

B16 Isotopes with a short half-life can be used in medicine because they decay quickly and therefore soon disappear from the body. Isotopes with medium half-lives are useful in industry. Isotopes with long, and very long half-lives can be used to date ancient objects and even rocks. ❑

Rearrange the following sentences by writing the letters in the correct boxes below to explain how ^{14}C can be used to date specimens that were once living.

a) The isotope decays by β emission at a known rate.
b) The level of ^{14}C in the body of an organism remains constant while it is alive.
c) ^{14}C is made constantly in the atmosphere by the action of neutrons on ^{14}N.
d) The count-rate gradually reduces over time.
e) ^{14}C is expelled from the body during respiration.
f) This replaces that lost by decay and the amount of ^{14}C in the atmosphere remains constant.
g) ^{14}C is taken into the body in food (or through photosynthesis).
h) From the present count-rate the time when the organism stopped respiring can be estimated.
i) After death the ^{14}C that decays is no longer replaced.

B17 Radioactive decay can be described by **nuclear equations**. A correct nuclear equation will show the type of radiation, the decay products and also account for all the protons and neutrons. The example below shows uranium-238 decaying by alpha emission. A nucleus of thorium-234 is produced. ❑

Check that all the protons and neutrons are accounted for in this nuclear equation by adding up the atomic numbers and the mass numbers on each side of the arrow.

$$^{238}_{92}U \rightarrow {}^{4}_{2}\alpha + {}^{234}_{90}Th$$

Write nuclear equations for the formation of ^{14}C in the atmosphere and also for its decay by ß emission.

C1 The **relative atomic mass (RAM)** of an atom of an element is its *average* mass. It is worked out by taking into account the abundance and mass of each of the element's isotopes. For example, natural chlorine is made of two isotopes. ❑

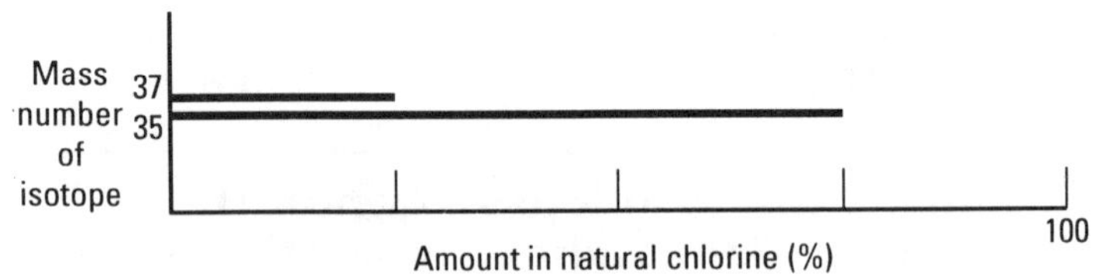

From the graph above, what is the average mass of a chlorine atom? (*Hint:* would it be nearer 35 or 37?)

C2 The RAM of chlorine is calculated as follows: ❑

$$\text{RAM} = \frac{(\text{mass of A} \times \%\text{ of A}) + (\text{mass of B} \times \%\text{ of B})}{100}$$

$$= \frac{(35 \times 75) + (37 \times 25)}{100}$$

$$= 35.5 \text{ amu (atomic mass units)}$$

Calculate the RAM of neon which contains two isotopes: $^{20}Ne(90\%)$ and $^{22}Ne(10\%)$.

C3 The **formula mass** of a substance is calculated by adding up the masses of all the atoms in the formula of the substance. For example,

$$\text{H—F} = 1 + 19 = 20 \text{ amu}$$ ❑

Examine the worked example and then complete the other examples:

Worked example:

calcium nitrate	hydrogen oxide	sodium fluoride	calcium carbonate
Formula: $Ca(NO_3)_2$			
RAM: 40 14 × 2 (16 × 3) × 2 = 40 + 28 + 96 = 164 amu			

C4 Single atomic particles are very small and impossible to weigh. We therefore use a quantity called the **mole** to measure the amount of a substance. The formula mass in grams of a substance contains 1 mole of particles, which is 6×10^{23}.

The number of moles, the mass and the formula mass are related. This triangle can be used to help you remember how: ❑

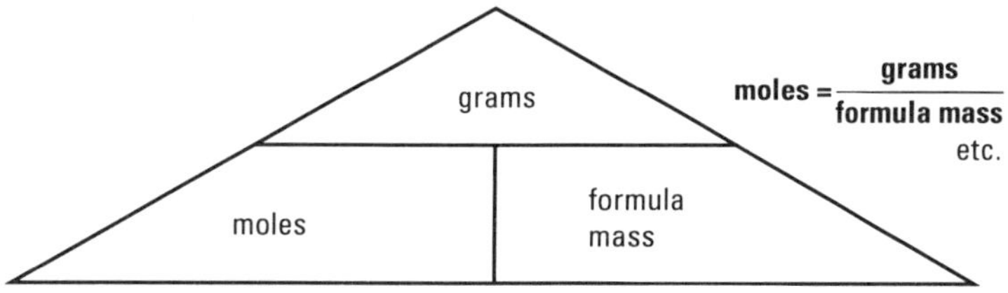

a) Work out how many grams there are in 2 moles of $CaCO_3$.

b) How many moles are there in 50 g of $CaCO_3$?

C5 The idea of the mole can be used with equations to calculate the quantity of product produced per mole of reactant. In any calculation from an equation you must always use the following steps:

● word equation:	carbon	+	oxygen	→	carbon monoxide
● balanced equation:	2C	+	O_2	→	2CO
	(2 atoms)		(1 molecule)		(2 molecules)
● moles:	2 moles		1 mole		2 moles
● in grams:	2×12 = 24 g		32 g		$2 \times (12 + 16)$ = 56 g

Note that:
- the moles do not balance on each side of the equation, but the grams do
- there is a line drawn across the page underneath the working. ❑

C6 The kind of working shown in C5 can be used to answer **calculation questions**. For example, how many grams of sodium oxide are produced by completely burning 2 moles of sodium?

word equation:	sodium	+	oxygen	→	sodium oxide
balanced equation:	4Na	+	O_2	→	$2Na_2O$
moles:	4 moles		1 mole		2 moles
in grams:	4×23 = 92 g		32 g		$2 \times (46 + 16)$ = 124 g

If the figures for Na are halved to become 2 moles then those for Na_2O will also be halved to become 62 g. ❑

Use the calculation on page 79 to work out how many grams of oxygen are required to burn:

2 moles of Na   10 moles of Na   46 g of Na   9.2 g of Na

C7 The **volume** occupied by 1 mole of a gas is the same for all gases at the same temperature and pressure. This fact can be used in equations where some of the substances are gaseous. For example:

	methane	+	oxygen	→	carbon dioxide	+	water
	CH_4	+	$2O_2$	→	CO_2	+	$2H_2O$
	1 mole		2 moles		1 mole		2 moles
For gases:	1 unit volume		2 units volume		1 unit volume		

This means that if there were 20 litres of methane, 40 litres of oxygen would be needed and 20 litres of carbon dioxide would be produced. ❏

Use the example given above to fill in the spaces:

If there were 15 cm^3 of methane, ... cm^3 of oxygen would be needed, and .... cm^3 of carbon dioxide would be produced.

C8 Calculate the mass of carbon dioxide produced when 50 g of calcium carbonate react with excess nitric acid.

word equation: calcium carbonate + nitric acid → calcium nitrate + carbon dioxide + water
balanced equation:
moles:
in grams:

If 50 g calcium carbonate react, ... g carbon dioxide are produced.

C9 In the example given in C8, assume 1 mole of a gas has a volume of 25 litres. How many litres of CO_2 would be produced?

C10 A mole of electrons has a total charge of 96 500 C. (This is known as the **Faraday constant.**) ❏

C11 During electrolysis, the positive metal ions gain electrons (are reduced). The negative ions lose electrons and are oxidised. The numbers that are gained or lost depend on the charges of the ions.

- **O**xidation **I**s **L**oss of electrons: **OIL**
- **R**eduction **I**s **G**ain of electrons: **RIG**. ❏

Write *R* for reduction and *O* for oxidation next to these equations:

$Zn \rightarrow Zn^{2+} + 2e^-$ ...... $4OH^- \rightarrow 2H_2O + O_2 + 4e^-$ ...... $NO_3^- + 2H^+ + e^- \rightarrow NO_2 + H_2O$ ......

$Ag^+ + e^- \rightarrow Ag$ ...... $Br_2 + 2e^- \rightarrow 2Br^-$ ...... $2H^+ + 2e^- \rightarrow H_2$ ......

C12 To produce 1 mole of an element from its ions during electrolysis, $\boldsymbol{n} \times$ **96 500 C** are needed, where n is the number of electrons involved in the oxidation or reduction reaction.

To produce copper: Cu^{2+} + $2e^-$ → Cu
1 mole, 2 moles, 1 mole
2 moles of electrons has a charge of 2 × 96 500 C.

To produce chlorine: $2Cl^-$ → Cl_2 + $2e^-$
2 moles, 1 mole, 2 moles
Again, 2 moles of electrons has a charge of 2 × 96 500 C. ❑

C13 The total charge passed during electrolysis is worked out by using the formula:

$$Q = I \times t$$

❑

Write down what the symbols in the formula above represent and what unit each variable is measured in.

C14 When the total charge that passes during an electrolysis has been worked out, we can use the relationship nF for 1 mole (see **C12** above) to calculate how many moles of substance are produced by this charge.

For example, in copper production:
$n\text{F} = 2 \times 96\ 500$ C,
which is 193 000 C for 1 mole.
If 1930 C are used during an electrolysis, then 1930 divided by 193 000 of a mole of Cu will be produced. ❑

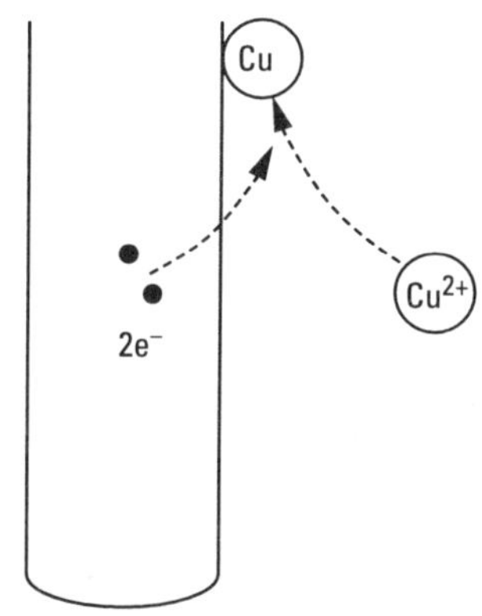

each Cu^{2+} takes two electrons, so one mole of Cu^{2+} takes two moles of electrons

C15 Atoms join together by forming chemical bonds. Energy is released when bonds are formed and energy is required when bonds are broken. Such **bond energies** are usually measured in kilojoules per mole. ❑

C16 A chemical reaction involves bond-breaking and bond-making.

- If the bond-breaking energy is greater than the bond-making energy then the reaction is **endothermic**.
- If the bond-making energy is greater than the bond-breaking energy then the reaction is **exothermic**.

In the example below, methane is burned completely to produce water and carbon dioxide.

Reactants			**Products**	
$CH_4 + 2O_2$		⟶	$CO_2 + 2H_2O$	
break 4 C–H = 4 × 414	= 1656		make 2 C=O = 2 × 724	= 1448
break 2 O=O = 2 × 497	= 994		make 4O–H = 4 × 458	= 1832
Total bond-breaking energy	= **2650**		Total bond-making energy	= **3280**

Overall energy = (energy in – energy out) = 2650 – 3280 = –630 kJ mol^{-1}

The minus sign shows that the reaction is exothermic. ❑

Complete an energy picture like the one in C16 on page 81 for the reaction $H_2 + Cl_2 \rightarrow 2HCl$.

Bond energies in kJ mol^{-1} are: H–H (436), Cl–Cl (243), H–Cl (431).

C17 A chemical reaction needs energy to get started. This is called the **activation energy** and it enables the particles to collide successfully. ❑

Mark the activation energy on the graph below (in the same way as the energy released in the reaction is marked).

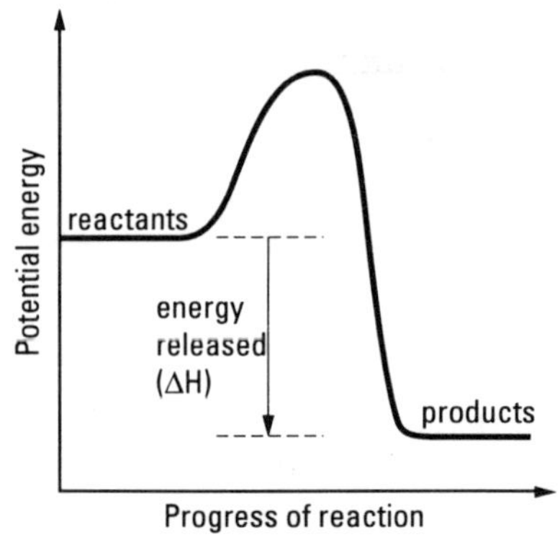

C18 Industry uses a wide variety of chemical processes to manufacture materials. Any chemical process should be **evaluated**, using a range of scientific information, for its effect on people and the environment, in addition to considering its economic importance. ❑

C19 The **chlor-alkali industry** uses salt as a raw material. Salt solution is electrolysed to produce sodium hydroxide solution, hydrogen and chlorine. ❑

Label the diagram of the membrane electrolysis cell to show where the three products form.

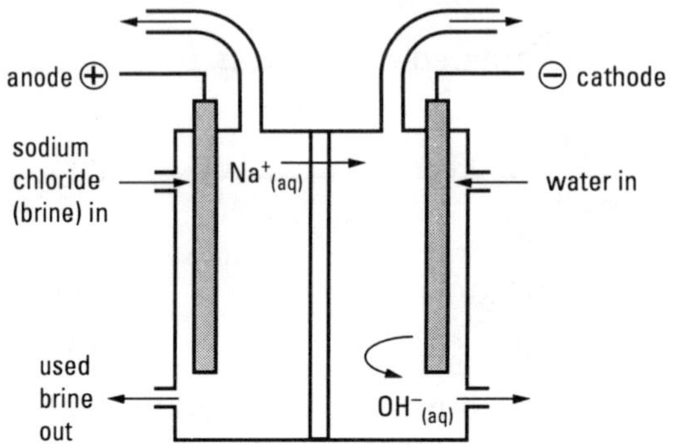

C20 The three products of the chlor-alkali process are sold to other companies who use them to make a variety of useful materials. ❑

From your knowledge of the chlor-alkali process, complete the table below.

Raw materials: salt, water

Cost of process: electricity, ..., ...

Product	Sold to make	Benefits	Drawbacks
	pesticides PVC bleach clean water		
	margarine hydrochloric acid		
	paper soaps/detergents synthetic materials		

C21 The fertiliser industry uses raw materials to manufacture chemical compounds that contain nitrogen, phosphorus or potassium (for example, ammonium nitrate).

For example **1** $N_2 + 3H_2 \Leftrightarrow 2NH_3$

then **2** $NH_3 + HNO_3 \rightarrow NH_4NO_3$ ❑

Identify the reversible reaction above and give three ways in which the manufacturers ensure that a high yield of product is maintained.

Number .... is reversible.

High yield of product maintained by 1 ....

2 ....

3 ....

D1 Air at ground level is compressed by the mass of air above it. Air is therefore more dense at sea-level and the air pressure is higher. **Infra-red radiation** from the Sun heats the ground, which in turn heats the air near to it causing the air to expand, become less dense and rise upwards. As a block of warm air rises, it also **spins** because of the spinning of the Earth. Warm air may also be damp, and a lot of energy is therefore trapped in it as **latent heat** (the energy needed to evaporate the water that it contains). ❑

Name three sources of energy that contribute to the energy of the atmosphere.

1 .... 2 .... 3 ....

D2 Warm, damp air rises and loses a lot of energy as it cools. The water vapour condenses and releases its latent heat; the fast-moving air molecules slow down. This release of energy can cause violent storms such as hurricanes. ❑

D3 Cold polar air flows to the hot equator and warm tropical air flows to the poles. Air at different temperatures does not mix easily and so high-level fast winds called the **jet-streams** are formed, travelling west to east as the Earth spins. ❑

Show on the diagram how the jet-stream over Britain can 'wobble' and give us highs (from warm tropical air) or lows (from cool polar air).

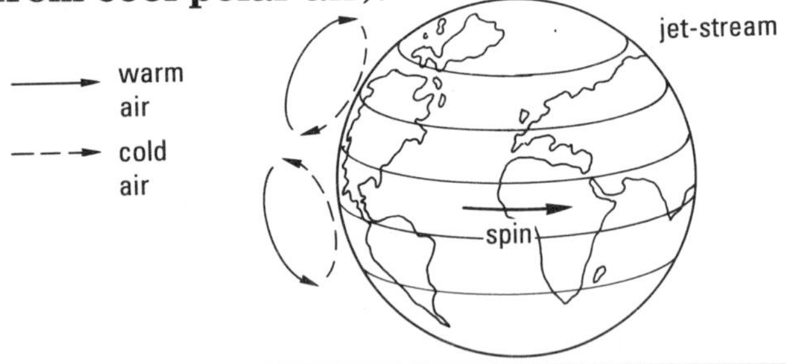

D4 The Earth is layered. ❑

Draw the Earth's layers on the cut-away diagram and add the following labels:

inner core (solid)   outer core (liquid)   crust   mantle

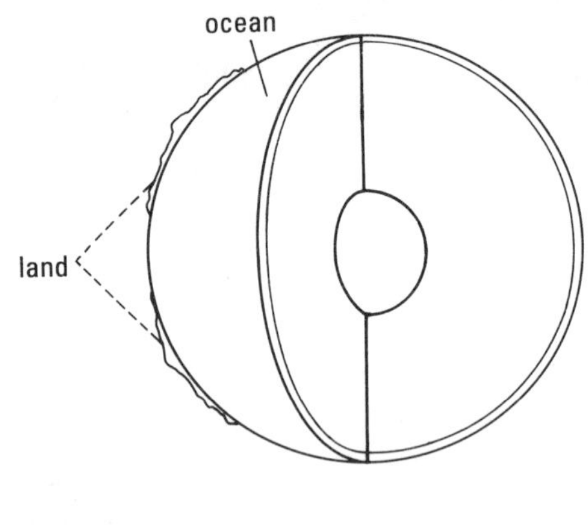

D5 **Earthquakes** produce energy waves which are recorded and analysed at **seismic** stations. These waves are refracted by different materials. This property has allowed scientists to establish that the core is metallic, probably largely iron and nickel, whereas the mantle is made of many compounds. The oceanic crust is mainly basalt and the upper continental crust contains a lot of granite. ❑

D6 The inside of the Earth is hot and much of it is molten. Energy escapes to the solid surface by **convection** currents which cause magma to ooze out and release heat. This magma then solidifies and forms new crust. Elsewhere, old crust sinks into the mantle and is reabsorbed. ❑

Label these features on the diagram:

mid-ocean ridge   ocean plate   hot magma   direction of convection current

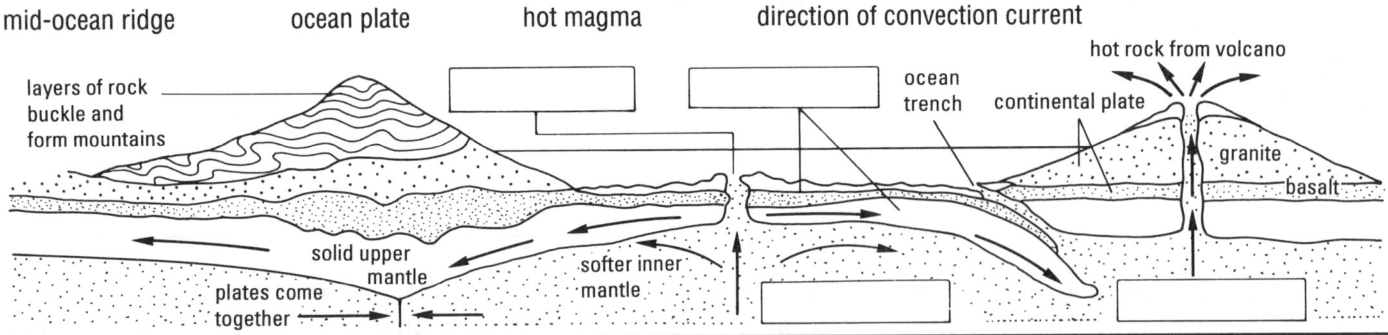

D7 The Earth's crust is divided into sections called **plates**. The plates move relative to each other because of the convection currents in the mantle. At the plate boundaries, several processes can lead to new features forming in the crust. **Plate tectonics** describe and explain this slow-acting yet dynamic change. ❑

Draw lines to match the processes with the features they create.

Process	Feature
plates slide past one another	fold mountains and trenches
plates collide and crumple at the edges	mid-ocean ridges
plates separate as new material is extruded	fault lines which are susceptible to earthquakes

ATTAINMENT TARGET 4

Physical processes

Big ideas

A Electricity and magnetism can be controlled to serve human needs.
B We face difficult energy choices; energy transfers take place in any process.
C Designing and building things requires an understanding of forces and their effects.
D How light and sound behave depends on the properties of waves.
D Theories and observations help to explain the Earth's place in the universe.

A1 Electric circuits are made up of a number of components. Circuits can be built by following a **circuit diagram** in which the components are shown as symbols. The flow of electric charges round a circuit is called the **current**. ❑

Draw lines to match each component and its symbol to its correct function.

Component

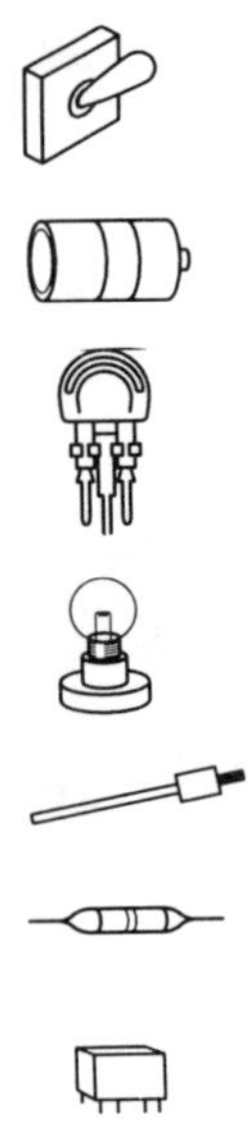

Symbol

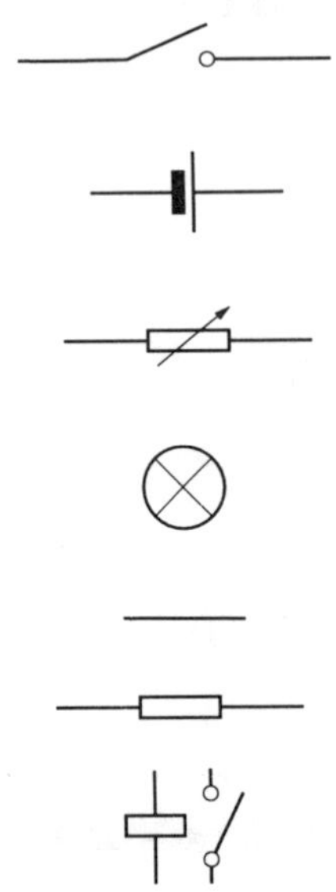

Function

changes electrical energy into light (and heat) energy

conducts electrical charges around a circuit

provides the energy to push the electrical charges round a circuit

opens or closes a circuit to stop or start the flow of electric charges

reduces the electric current by a fixed amount

varies the size of electric current as it is adjusted

a switch turned on or off by an electric current

A2 Circuits can be set up with all the components on a single loop or branch – a **series circuit** – or with components on several different branches – a **parallel circuit**. ❑

Label each circuit *series* or *parallel*. Describe what happens in each circuit when the switch is closed.

....

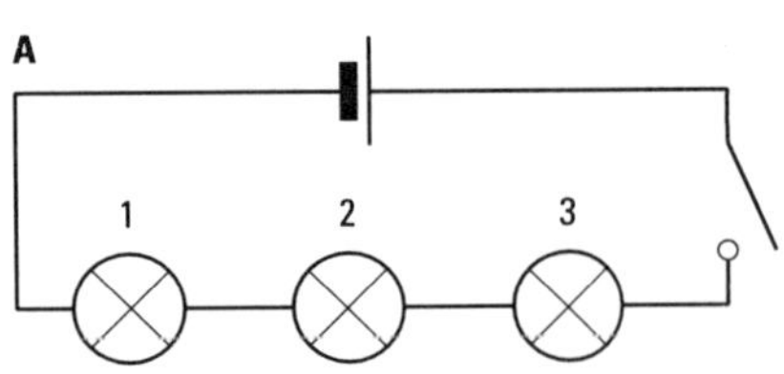

....

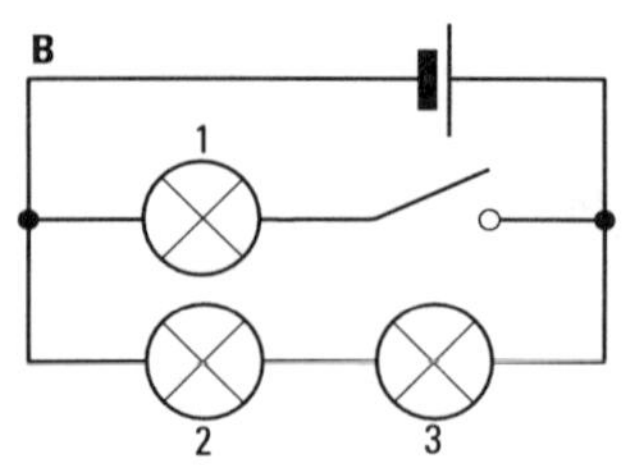

A3 In a series circuit, if one bulb fails the current stops. In a parallel circuit, if a bulb fails on one branch the current can flow through the other branch of the circuit. ❑

Look at the two circuits in A2 on page 86 again. Describe what happens to bulbs 2 and 3 in each circuit, with the switch closed, if bulb 1 fails.

In circuit A

In circuit B

A4 Some electrical components conduct electricity better than others. They have a lower **electrical resistance**. For example, a thick wire has a lower resistance than a thin wire. ❑

A5 The energy needed to make electric charge or current flow in a circuit is measured in **volts**. The **voltage** in a simple circuit is supplied by the cell or battery. The more cells there are in a circuit the higher the voltage will be, and the higher the current. ❑

A6 Components such as bulbs offer resistance to the current. The more bulbs there are in a circuit the higher the resistance will be, and the lower the current. If the current through a bulb increases the bulb glows more brightly. ❑

Complete the sentences to say what you could do to alter the current in the circuit shown.

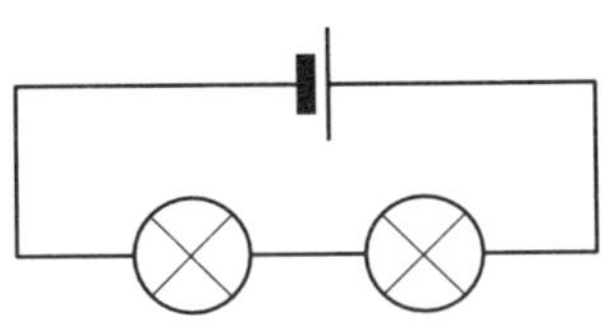

Increase the current by adding .... or by removing .... .Decrease the current by .... or by ....

A7 The electric charges that move in a circuit are **electrons** – part of the atoms of the conductor. Electrons have a negative charge. ❑

A8 When some materials are rubbed together, such as plastic being rubbed with a cloth, electrons are moved from one object to the other. The object that gains electrons becomes negatively charged. The object that loses electrons becomes positively charged. This causes **static electricity**. ❑

Label the diagrams below using the terms *balanced charges* and *unbalanced charges*.

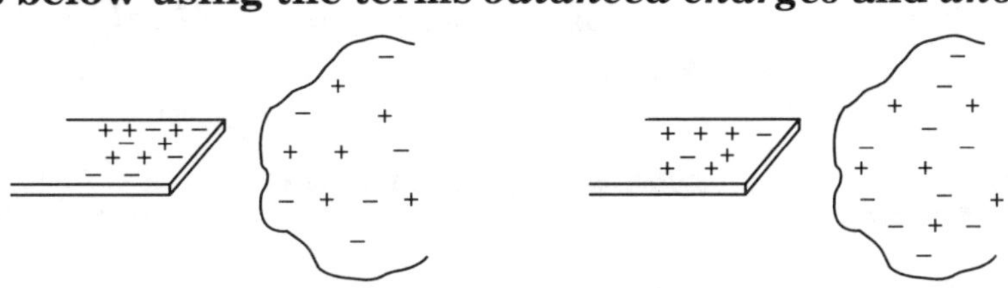

A9 Static electricity can move (**discharge**) onto a conductor causing a spark. This can be dangerous, for example if an object discharges near petrol or explosive gases. ❑

Give two common examples of static electricity discharging.

1 .... 2 ....

A10 Electrical **appliances** are made safe by
- wiring the plug correctly
- having a fuse in the plug to prevent too high a current flowing
- having an earth wire to conduct any charge that builds up to earth
- double insulating – making sure that no wires touch any metal part of the appliance. ❑

Label the three wires in the plug *live, neutral, earth.* Colour the wires correctly.

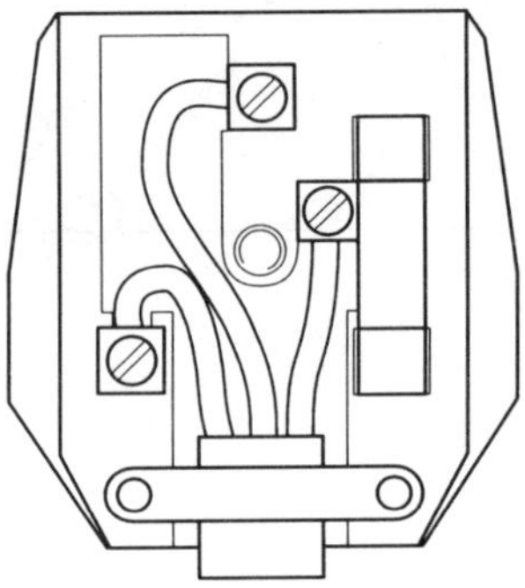

A11 **Electronic systems** have three parts: **input**, **processor** and **output**. The input can be a sensor and the processor can be made up of logic gates. ❑

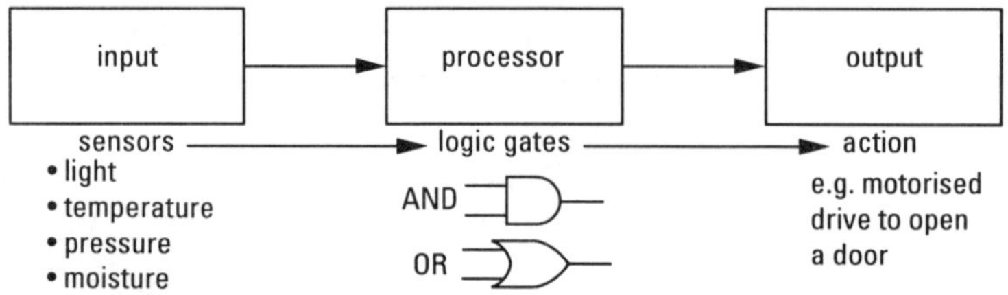

Design two circuits using the system shown above. *Circuit 1:* doors open when it becomes light or the temperature rises; *Circuit 2:* a light goes on when it gets dark or someone stands on a pressure pad.

Circuit 1

Circuit 2

A12 Electronic circuits may also contain **capacitors** and **transistors**. Capacitors are used to delay the processing part of a system and transistors act as switches or amplifiers. An **electronic chip** can contain a large number of transistors joined together to form **logic gates**. ❑

Complete the table.

Electric component	Symbol	Function in electronic circuits
capacitor		
	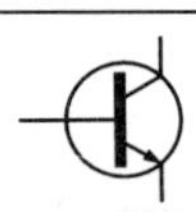	

B1 **Energy** is transferred from one form to another in any process. For example, when
- a light goes on: electrical to light
- a clockwork toy starts: potential (stored) to kinetic (movement)
- a solar panel drives a motor: light to electrical ❑

Complete the energy transfers in the two processes below. Choose the energy forms from this list:

heat light sound nuclear electrical kinetic potential chemical

1 boiling water in a kettle: .... to ....

2 photosynthesis: .... to ....

Suggest a process in which each of the following energy transfers takes place.

3 electrical → sound: ....

4 kinetic → electrical: ....

B2 In many processes there are several **energy transfers**. For example, in a hydroelectric power station:

potential → kinetic → electrical ❑

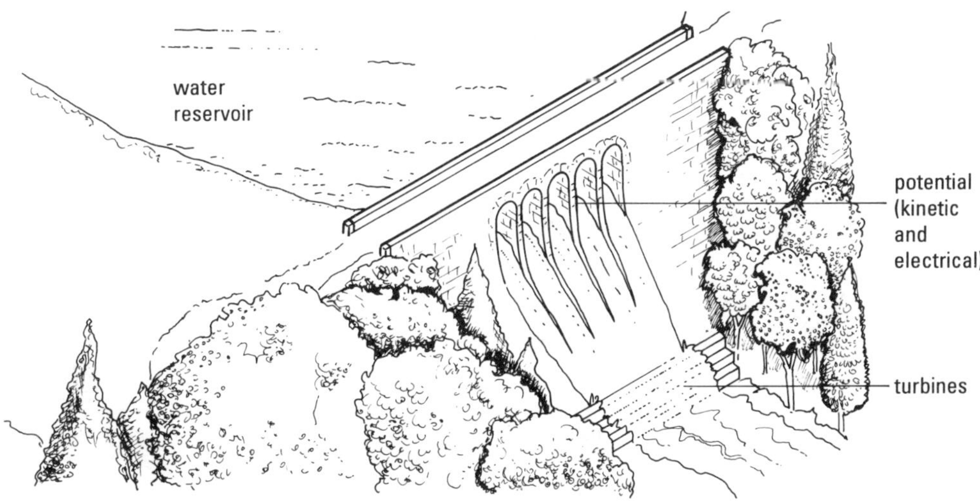

Write down the energy transfers in a power station that uses fossil fuels.

coal, oil or gas burned	→	water turned to steam	→	steam turns turbine	→	electricity generated
....	→	....	→	....	→	....

B3 No energy is lost in any energy transfer but some is wasted (changed to a form that is not useful). Because energy is **conserved** the total energy input always equals the total energy output. ❑

Underline or highlight the waste energy below.

1 chemical reactions, e.g. combustion:

chemical → heat + light + sound

2 food chains:

chemical → chemical + heat + kinetic

Complete the following energy transfers, then underline or highlight the wasted energy.

1 playing a radio: electrical → .... + ...

2 battery-powered car: .... → .... + heat

B4 Electrical energy can be generated from **energy sources** that are either **non-renewable** or **renewable**. ❑

Write the correct heading – *renewable* or *non-renewable* – above each column in the table. Then write the correct energy sources from the list under each heading.

______________________	______________________
energy sources that will eventually run out	energy sources that are not used up

Energy sources list

coal	oil
wind	sunshine
gas	water
nuclear fuel	waves

B5 The Sun is the starting point for many of our energy sources. Energy flow in a **food chain** depends on plants using solar energy in **photosynthesis**. Coal, oil and gas are all **fossil fuels** produced over millions of years from dead plants and animals. These were once part of food chains and were therefore ultimately dependent on the Sun. ❑

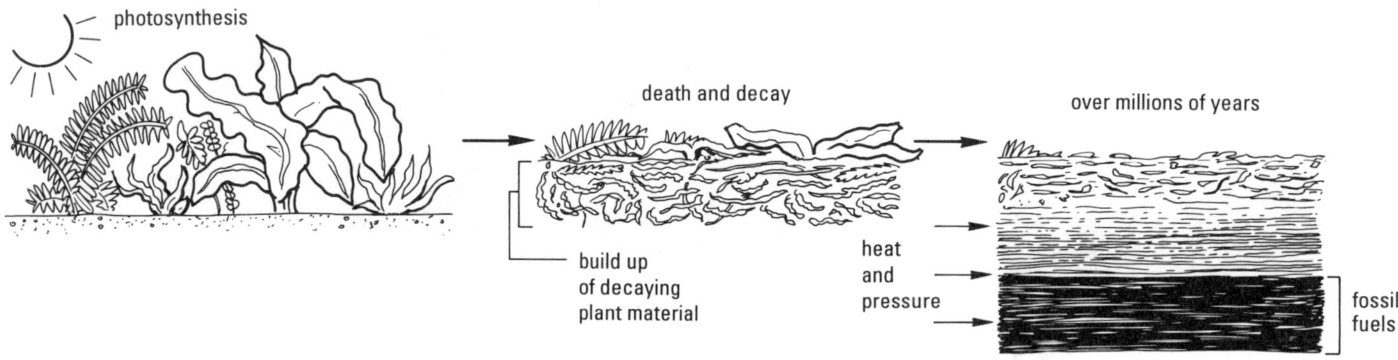

Use the information below to draw a bar chart using the axes provided. Give the chart a suitable title.

If fossil fuels continue to be used at the present rate oil will last about 60 years, coal about 300 years and gas around 50 years.

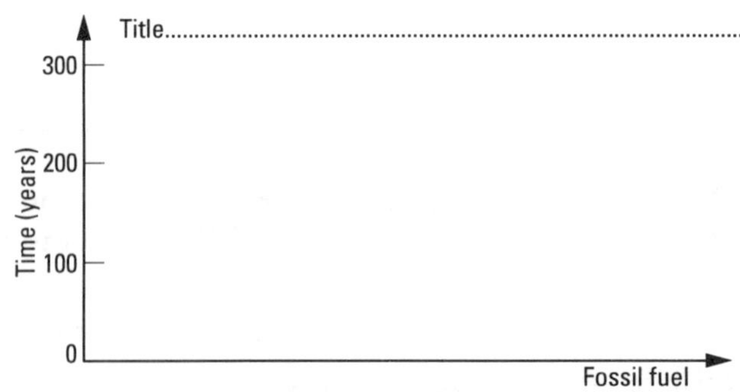

B6 Solar energy can be used directly as an energy source. It is also involved in creating weather changes that affect winds and waves. ❑

B7 Energy is measured in **joules** (J). 1000 joules = 1 kilojoule (kJ) ❑

C1 **Force** is measured in **newtons** (N). ❑

C2 There are several different types of forces:
● pushing or bending ● squashing ● pulling or stretching ● twisting ● tearing. ❑

What is the main force acting in each of these situations?

friction slowing a car	....	rolling a snowball	....
jumping on a sandcastle	....	magnet attracting a nail	....
charged comb attracting paper	....	ripping up paper	....
opening a jam jar	....	gravity acting on a ball	....

C3 An object can be affected by more than one force, and forces can act in different directions. A bridge is a good example. ❑

C4 Living organisms have features that allow them to withstand damaging forces. Man-made objects are also designed to withstand damaging forces. ❑

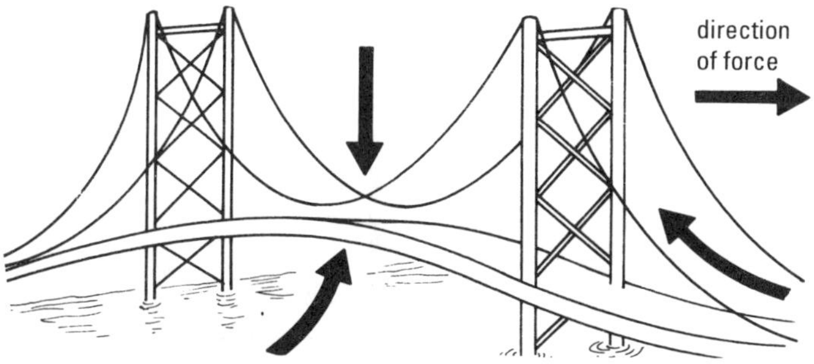

Write down the type of force that each feature is designed to withstand.

hollow stems in waterweeds

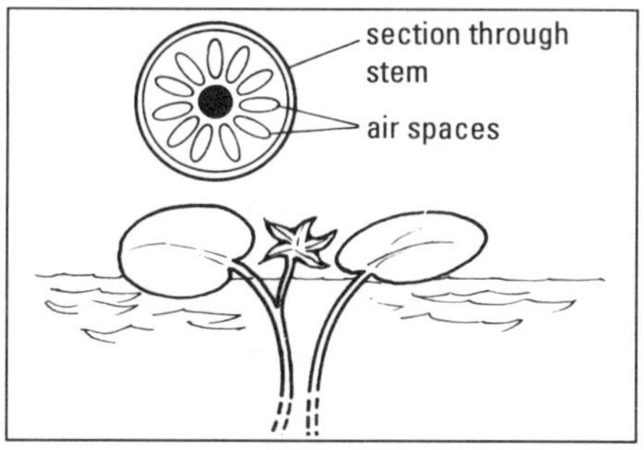

....

pillars supporting a roadway

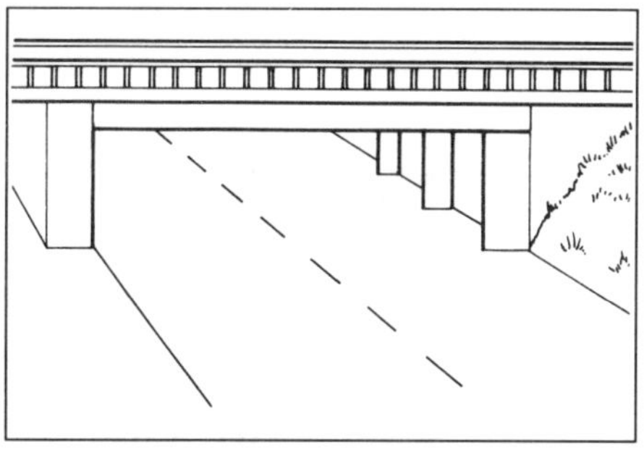

....

ropes to hold down a tent

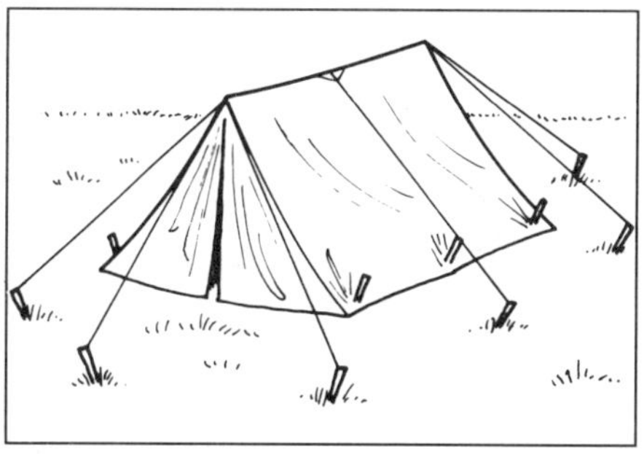

....

C5 When the forces on an object are **balanced** the object will be:
- at rest
- floating
- moving at a steady speed. ❑

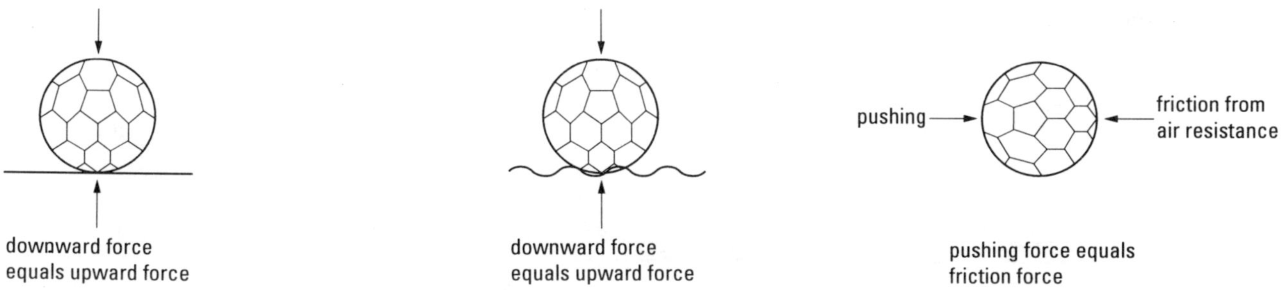

balanced forces acting on a ball

C6 When forces do not balance the **resultant force** will make the object:
- move more slowly (decelerate)
- move more quickly (accelerate)
- change direction.

For example, when a parachutist jumps from a plane. ❑

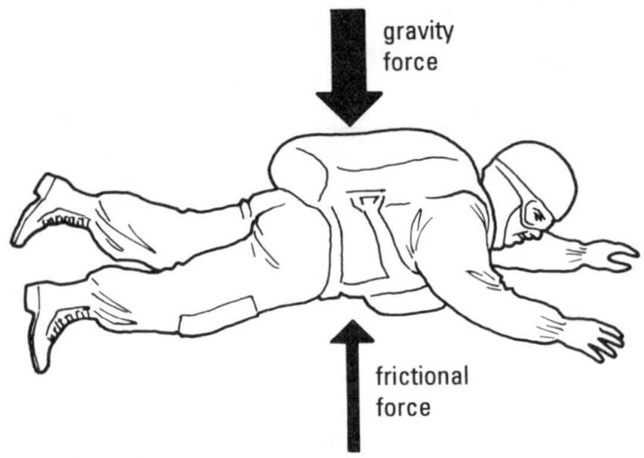

at first the parachutist accelerates because the force of gravity is bigger than the frictional force of air resistance

when the parachute opens the force of friction is bigger than the force of gravity. The parachutist decelerates

Write *accelerate, decelerate* or *change direction* above each diagram.

....

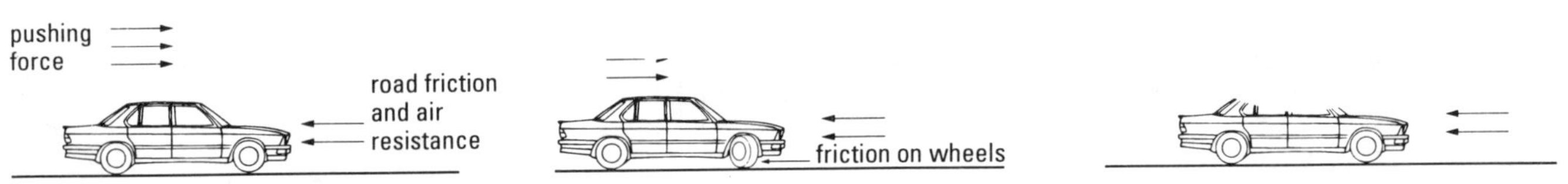

C7 The **average speed** of an object depends on the distance travelled and the time taken.

$$\text{average speed } (v) = \frac{\text{distance travelled } (s)}{\text{time taken } (t)} \quad \text{or} \quad v = \frac{s}{t}$$ ❑

Write down the formula for *time taken* and *distance travelled*. Calculate the answer to the problem.

time taken, t =

distance travelled, s =

What is the average speed of a car travelling 720 km in 4.8 hrs?

C8 When a force presses on a small area, it exerts a large **pressure**. The same force applied to a larger area exerts less pressure. For example, the same person exerts a different amount of pressure on the ground depending on the shoes they wear. ❑

C9 Pressure is measured in units called **pascals** (Pa). ❑

the force spread over a smaller area

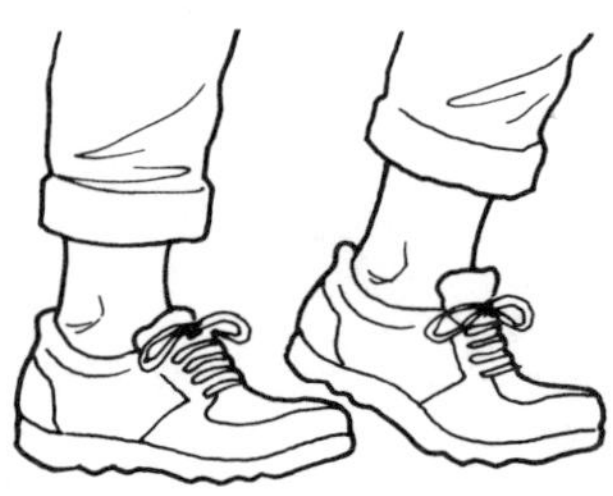

the force spread over a large area

Cross out the two incorrect formulae for calculating pressure. Calculate the pressure in the example given.

pressure = force × area

$$\text{pressure} = \frac{\text{force}}{\text{area}}$$

$$\text{pressure} = \frac{\text{area}}{\text{force}}$$

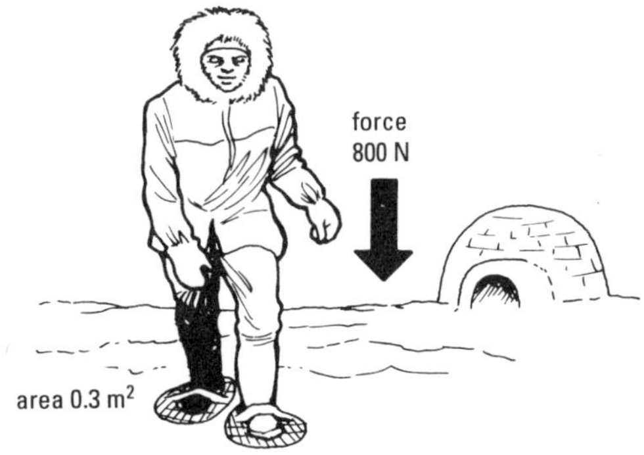

D1 When light strikes an object some light is absorbed by the object, some light passes through the object and some light is **reflected**. The reflected light is detected by our eyes and this allows the object to be seen. ❑

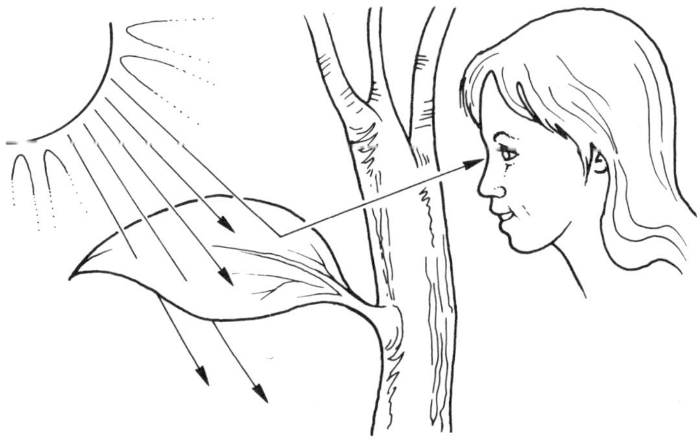

D2 Both light and sound travel through the air as **waves**. However, their speeds are very different:
- light travels at 300 million metres per second (3×10^8 m/s)
- sound travels at 340 metres per second (340 m/s). ❑

Explain *one* of the following:
a) why you can see a ball leaving a cricket bat before you hear the thump, *or*
b) why you see the flash of a gun before you hear the bang.

D3 Sounds are produced when an object vibrates. The **vibrations** cause tiny pressure changes in the air, which are **transmitted** (passed) through the air in a straight line. ❑

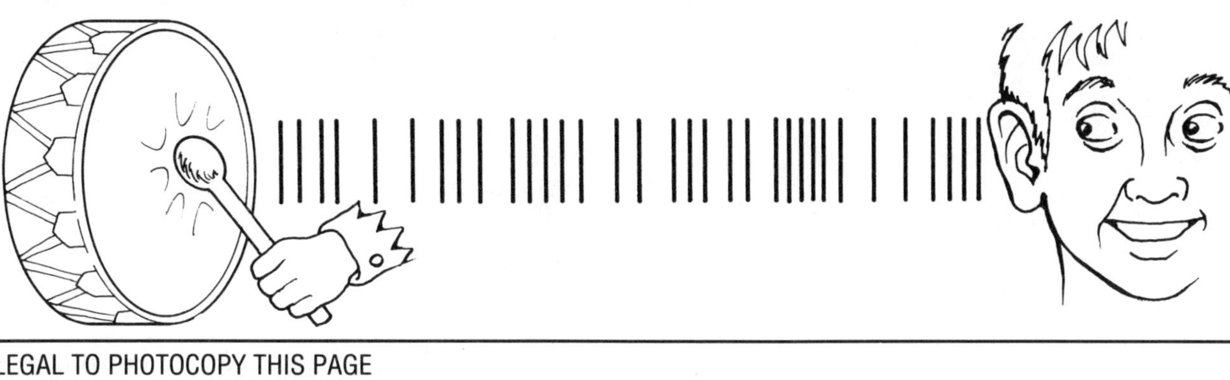

D4 An **oscilloscope** produces a graph of the changes in pressure caused by sound. Two important characteristics of sound can be compared using these graphs:

- loudness depends on the energy of the sound wave. The amount that the pressure of the air changes above or below the normal is called the **amplitude** of the change;
- how high or low the sound is (the **pitch**) depends on the number of vibrations per second. This is measured in units called **hertz** (Hz). ❑

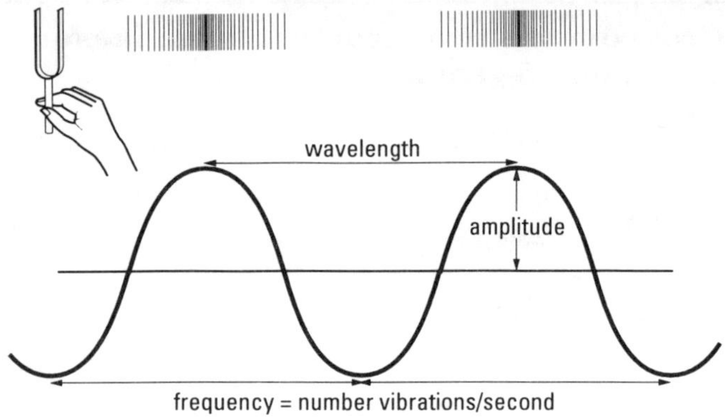

Label the pairs of oscilloscope graphs correctly. Choose from:

same pitch, different loudness   different pitch, different loudness   different pitch, same loudness

Describe the sound in each diagram by writing *high* or *low*, and *loud* or *soft* under each graph.

....

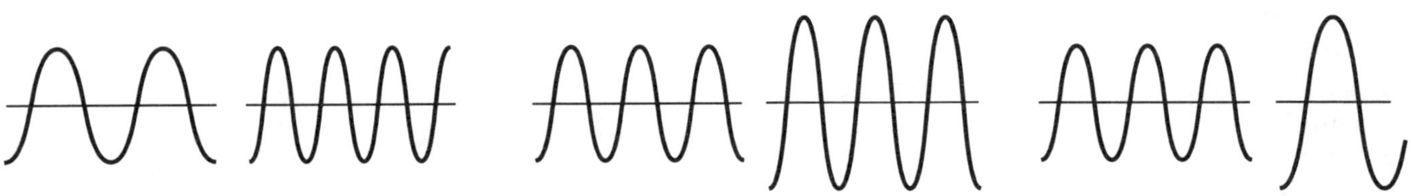

sound ....

D5 In woodwind or brass musical instruments a column of air vibrates to create sound. In stringed instruments the strings vibrate, whereas in percussion instruments it is the skin or metal that vibrates. Altering the length of the vibrating string or air column alters the pitch of the note produced. The shorter the length the higher the pitch. ❑

Put an *H* beside the instrument in each pair that would produce the higher note.

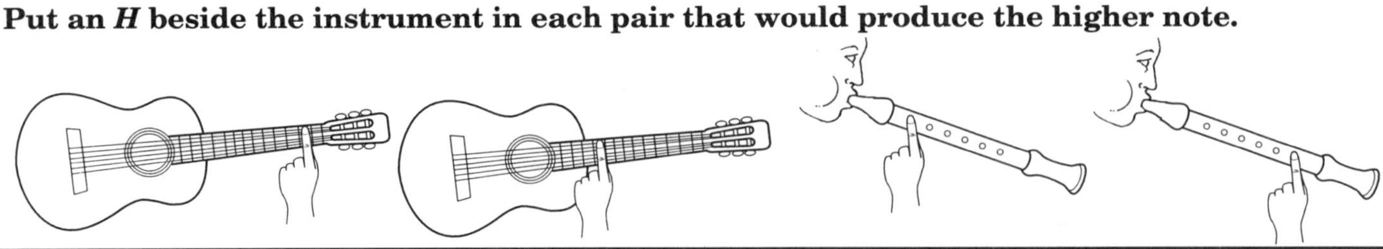

E1 The **Solar System** is the name we give to the Sun and the nine planets (one of which is the Earth) that **orbit** it. There are four inner planets and, much further away, five outer planets. For most of its orbit, Pluto is the outermost planet but at some points in its orbit it comes closer to the Sun than Neptune. All of the planets orbit the Sun on approximately the same plane or level. ❑

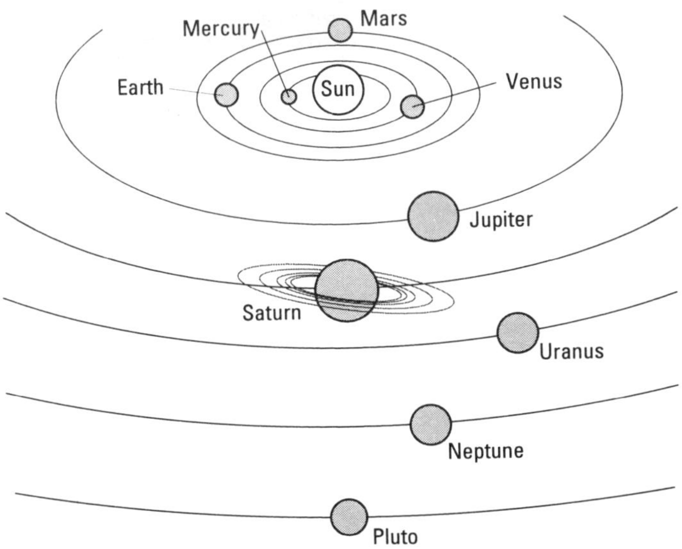

Write the names of the planets in the table below.

Planet	Time for 1 revolution of the Sun
	88 days
	224 days
	365 days
	687 days
	11.9 years
	29.5 years
	84 years
	165 years
	248 years

E2 The Earth spins or rotates from west to east as it orbits the Sun. It is tilted on its **axis** as it spins. This explains why we experience:

- differences in daylength at different points on Earth
- night and day
- the four seasons. ❑

On the following diagram, shade in the night side of Earth. Label *night* and *day*.

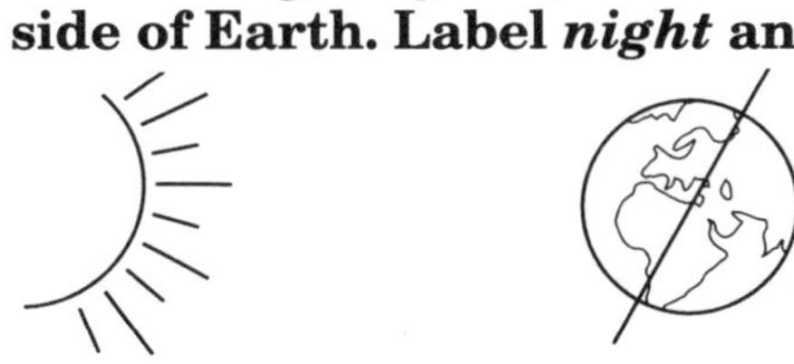

On the diagram below, label *summer in northern hemisphere* and *winter in northern hemisphere*.

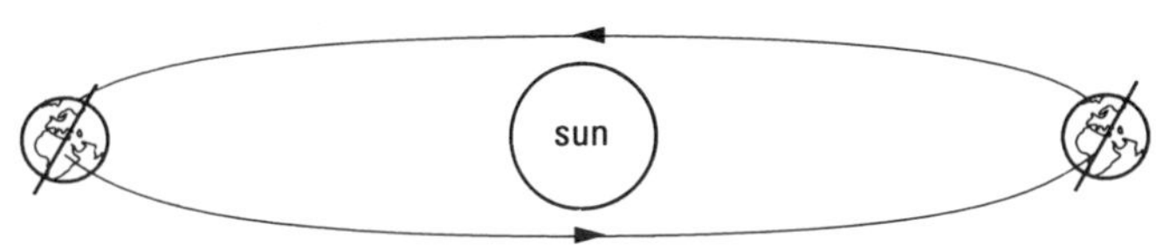

E3 The Solar System forms part of a **galaxy** known as the **Milky Way**, which is part of a large system called the **universe.** There are millions of stars in our galaxy, which is in a local cluster of about 19 galaxies, and there are millions of galaxies in the universe. ❑

Write the following in order of increasing size:

galaxy   planet   Solar System   Sun   universe

....

smallest   largest

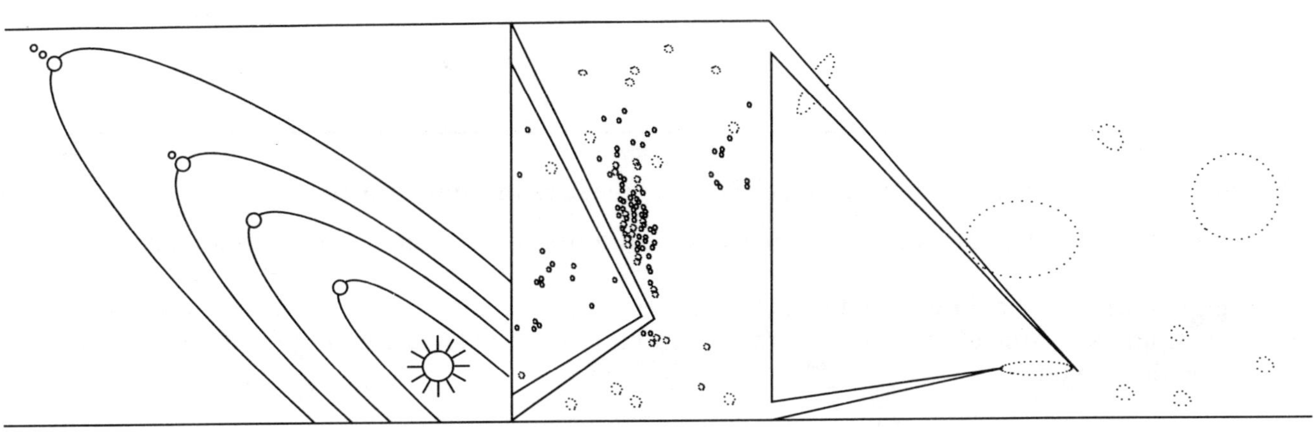

Our solar system   The Milky Way   A cluster of galaxies in the Universe

A1 Electricity needs:

- an electric charge that is free to move – this is the current, measured in **amperes** (amps) using an **ammeter**
- energy to move the electric charge – this is the voltage, measured in **volts** using a **voltmeter**
- an electrical conductor that will have a low resistance, measured in **ohms**. ❏

A2 The rule that connects current, voltage and resistance in metals and carbon (but not in any other materials) is called **Ohm's law**.

voltage (V) = current (I) × resistance (R) or $V = IR$ ❏

Write down the formulae for current and resistance in a circuit. Calculate the current flowing in the series circuit shown.

current, I =

resistance, R =

current flowing:

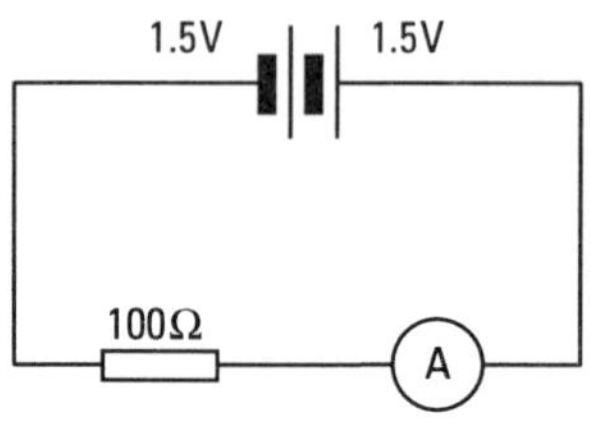

A3 Total resistance is calculated differently in series and parallel circuits.

In this series circuit:
total resistance $R = R_1 + R_2 + R_3$

In this parallel circuit:
total resistance $1/R = 1/R_1 + 1/R_2 + 1/R_3$ ❏

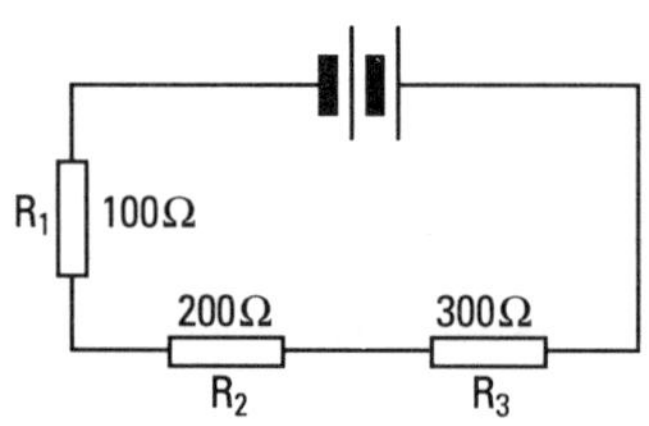

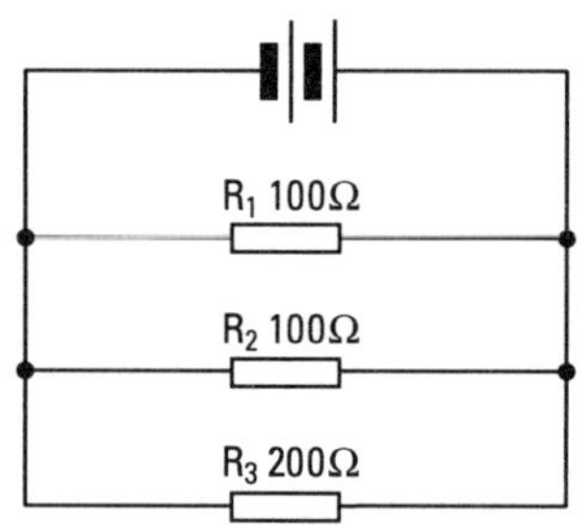

Calculate the total resistance in each of the circuits above.

series circuit:

parallel circuit:

A4 The total **electric charge** moved in a circuit is measured in **coulombs**.

charge moved (Q, in coulombs) = current (I, in amperes) × time (t, in seconds) or $Q = It$ ❏

A5 Voltage is a measure of how much energy is given to 1 coulomb of charge. When or if 1 coulomb of charge supplies 1 joule of energy as it goes round a circuit, then the voltage is 1 joule per coulomb. This is called 1 volt. ❏

Calculate the total charge flowing in a circuit carrying 4 amperes through a car headlamp for 1.5 hours.

A6 The electrical energy passing round a circuit is transferred to the components in that circuit. For example, the electrical energy in a car headlamp circuit is transferred to the filament of the lamp. The filament heats up and glows to produce light. ❑

A7 A **magnetic field** forms around any conductor carrying an electric current. This effect is used to produce **electromagnets.** An electromagnet is useful because it can be switched on and off. It can also be made stronger or weaker by:

- altering the number of coils of wire
- altering the size of the current in the wire
- adding a soft iron core to the centre of the coil of wire or by removing the iron core. ❑

Redraw the electromagnet below with three alterations to make it stronger.

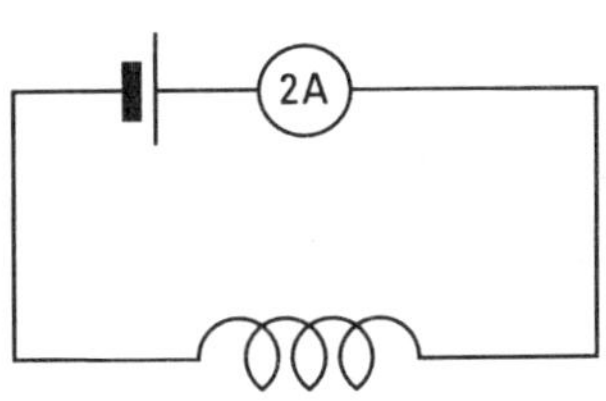

Your stronger electromagnet

A8 Electromagnets are found in many everyday appliances such as telephones, loudspeakers, relays (magnetic switches) and electric motors. ❑

Circle the electromagnet in each device.

Reed relay
The current in the control circuit passes through the coil of wire or solenoid. The metal reeds become magnetised and the current in the main circuit is switched on.

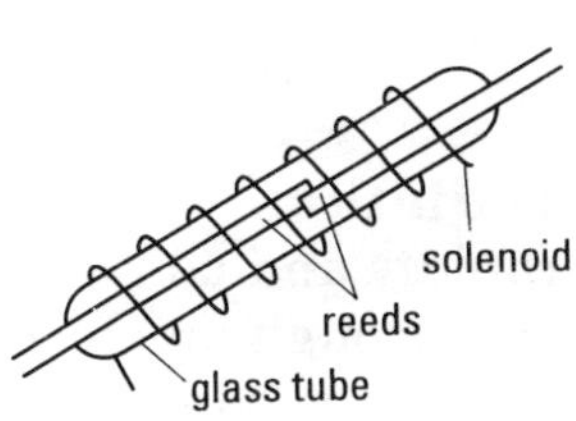

Loudspeaker
A paper cone attached to the coil of wire moves in and out as current passes through the wire. This makes the air vibrate creating sound.

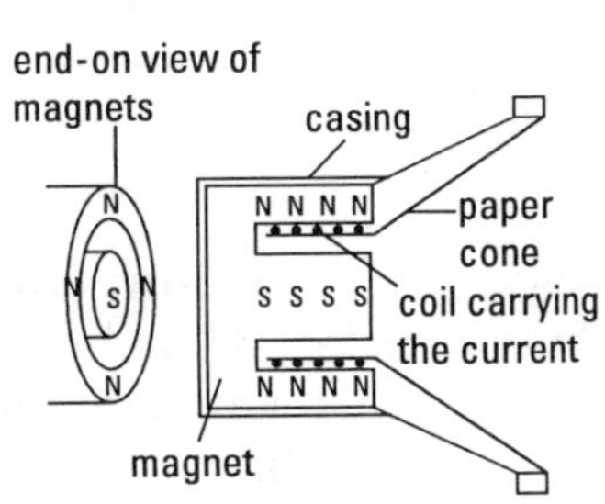

Electric motor
A soft iron core with a coil of wire around it is placed in the field of a permanent magnet. When the electromagnet is on its field reacts with that of the permanent magnet. The force produced makes the coil and iron core spin.

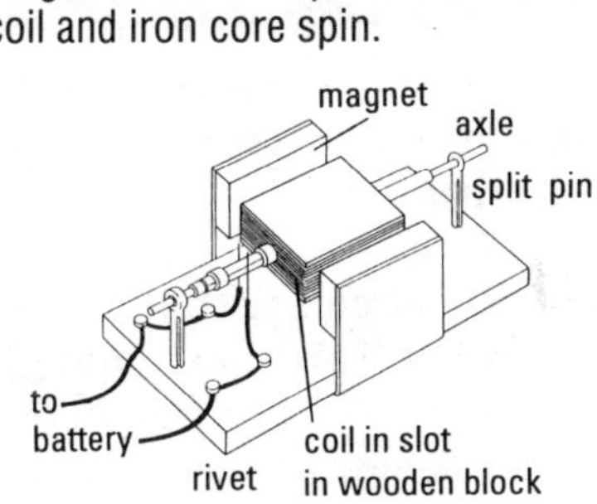

A9 Electronic circuits contain **logic gates** made up of switches with inputs and outputs. A **truth table** can be used to show what happens at the output for all possible inputs to a logic gate. ❑

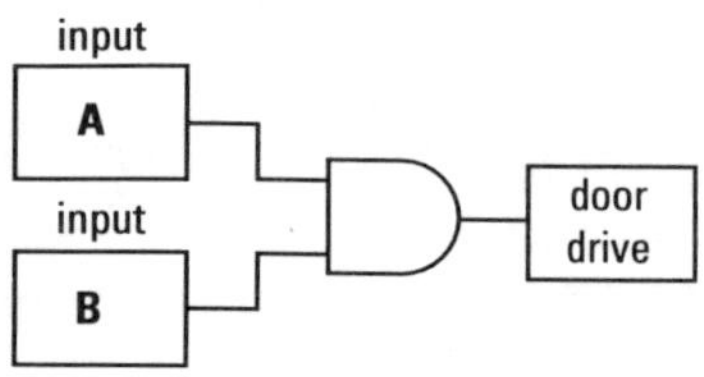

0 = off, 1 = on

Input A	Input B	Output	Result
0	0	0	nothing happens
1	0	0	nothing happens
0	1	0	nothing happens
1	1	1	door opens

Complete the truth table for the logic gate shown below.

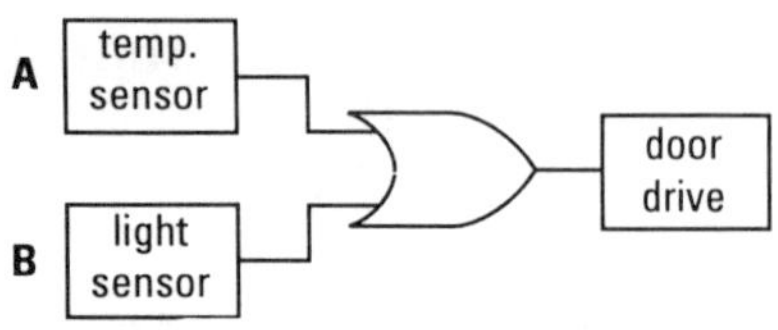

Input A	Input B	Output	Result

A10 NOT gates have a single input and a single output. They reverse the original signal. NOT gates can be combined with AND gates (NAND) and OR gates (NOR). ❑

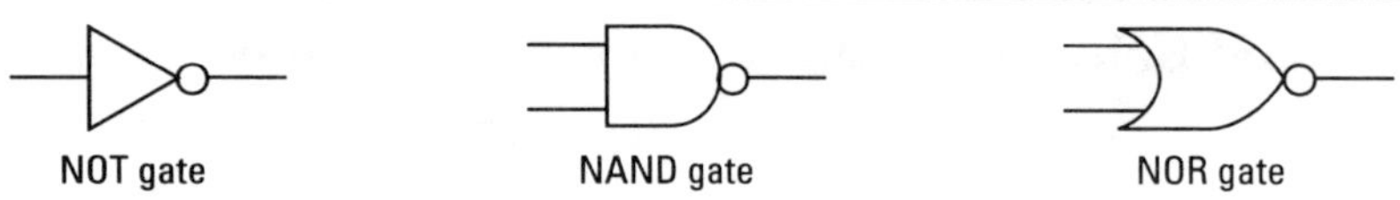

Describe the conditions under which the lamp will light in the systems below.

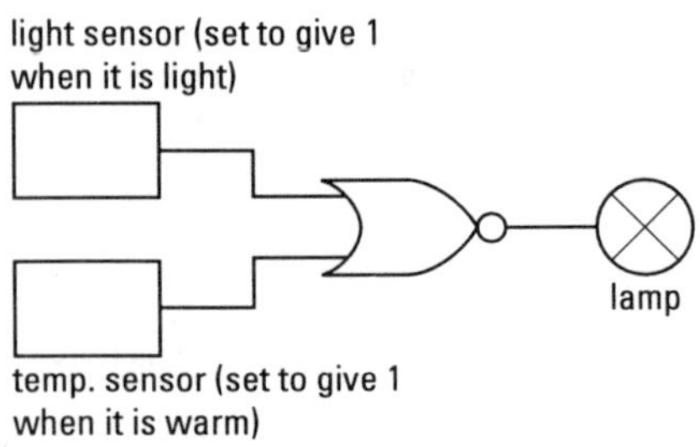

A11 An OR gate, with its output connected in a feedback loop to one of its inputs, stays on once it has been triggered. The circuit stays in the 'on' state whatever happens until it is reset. This **latch** circuit 'remembers' the first input and locks or latches 'on' until reset. Latch circuits are simple memory circuits and are the basis of memory chips in computers. Latches are also called **bistable circuits**. ❑

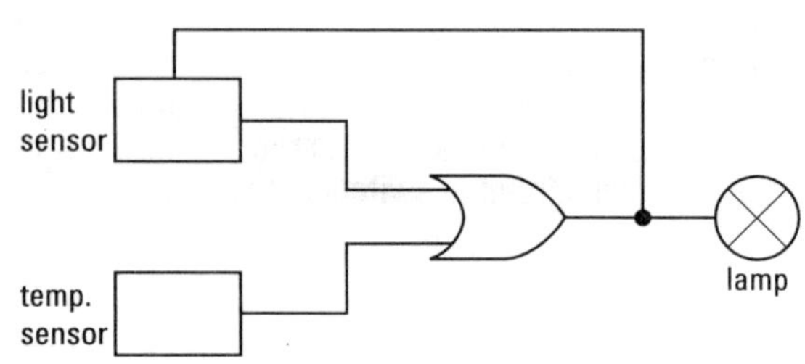

B1 A hot object can transfer heat in three ways: **conduction, convection** and **radiation**.
● **Conduction** takes place in solids. The particles of the hot object vibrate rapidly and pass some of this energy on to neighbouring particles. In this way heat can be transferred through an object or to other cooler objects that it is in contact with. Some materials, such as metals, are good thermal conductors; others, such as glass, wood and air, are poor thermal conductors. Heat is conducted well

through metal cooking pots.

● **Convection** takes place in liquids and gases. As a liquid/gas becomes hotter, it also becomes less dense. As this hotter liquid/gas rises through the cooler, denser liquid/gas, convection currents are set up. Water is brought to the boil in an electric kettle in this way.

● **Radiation** takes place through air or space. As particles vibrate they transmit some of their heat energy in the form of waves. These can pass through a vacuum, and this is how heat reaches us from the Sun through space. ❑

Summarise the information above in the following table.

	Radiation	Convection	Conduction
Heat transfer through		liquids/gases	
Heat transfer by			passing vibrations through neighbouring particles
One example			

B2 Objects designed to reduce heat loss must prevent conduction, convection and radiation. For example, in a vacuum flask:

● the internal mirror surface reflects radiated heat back into the liquid

● the inner container is made of glass – a poor conductor

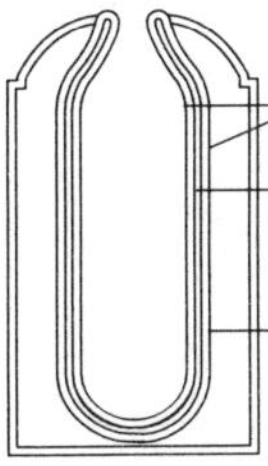

● the system is closed, avoiding heat loss by convection

● the internal vacuum prevents heat loss by conduction or convection. ❑

Houses are designed to prevent heat loss. Which type of losses – convection, conduction or radiation – are avoided by the measures shown below?

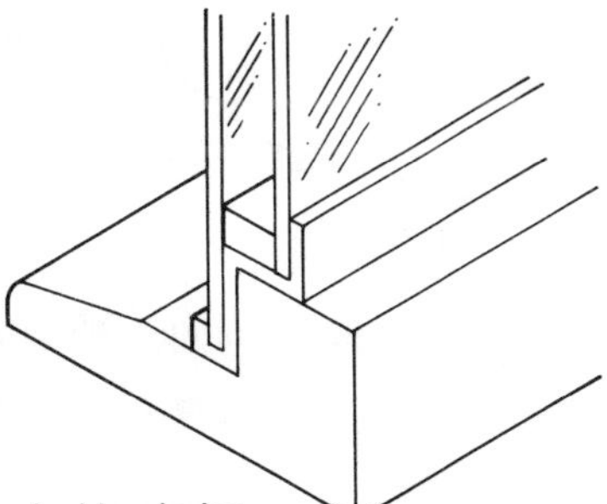

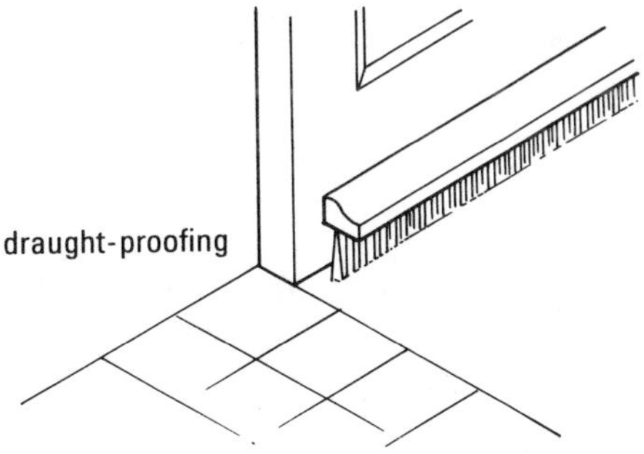

....

B3 Energy **efficiency** depends on the amount of useful energy that comes out of a system compared with the amount put in. Some energy is always wasted in the **transducer** (the energy changer), often as heat produced by friction and as sound.

$$\% \text{ energy efficiency} = \frac{\text{energy output}}{\text{energy input}} \times 100$$

❑

Calculate the efficiency in these two systems.

Energy input	Transducer	Energy output	Efficiency
chemical 2800 J	human muscle	kinetic 1120 J	
electrical 1500 kJ	electric fire	heat 1425 kJ	

B4 The heat energy wasted in energy transfers can be reduced by:
- insulating the transducer
- reducing friction in the transducer
- capturing the heat energy and using it. ❑

B5 **Power** is a measure of the rate of energy transfer or **work done**. It can be calculated from:

$$\text{power (watts)} = \frac{\text{energy transferred (joules)}}{\text{time (seconds)}}$$ ❑

B6 The power rating of an electrical appliance tells us how much energy it uses each second.
- 1 watt = 1 joule per second
- 1 kilowatt = 1000 joules per second

The power rating of a device depends on the supply voltage and the current through the device. The supply voltage in our homes is 240 volts.

power (watts) = voltage (volts) × current (amperes) or $P = VI$ ❑

Rearrange the formula given in B6 to show the formulae for calculating current and voltage.

I =

V =

What is the power rating of an electric kettle taking 9.6 amps at 240 volts?

What is the power rating of a 3-bar electric fire taking 12.5 amps at 240 volts?

What current flows in a refrigerator off a supply voltage of 240 volts with a power rating of 120 watts?

B7 A **joulemeter** can be used to measure the energy used by electrical appliances. Domestic electricity meters act as joulemeters. ❑

B8 The **specific heat** (thermal) capacity of a substance is the amount of energy required to raise the temperature of 1 kg of the substance by 1 degree Celsius. The specific heat capacity of water is 4200 joules per kilogramme per degree Celsius.

The energy transferred by heating can be found using:

energy transferred = mass of substance × specific heat capacity × rise in temperature

E (J) = m (kg) × s × t (°C) ❑

Rearrange the formula given in B8 to calculate the temperature rise and the mass of substance heated.

$t =$ $m =$

B9 If a heating device like a kettle is thermally insulated the efficiency of energy transfer will be closer to 100 %.

To calculate the temperature rise of 2.5 kg of water in a 2.5 kW tea-urn in 2 minutes:

energy supplied = 2500 joules/second or 2500 × 120 joules in 2 minutes

$$t = \frac{E}{ms} \quad \text{or} \quad t = \frac{2500 \times 120}{2.5 \times 4200}$$

$$= 28.6\ °C$$

❏

Calculate the mass of water which could be raised by 10 °C in 5 minutes in the tea-urn described opposite.

C1 Work is done when a force produces movement. Power is a measure of the rate at which work is done or energy is transferred. These formulae are used to calculate work done and power:

- work done = force × distance
- $\text{power} = \frac{\text{work done}}{\text{time}}$

For example, when a 30 kg girl runs to the top of 3 m high stairs in 12 s:
work done = 300 × 3 = 900 joules
power = 900/12 = 75 watts ❏

Calculate work done and power.

work done = power =

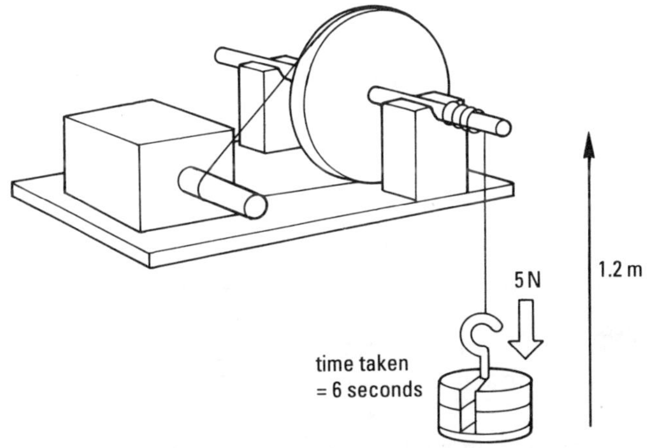

C2 The **lever** is a simple machine made up of a **bar** and a **pivot**. A force applied at one end of the bar makes it turn around the pivot. This turning effect is called the **moment**. ❏

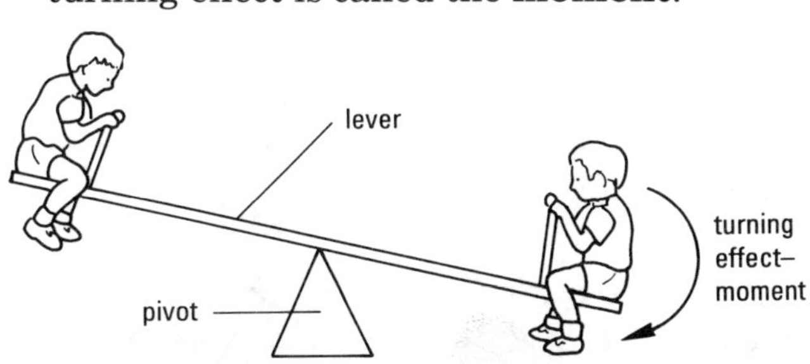

C3 The law of moments states that when the turning effects on both sides of the pivot balance, then:
force × distance from pivot on left =
force × distance from pivot on right

This law is important in the design of cranes. The counterbalance is moved to balance the turning effect of the load. ❏

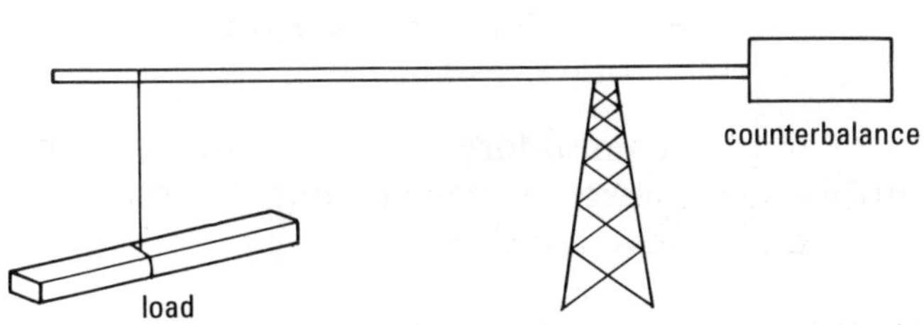

Mark on the diagram where you would place the child to balance the lever.

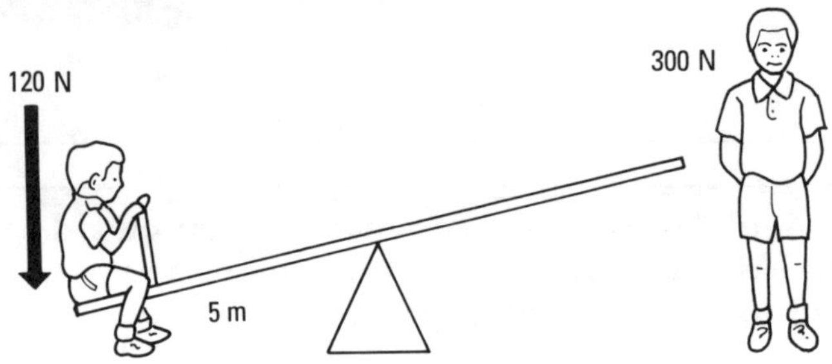

Write on the diagram the amount of force that would be needed to keep the paving slab in this position.

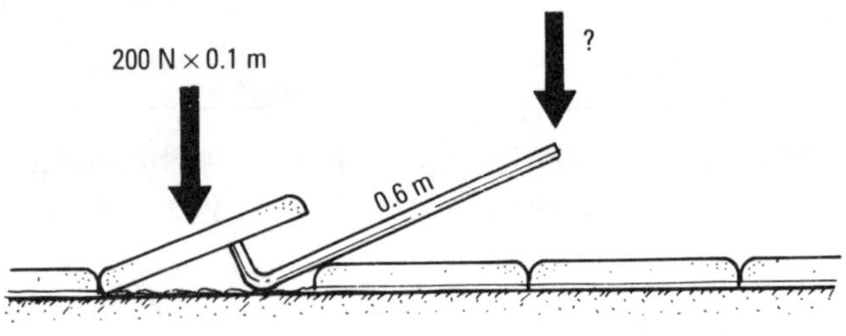

C4 Unstable objects fall over easily. They can be made more stable by lowering their centre of mass. ❑

C5 When an object speeds up it is accelerating. **Acceleration** is a measure of the change in speed per second.

$$\text{acceleration (m/s/s)} = \frac{\text{final speed or velocity (m/s)} - \text{starting velocity (m/s)}}{\text{time taken (s)}} \quad \text{or} \quad a = \frac{v - u}{t}$$

For example, for a car going from 25 m/s to 39 m/s in 7 s,

$$\text{acceleration} = \frac{39 - 25}{7} = 2 \text{ m/s/s}$$

Calculate the average acceleration of a sprinter running 100 metres in 10 seconds. Her final velocity is 12 m/s.

C6 To change the speed of an object an unbalanced force must act on it.

$$a = \frac{F}{m} \quad \text{or rearranged} \quad F = ma$$

where F = force (N), m = mass (kg) and a = acceleration (m/s/s).

For example, a small force is needed to start an empty supermarket trolley moving. A larger force is needed to move a full trolley.

C7 When an object falls it accelerates owing to the force of **gravity**. Two different objects dropped at the same time will hit the ground at the same time because the acceleration of **free fall** is the same for both. (This assumes the objects have the same air resistance.) The force of gravity is normally rounded up to 10 N per kg. ❑

Calculate the acceleration acting on each parachutist.

C8 The force of gravity also acts on an object thrown or fired horizontally. It will strike the ground at the same time as it would if it had been dropped vertically. ❑

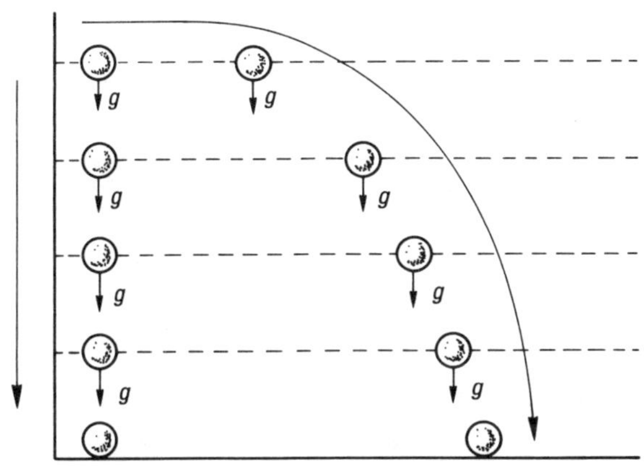

C9 Car seat belts are designed to reduce the deceleration on the body by yielding a little when a car stops, and so reducing the stopping force on the body.

force (F) = mass (m) × acceleration (a)

substituting $a = \dfrac{v - u}{t}$

stopping force $= \dfrac{m\,(v - u)}{t}$

Any increase in time reduces the stopping force and helps to prevent injury. ❑

C10 Car design also includes crumple zones around the front and rear bumpers. On collision these reduce the stopping time fractionally and so reduce the risk of injury. ❑

Calculate the stopping force for a 1000 kg car without crumple zones crashing to a stop from 30 m/s in 0.1 s

Calculate the stopping force for a 1000 kg car with crumple zones crashing to a stop from 30 m/s in 0.15 s

D1 Light consists of waves that carry electric and magnetic energy through space. Light is one type of **electromagnetic radiation**. Light has a range of wavelengths that our eyes can detect. Sunlight also carries ultra-violet and infra-red radiation, which we cannot see. ❑

D2 The speed of a wave is related to its frequency and wavelength:

speed (velocity) (m/s) = frequency (Hz) × wavelength (m) or $v = f\lambda$

This is true for all waves. ❑

Write down the *formula for wavelength* and the *formula for frequency.*

....

D3 Visible light is one part of the electromagnetic spectrum. This spectrum is made up of radiations of different wavelengths, from the shortest (gamma radiation) to the longest (TV and radio waves). All electromagnetic radiation travels through space at 300 000 kilometres per second. ❑

Label the positions of *gamma radiation, visible light* and *TV and radio waves.*

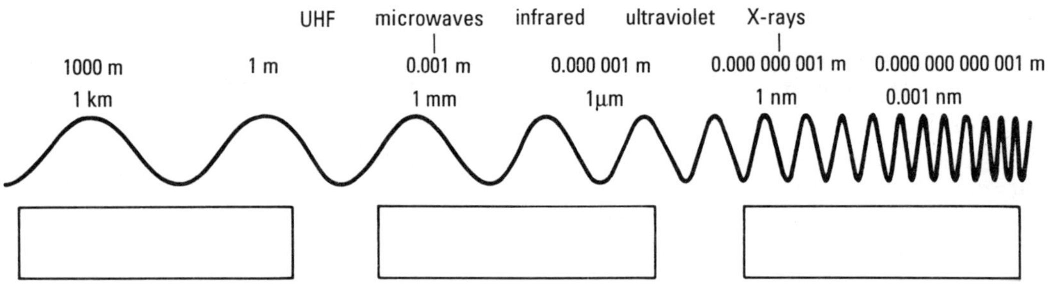

D4 When light passes from one material to another it changes speed and wavelength, but frequency stays the same. Speed and wavelength decrease as the density of the material increases. If light enters a different material at an angle it changes direction. This is called **refraction**. ❑

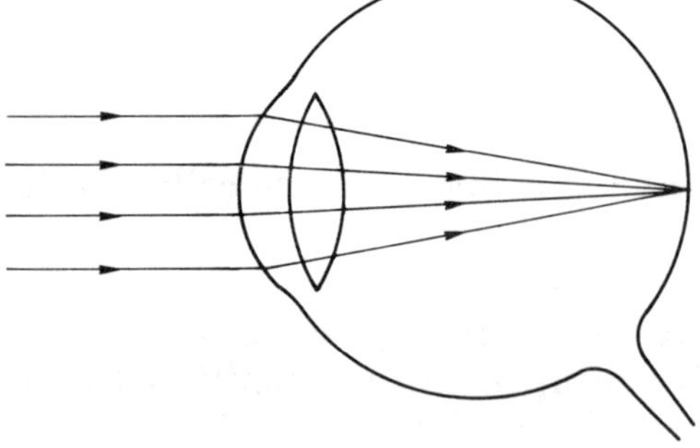

the lens of the human eye depends on refraction to focus light on the retina

a pencil in a glass containing water looks broken because of light refraction

Complete the diagram to show the path of light through a prism. Write *refraction* in the correct places.

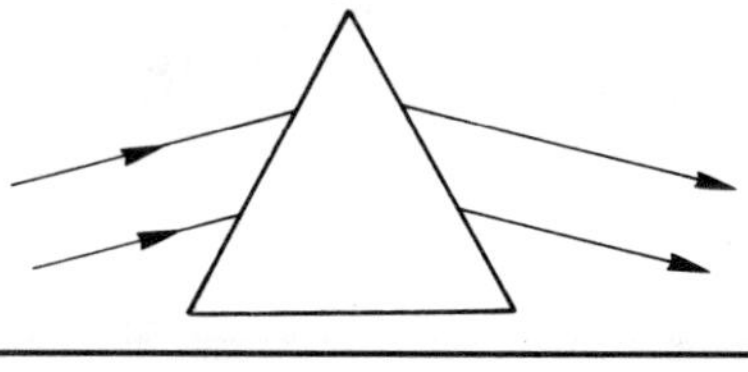

D5 Different sounds have a different pitch, quality and loudness. These features depend on the frequency, wavelength and amplitude of the sound wave. ❑

D6 The vibrations from musical instruments can produce simple or complex waveforms. The simplest way a string or column of air vibrates is called its **fundamental frequency** (fundamental mode). This is the lowest frequency of the instrument. The quality of sound depends on complex vibrations made up of the fundamental frequency plus **overtones**. Overtones are multiples of the fundamental frequency. ❑

Label each wave correctly using the terms: ***overtones*** **or** ***fundamental frequency.***

D7 In musical instruments the strings or air column vibrate at a **natural frequency**. The instrument is designed to vibrate in time with this frequency. This produces **resonance**. ❑

D8 An object can pick up energy from the sound waves in the air. If the frequency of the sound matches the natural frequency of the object it begins to resonate. The energy transferred to the object continues to build up and the resulting vibrations may damage it. ❑

a note from a singer could smash a glass

vibrations in a washing machine could match the machine's natural frequency. The resulting vibrations could damage it

D9 It is important to control noise in the environment to prevent damage to objects and to our hearing. ❑

D10 Electronic sound is used socially, in medicine and in industry. ❑

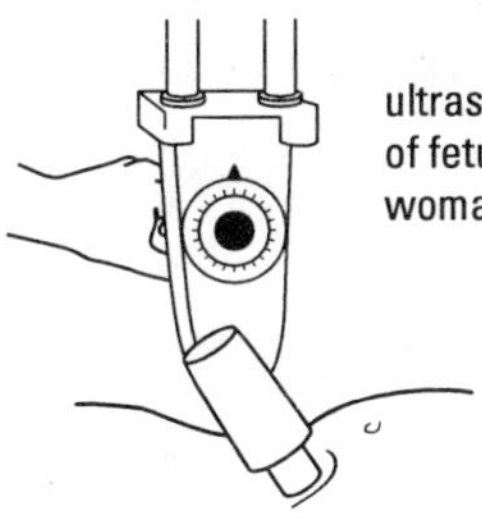

ultrasound examination of fetus in a pregnant woman

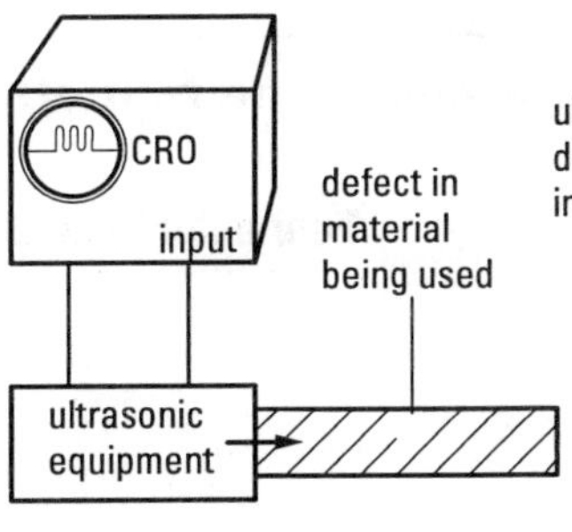

ultrasound is used to detect defects in industrial materials

radio

E1 The force of gravity acts between all objects but is negligible if the objects are small. Gravity between massive objects such as planets depends on:

- the mass of the objects
- their distance apart. ❑

Complete the sentences with the words *increases* and *decreases*.

The force of gravity .... as the mass of the objects increases.

As the distance between the objects increases the force of gravity between them ....

E2 Gravity pulls all objects towards the centre of the Earth. This force on an object is called its **weight**. The Earth's gravity field pulls with a force of 9.8 N per kilogram – usually rounded up to 10 N/kg. ❑

E3 The gravity field of the Sun is so great that it has an influence throughout the Solar System. For example, it:

- keeps the planets in orbit
- deflects the path of comets entering the Solar System
- affects tides on Earth. ❑

E4 The Sun generates heat by **nuclear fusion** and influences many features of the planets, for example day length and surface temperature. ❑

Plot a line graph of surface temperature against distance from Sun. Label each point with the name of the planet.

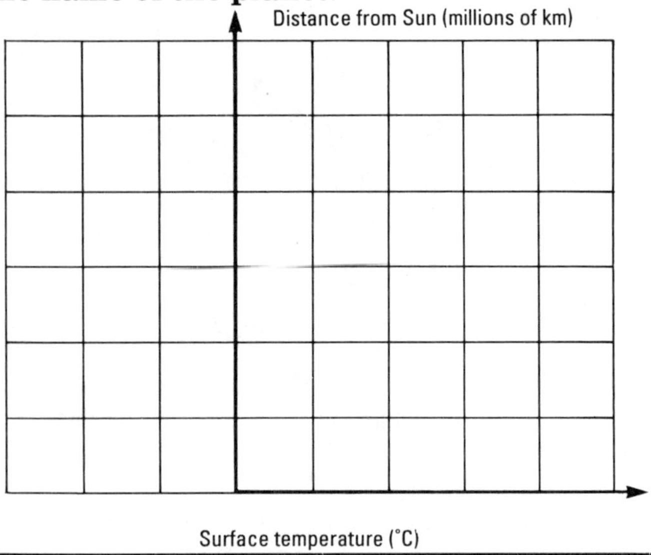

Planet	Distance from Sun (millions of km)	Surface temp. (°C)
Mercury	60	350
Venus	110	460
Earth	150	20
Mars	230	–23
Jupiter	780	–120
Saturn	1400	–180
Uranus	2900	–210
Neptune	4500	–220
Pluto	5900	–230

E5 Eight of the planets in the Solar System fall into two groups with common features. Pluto is the odd planet out and may be a former moon of Neptune. ❑

Complete the following by writing the names of the planets in each group in the correct boxes:

Four inner planets

- solid surfaces made of similar materials
- high density
- thin atmospheres

Four outer planets

- fluid (gas or liquid) surfaces
- low density
- very dense atmospheres

E6 Distances in space are measured in **light years** – the distance light moving at 300 000 km/s would travel in one year. The nearest star to the Sun is 4.2 light years away. Such vast distances limit the amount of data that can be obtained from outer space by spacecraft. ❑

Read A1 to A11 again. List all the formulae to do with electricity.

Read B1 to B9 and C1 to C10 again. List all the formulae to do with energy and movement.

A1 A voltmeter is used to measure the **potential difference** (p.d.) between two points in a circuit. The voltmeter has a high resistance and is placed across (in parallel with) the circuit component. The positive terminal of the voltmeter is always connected to the positive side of the circuit. ❑

Draw two voltmeters in this circuit – one to measure the p.d. across the resistor and one to measure the p.d. across the bulb.

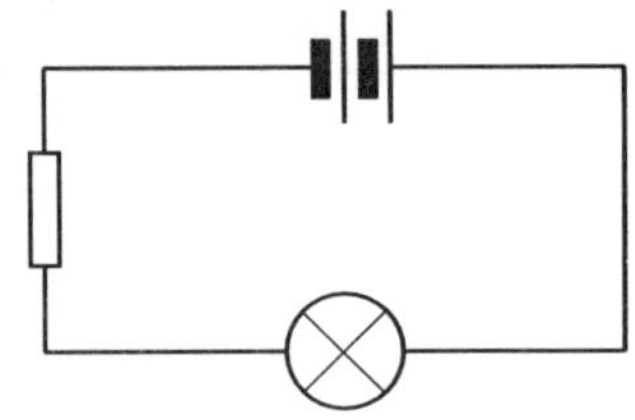

A2 The **power rating** of an electrical appliance is given in watts or kilowatts. This shows how much energy it uses per second.

- 1 watt = 1 joule per second
- 1 kilowatt = 1 kilojoule per second

The power rating of an appliance is found using:

$$\text{power} = \text{voltage} \times \text{current} \quad \text{or} \quad P = VI$$

$$\text{substituting } V = IR \text{ gives } P = I^2R$$

$$\text{substituting } I = \frac{V}{R} \text{ gives } P = \frac{V^2}{R}$$

❑

Complete this table.

Appliance	Power rating	Voltage	Current	Resistance
car headlamp		12 volts	3 amps	
electric drill	240 watts	240 volts		

A3 Domestic electricity bills are calculated on the number of units of electricity used. One unit is 1 kilowatt hour. The immersion heater in a hot water tank has a power rating of 9 kilowatts. This means it uses 9 units of electricity per hour. A 100 watt electric light bulb uses 0.1 units per hour. ❑

A4 When a coil of wire is moved between the poles of two magnets, an electric current flows in the wire. This is called **electromagnetic induction**. The same thing happens if the coil is held steady and the magnets are moved. If the coil is rotated in the magnetic field the current changes in size and direction. This is called **alternating** or **a.c. current**. ❑

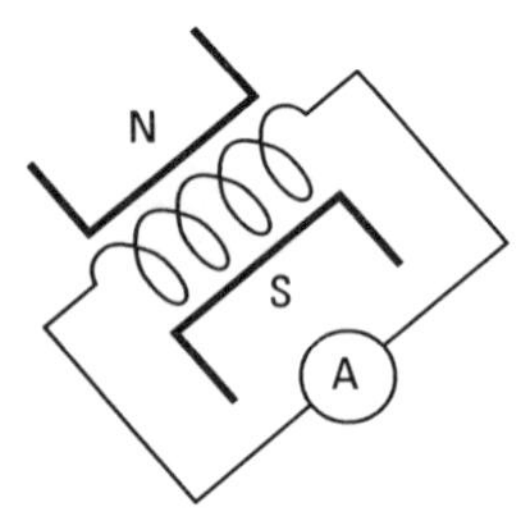

A5 The induced current can be increased by:

- using a coil with more turns
- using stronger magnets
- winding the coil on a soft iron core
- moving the coil faster. ❑

Complete the diagram to produce a higher induced current than that in A4 above.

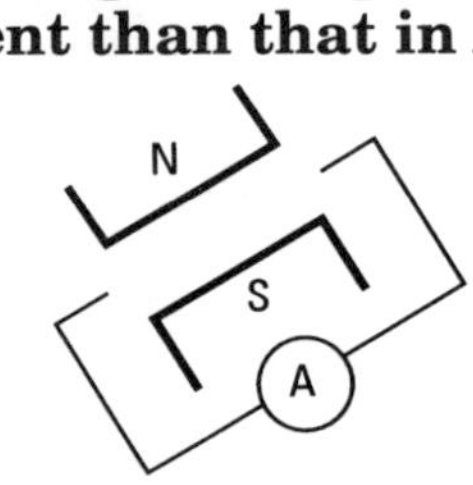

A6 A simple bicycle **dynamo** has the same basic parts as an electric motor – a fixed magnet and a moving coil. ❑

Complete the boxes in each flow diagram using the list of statements.

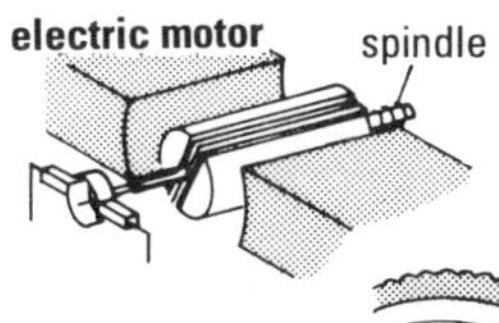

Electric motor: [ ] → [ ] → [ ]

Bicycle dynamo: [ ] → [current induced in coil] → [ ]

- current passed through coil
- coil spins round
- as wheel turns coil spins round
- rotating spindle raises load
- induced current lights bulb

A7 A **transformer** is made of two C-shaped soft iron cores each with a coil of wire wound round it. When a current is switched on in circuit 1 an electric current is momentarily induced in circuit 2. If the current in circuit 1 is steadily changed, a steady direct current is induced in circuit 2. If the current in circuit 1 is switched on and off, a steady alternating (a.c.) current is produced in circuit 2. ❑

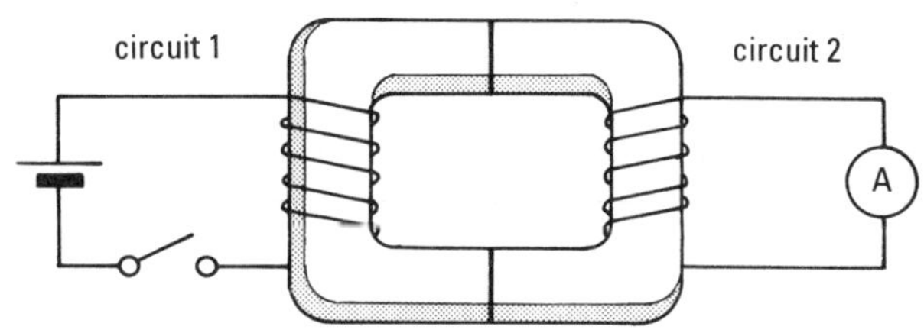

Label each circuit correctly using the terms *direct current produced* and *alternating current produced.* Make a key for these components: *ammeter, transformer, variable resistor, cell.*

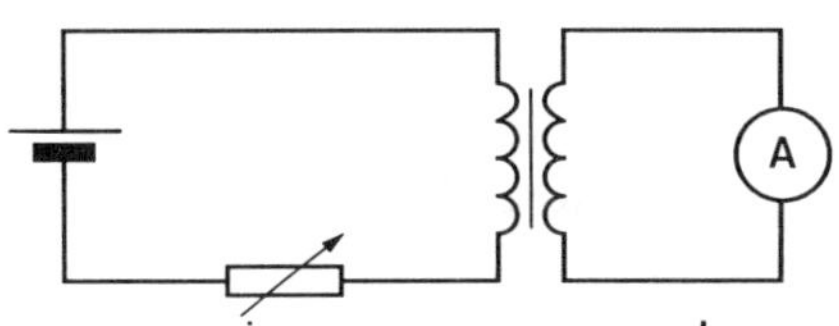

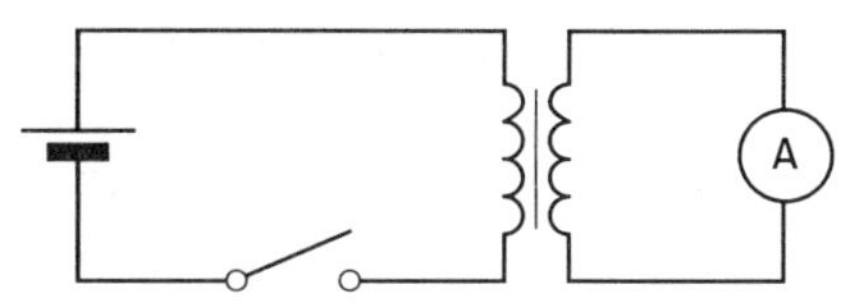

....

Key:

A8 Transformers can be used to alter the supply voltage by **stepping** it up or stepping it down. The voltage in the secondary circuit depends on the ratio of the number of coils in the primary to the number of coils in the secondary.
Because transformers are nearly 100 % efficient: ❑

electrical power of the primary circuit = electrical power delivered by the secondary circuit (supply)

$$V_{\text{primary}} \times I_{\text{primary}} = V_{\text{secondary}} \times I_{\text{secondary}}$$

Calculate the missing values in diagrams b) and c). Complete the final sentence.

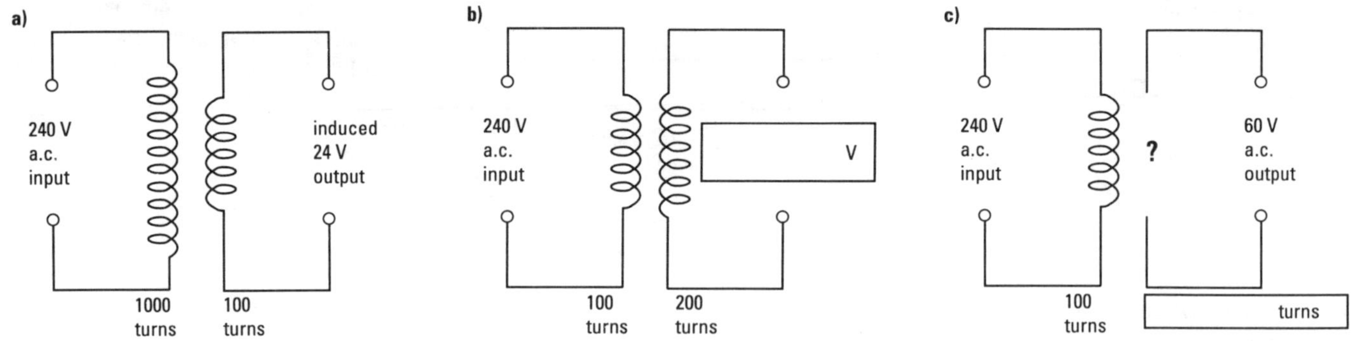

When the voltage is stepped up the current is stepped .... and vice versa.

A9 Electromagnetic induction is very important in the electricity industry for:
- producing electricity with **a.c. generators**
- stepping up the voltage using transformers before transmission. ❑

A10 In **a.c. generators** a central electromagnet rotates between fixed coils of wire where an alternating current is induced.

The shaft of the electromagnet is attached to a steam turbine. The turbine shaft rotates when steam is forced through the turbine blades. The steam is produced from water heated by burning fossil fuels in a furnace or by the heat from a nuclear reactor. ❑

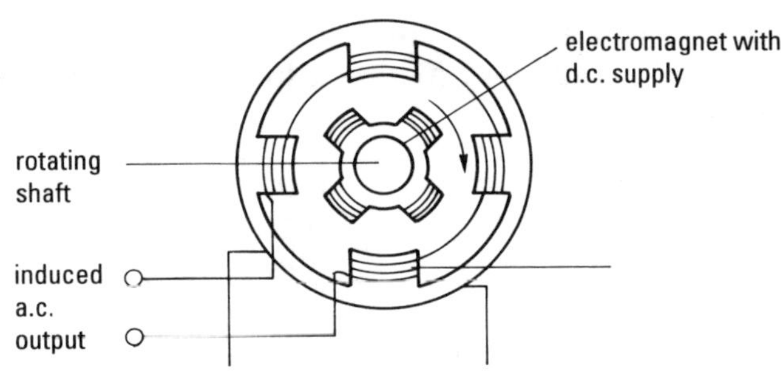

Complete the flow diagram using the words below.

a.c. current induced a.c. generator turbine shaft rotates turbine produce steam

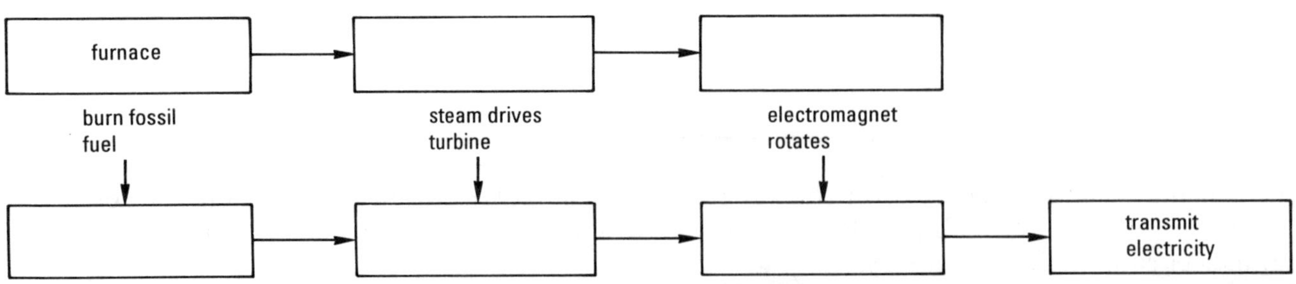

A11 Power stations produce electricity at very high voltage and high current. If it were transmitted like this, a great deal of energy would be wasted as heat in the electricity cables. The heat loss can be calculated from the formula $P = I^2R$. Any reduction in current will reduce energy loss. A step up transformer allows electricity to be transmitted through the supergrid at 400 000 volts and very low current. Transformers in local substations step down the voltage to 240 volts for domestic use. ❑

B1 We are faced with a number of different energy options and choosing the best one can be difficult. The choice of energy source depends on balancing
- availability
- need for conservation
- financial cost
- environmental impact
- social cost. ❑

Give:

a) one social cost of not using coal

b) one environmental effect of mining

c) one reason for conserving fossil fuels

B2 In any process, 'waste' energy spreads out into the surroundings. It is distributed amongst many particles and cannot be collected easily and put to use. For example, the internal combustion engine is only about 15 % efficient. 85 % of the energy in petrol is lost to the surroundings. ❑

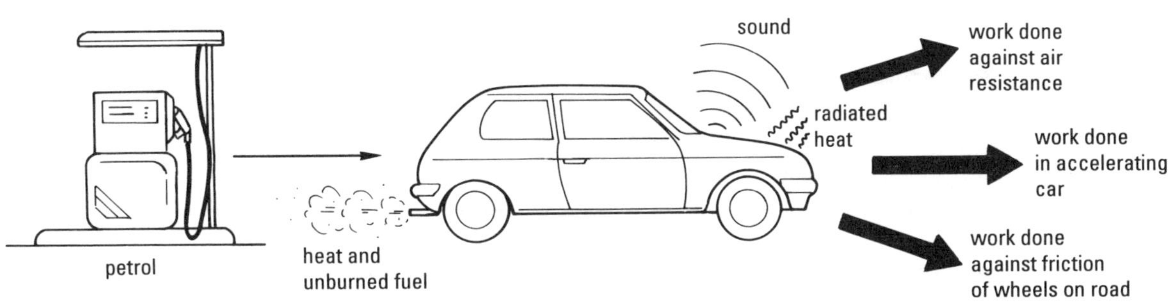

B3 There is a move towards the use of renewable energy sources such as

● tidal energy ● wave energy ● solar energy ● wind ● biomass.

Biomass is organic material – plants, animals and their wastes. Biomass can be digested by bacteria to produce methane gas for burning or converted to pellets that can be burned. ❑

Write the headings *advantages* and *disadvantages* in the correct place in the table.

Renewable energy sources

plentiful supply	supply seldom continuous
non-polluting	technology for collection still being developed
free	expensive to collect

C1 The combination of velocity and mass is called **momentum.**

$$\text{momentum} = \text{mass (kg)} \times \text{velocity (m/s)}$$

The faster moving of two identical cars has the larger momentum. If two cars of different mass are travelling at the same velocity the heavier of the two has the most momentum. ❑

Complete the momentum calculations for each pair of cars, then circle the car with the bigger momentum of each pair.

Pair 1 Mass	Velocity	Momentum	Pair 2 Mass	Velocity	Momentum
1000 kg	30 m/s		1000 kg	40 m/s	
1000 kg	35 m/s		1200 kg	40 m/s	

C2 In collisions, total momentum is conserved:

total momentum before collision = total momentum after collision. ❑

Calculate the total momentum after the collision in examples b) and c). Calculate the final speed after collision in c).

a)

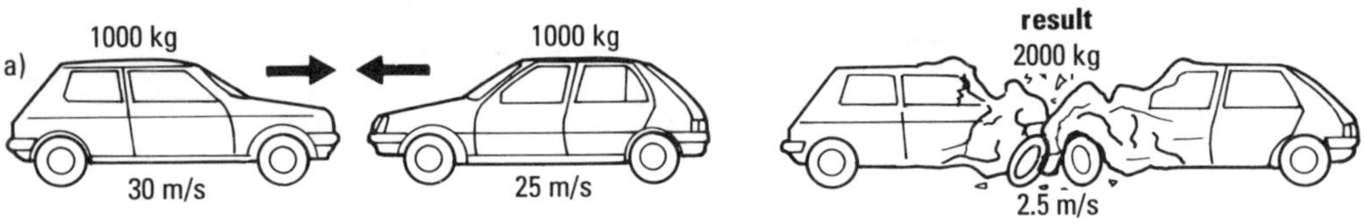

momentum before = 30 000 – 25000 = 5000
momentum after = 5000
mass after = 2000 kg
speed after = 2.5 m/s

b)

c)

C3 An unbalanced force can change the momentum of an object. A large force acting for a short time can have the same effect as a small force acting for a longer time. This idea is important in road safety.

Force (N) x time (s) = change in momentum (momentum at end – momentum at start)

$$\text{or } Ft = mv_{(\text{end})} - mv_{(\text{start})}$$

Ft is called **impulse**. Stopping force can then be calculated from

$$F = \frac{\text{change in momentum}}{\text{time}}$$ ❑

Calculate the stopping force in each situation below.

a) a 1000 kg car braking to a halt from 35 m/s in 6 seconds

b) a 1000 kg car stopping from 35 m/s in a collision in 0.1 seconds

C4 When a rocket takes off there is a change in momentum. The mass of gas leaving the engines exerts an equal and opposite force called **thrust** which pushes the rocket forward.
Since force × time = change in momentum

$$\text{Force (thrust)} = \frac{\text{change in momentum}}{\text{time}}$$ ❑

Calculate the thrust provided by a rocket with a mass of 3×10^6 kg if the speed after 50 s is 30 m/s.

$F \times t = mv_{(end)} - mv_{(start)}$

velocity at start = 0

velocity after 50 s = 30 m/s

thrust = change in momentum/time

=

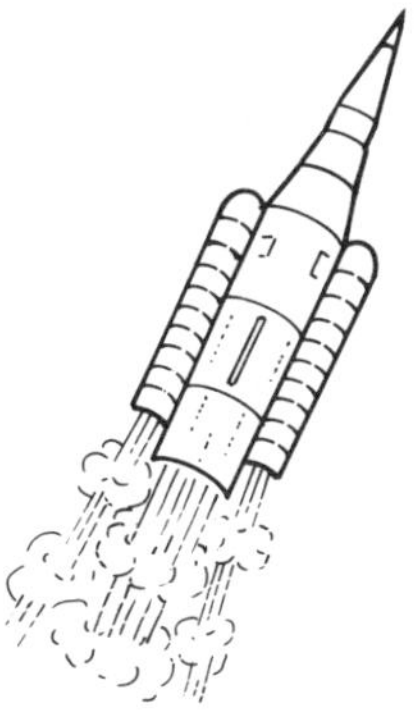

C5 When work is done against gravity there is always an increase in **potential energy.** The potential energy of an object depends on the mass of the object (m), the gravity force acting on it (g) and the height it is moved (h).

Energy transferred as potential energy, $E = mgh$ ❏

A 0.5 kg tub of margarine is moved from the floor to a shelf in the fridge 0.5 m higher. Calculate the potential energy of the tub of margarine.

C6 The energy of a moving object depends on its mass and velocity. These are related by the formula:

$E = \frac{1}{2}mv^2$ where E = kinetic energy (J), m = mass (kg) and v = velocity (m/s). ❏

C7 A falling object loses potential energy and gains kinetic energy.

potential energy lost = kinetic energy gained or $mgh = \frac{1}{2}mv^2$

This can be rearranged to give $v^2 = 2gh$ or $v = \sqrt{2gh}$ and allows the velocity of the object at any point in its fall to be calculated. ❏

Calculate:
a) the potential energy of a 2.5 kg book on a shelf 2 m high

b) the kinetic energy when it just hits the ground

c) the velocity of the book when it has fallen 1 m.

C8 The stopping distance of a car is proportional to the square of the velocity: ❑

$$d \propto v^2$$

D1 Each part of the electromagnetic spectrum has different properties that are related to the wavelength of the radiation, and can be detected in different ways. Each type of radiation has its uses. ❑

Write the name of each type of electromagnetic radiation in the word bank in the correct place below.

gamma rays   infra red   microwaves   radio waves   ultra violet   visible light   X-rays

Electromagnetic radiation	Wavelength	Properties	Detected by	Uses
	0.1–1 km	formed by electrons moving rapidly up and down aerial	tuned circuit or receiver	radio and TV transmission
	10^{-2} m	moving electrons produced by magnetron	tuned circuit	radio and TV transmission via satellite, radar, microwave ovens
	10^{-4} m	lamps, fires, sunlight	heating effect	heating, cooking
	5×10^{-7} m	lamps, lasers, sunlight	visible	seeing, photography
	10^{-8} m	lamps, sunlight	tanning effect on skin	sunbeds, skin treatment, killing bacteria
	10^{-9} m	X-ray tube rays penetrate soft tissue, reflected by bone	photographic plate	X-rays and CAT scanners
	10^{-12} m	radioactive sources, highly penetrative	photographic plate	killing cancers

D2 When a wave passes through a small gap in a barrier it spreads out. This is called **diffraction** and applies to sound waves as well as all types of electromagnetic radiation. ❑

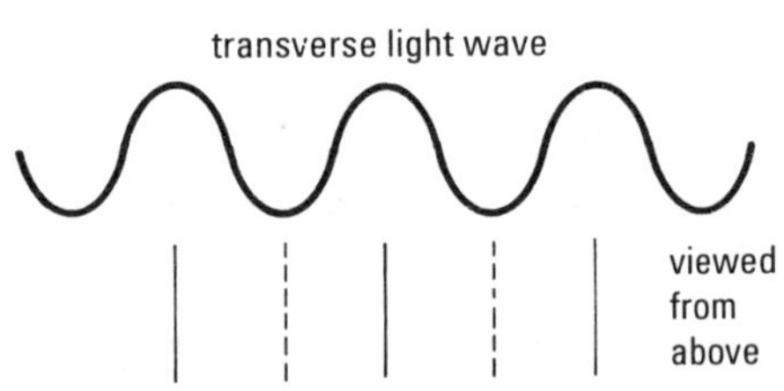

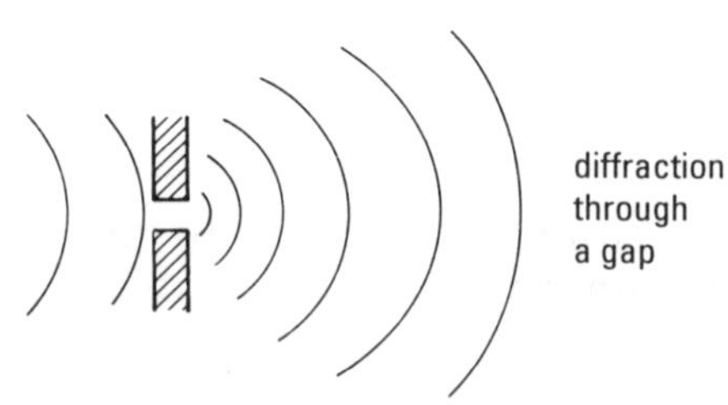

D3 **Interference** effects occur when waves meet. When two troughs or two crests meet in phase (together) they combine to form larger troughs or crests. If a trough and crest meet they cancel each other. ❑

Draw the results of the two types of interference shown below.

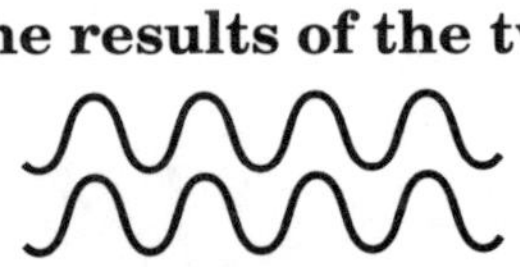

constructive interference – waves in phase

destructive interference – waves out of phase

D4 A ray of white light is made up of many different wavelengths vibrating at different angles to each other. A **polarised** substance only allows light waves that are vibrating at one particular angle through. The result is **polarised light**. Polarised sunglasses prevent some reflected light from reaching the eyes on bright days and so cut down on glare. ❏

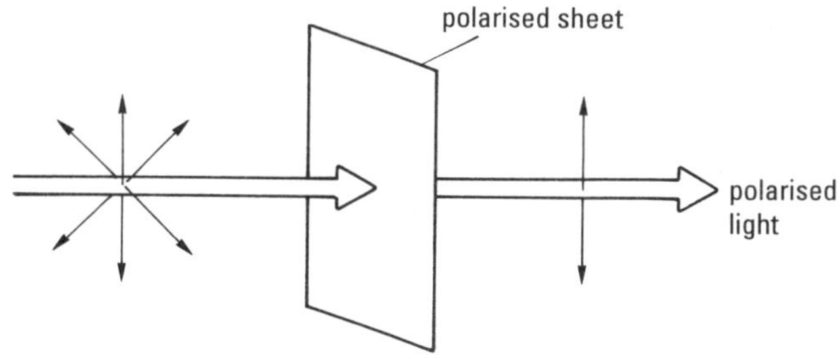

D5 TV and some radio signals are transmitted at ultra-high frequencies (UHF) and short wavelengths because these waves travel in straight lines and give a better quality of picture and sound than medium- or long-wave transmissions. A disadvantage is that they do not follow the curvature of the Earth and so are only suitable for transmission over short distances.

Transmitters and receivers must be positioned carefully for good communication. There have to be many transmitters, each operating over a slightly different frequency band to avoid interference. ❏

E1 Gravity forces occur in pairs, and both objects involved exert an equal but opposite pull on each other. This results, for example, in the planets staying in orbit around the Sun. ❏

E2 The force that keeps an object moving in a circle is called the **centripetal force**. This can be calculated from:

$$\text{force} = \frac{mv^2}{r}$$

where r is the radius of the circle.

This formula shows that doubling the speed increases the force required to keep the object travelling in a circle by a factor of 4. ❏

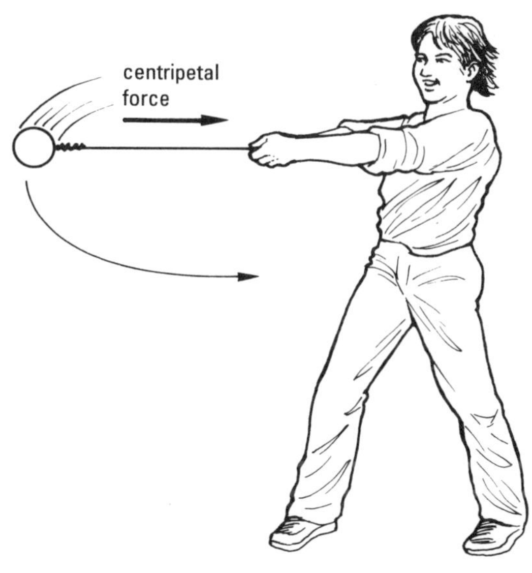

E3 Artificial satellites move in a circle round the Earth. The centripetal force that keeps them in orbit is gravity. There are low-orbit and **geostationary** (**geosynchronous**) satellites. Low-orbit satellites are on high-velocity orbits and are out of contact with their Earth tracking stations for some of the time. They are used for spying, surveying and studying the weather. Communications satellites and some weather stations are on geosynchronous orbits. These satellites are in high orbits travelling at a speed that keeps them over the same place on the Earth's surface.

The forces on low-orbit satellites are much greater than those on geostationary satellites because their speed is much greater and their orbit height lower. ❏

Label the two geostationary satellites and the low-orbit satellite below.

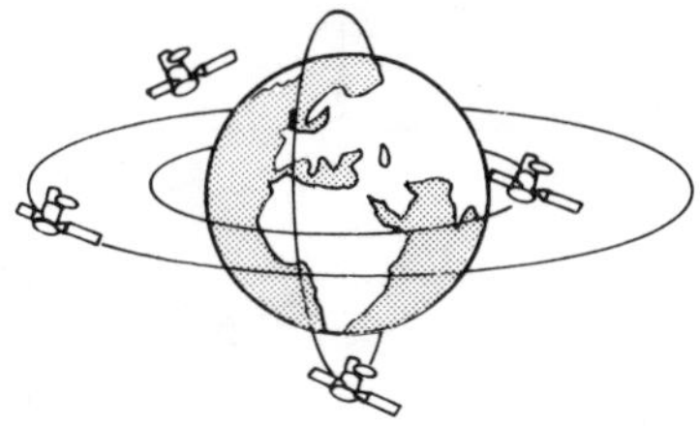

E4 Many scientists believe in the **big bang theory** to explain the origin of the universe about 15 billion years ago. This theory suggests that the universe began with the explosion of a very dense, very hot fireball, which threw matter out in all directions. ❑

E5 Evidence for the big bang theory comes from:
- observations of the positions of stars which suggest they are moving away from each other
- examining the quality of light from distant stars and galaxies. The **spectra** have longer wavelengths than expected. This **'red shift'** indicates that these bodies are moving away from Earth. ❑

E6 Scientists suggest that one of three things will happen to the universe:
- the universe will keep on expanding for ever
- the universe will stop expanding and reach a steady state
- the universe will stop expanding then contract in on itself. ❑

E7 Stars are thought to follow a 'life cycle':
1. clouds of hydrogen gas are drawn together by gravity
2. nuclear fusion occurs when hydrogen atoms collide and combine to form helium and release light energy
3. eventually all the hydrogen is used up and the star becomes a **red giant**
4. depending on its size, the red giant can explode in a **nova** and form a **white dwarf**, explode in a **supernova** and become a **pulsar**, or collapse in on itself to become a **black hole**. ❑

Summarise the points above by completing the flow chart to describe the life cycle of a star.

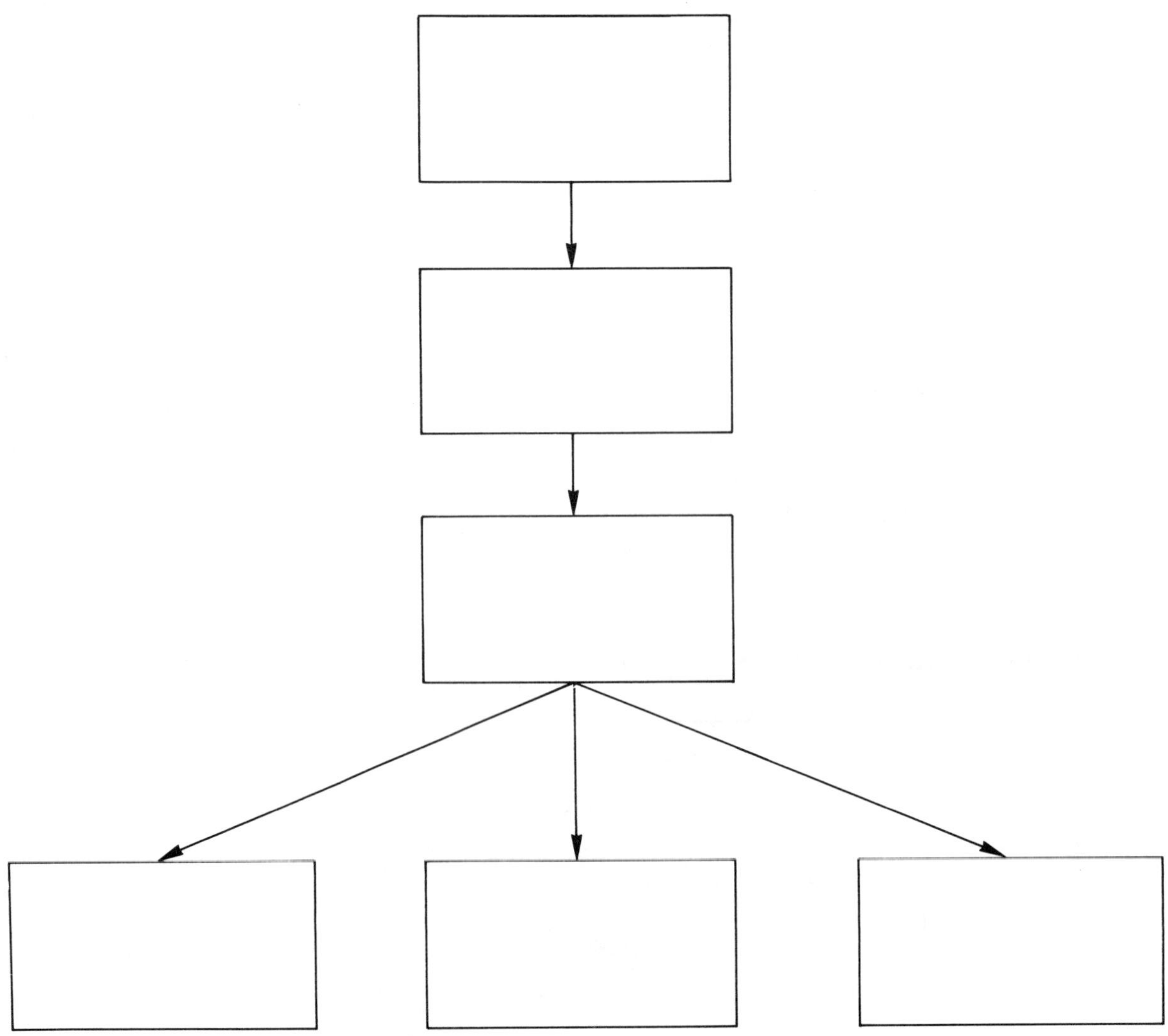

Read A1 to A11 again. List all the formulae to do with electricity.

Read B1 to B3 and C1 to C8 again. List all the formulae to do with energy and movement.

Answers

answers

AT1 Levels 4, 5 & 6 (pages 2–5)

AT1 encourages investigation, and as a result, there can be several correct responses to a question. The answers to AT1 are a guide only.

A1

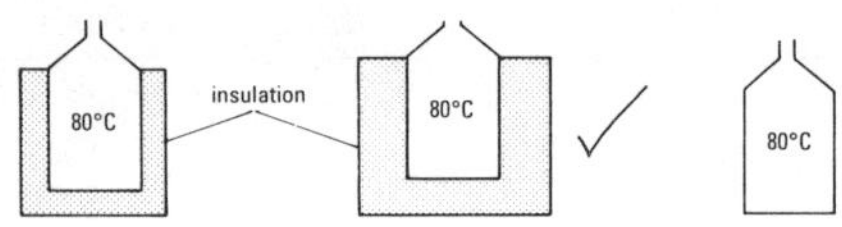

A2 1 **wool** 2 **fur.** Or anything suitable.

A3 **Using equal quantities of dough in identical containers, place one container in a controlled temperature area of 35 °C, and one container in an identical area at a different temperature. Use a ruler to measure the height the dough rises over a defined period of time. Different temperatures above and below 35 °C should be tested, each time using a control.**

A4, A5

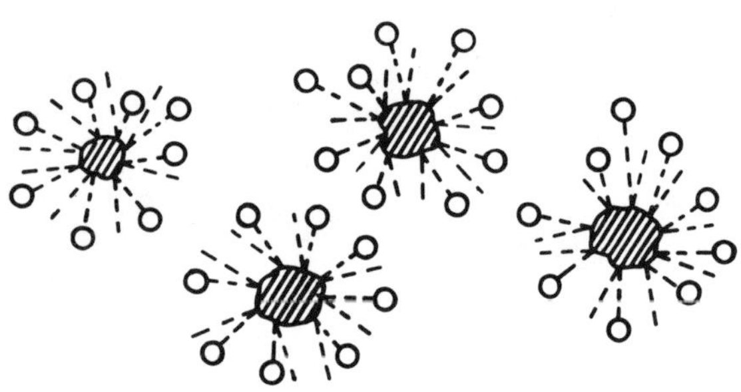

B1 **There would be fizzing around the chalk, which would dissolve, leaving a colourless solution.**

B2 **temperature size of chalk pieces.**

B3 **34 °C; 40 °C.**

B4

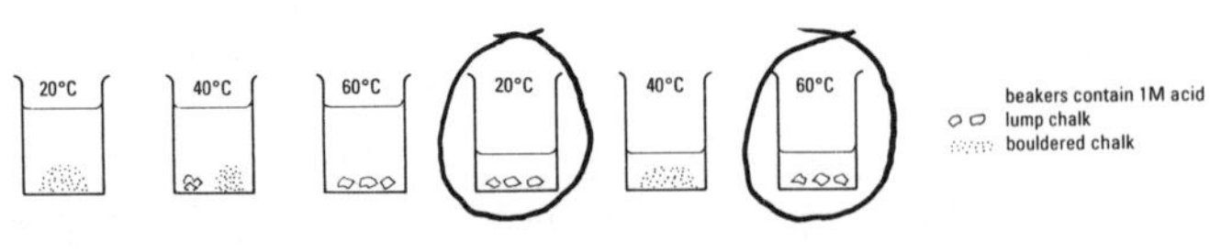

B5 **concentration of acid size of chalk particles temperature type of container.**

B6 **smell; feel; sound.** Or anything suitable.

B7 **weight; width; density.** Or anything suitable.

B8, C1 **The woollen cover is a good insulator. The nylon cover is not a good insulator.**

C2 a)★★★ b) ★ c) ★★ d) ★.

C3

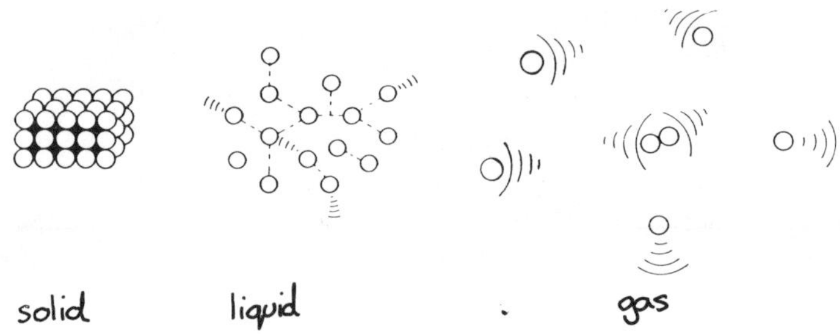

C4

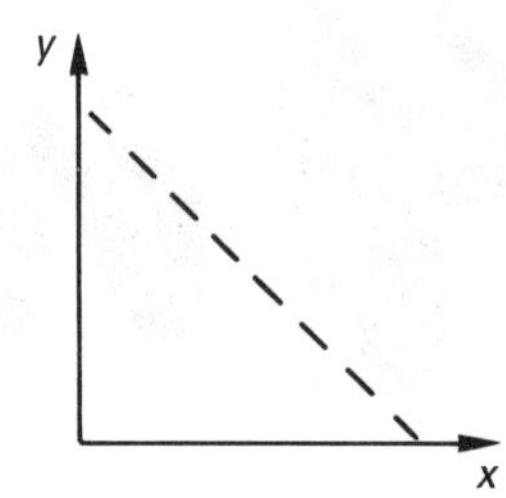

C5

As the thickness of the insulator increases, its insulation effect increases.	**Wool is the best insulator, followed by cotton, rayon and nylon in descending order of effectiveness.**	**The temperature decreased over time.**

AT1 Levels 7 & 8 (pages 6–7)

A1 **The control plant should be grown in exactly the same conditions as the plants in the greenhouse. Each batch of plants in the greenhouse should be exposed to a change in one variable, for example; temperature, moisture, light, carbon dioxide concentration. Indications of growth could be height increase of the plant, increased foliage, or increased dry weight.**

A2 **2 6 3**
1 4 5

A3 Type of food supply: **proteins, fats, carbohydrates**
Amount of water: **more than 50 litres/day (including washing and toilet)**
Temperature: **0 °C–35 °C, (internal 37 °C)**
Climate: **no extreme conditions**
Other factors: **social structure**
Shelter: **to protect from harsh weather, predators, etc.**

B1 **Remove a panel of glass to cool the greenhouse; add a heater to heat the greenhouse. Use an accurate thermometer for measurements.**

B2

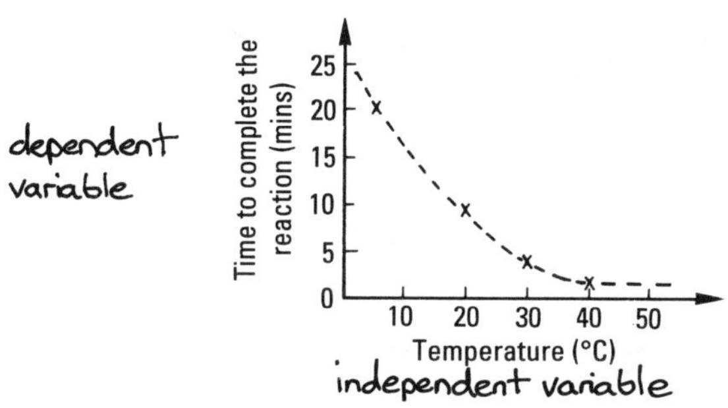

B3 height of a pot plant — micrometer
height of a fir tree — 30 cm ruler
length of a leaf — metre stick
thickness of a leaf — 10 m tape

C1, C2 **Lack of fine discrimination in instruments. Not carrying out a fair test. Not planning an experiment sufficiently before beginning. (The experimenter.)**

AT1 Levels 9 & 10 (pages 8–12)

A1 **amount of corrosion at temperatures in the range 200–400 °C.**

A2, A3 **That inheritance depends on the combination of two alleles which are either double recessive, double dominant or heterozygous for a character; and that inheritance is in the ratio of 3:1. (Mendel's First Law).**

A4, A5

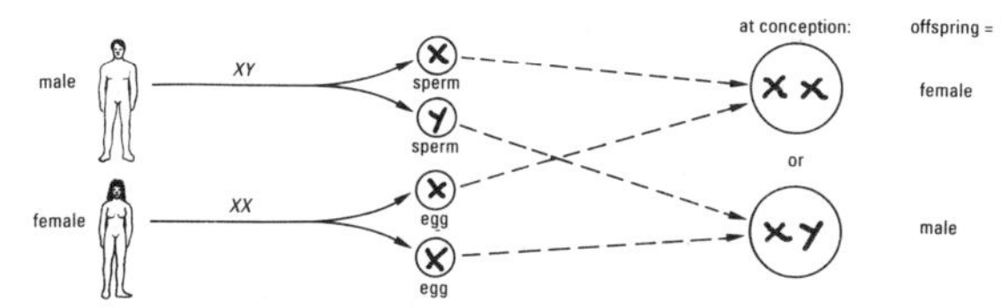

A6 **atom ion pH.**

B1 **Investigate parent populations of *WW* and *ww* and count the number of offspring in the first generation, and then the second. Look for the ratio 1:2:1 in the second generation.**

B2 **Readers were not sampled. Instead they chose whether or not to take part. Only a small number did so. Health problems were to be identified by the person rather than a medical practitioner.**

B3 1 **age group defined** 2 **social group defined.**

B4 **Use a larger sample group. Use health data from a medical practitioner. Ensure the sample population is chosen at random.**

C1 **Aluminium corrodes most at pH 2, 4 and 5. At pH 3 and pH 6 to 8 corrosion is minimal, while at pH 9 and 10 no corrosion occurs.**

C2 **Aluminium corrodes in very acidic conditions, and weakly acidic conditions.**

C3 **pH 3.**

C4 **living cells contain water sickle cell anaemia is inherited.**

C5 1 **extent of harmful effects of radiation exposure**
2 **type of diet affects cholesterol levels in the body.**
Or anything suitable.

C6 **a) 1 in 4 b) 1 in 1000 c) 1 in 10 d) 1 in 1.**

AT2 Levels 4, 5, 6 (pages 14–25)

A1, A2 animal cells:

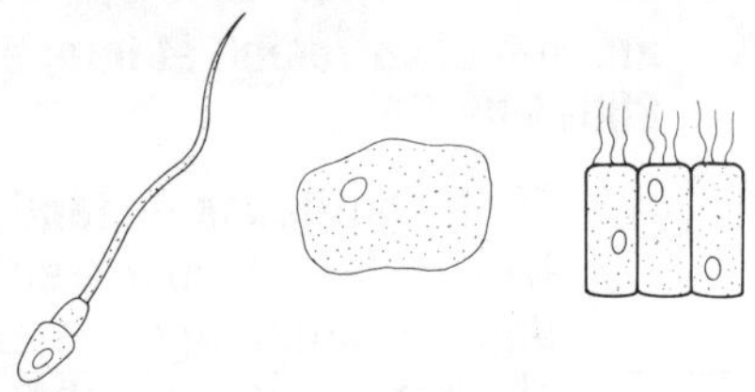

plant cells:

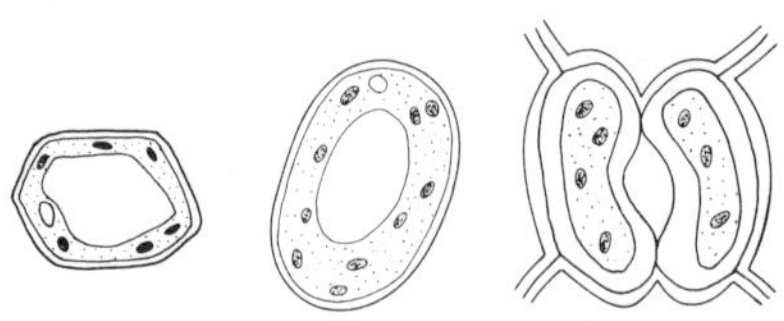

A3 **cell membrane cytoplasm nucleus chloroplasts vacuole cell wall.**

A4

tissue	a group of organs and tissues carrying out one life process
organ	a group of cells with the same structure and function
system	a structure, made up of several different tissues, which carries out one particular function

A5

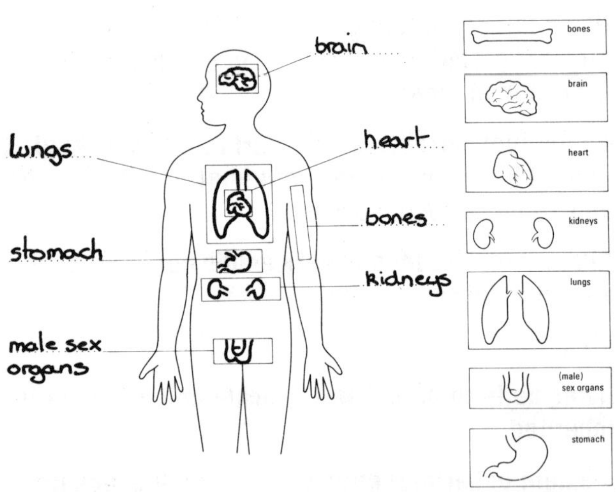

A6 brain — nervous — sensing and responding;
bones — skeletal — support and movement;
heart — transport — supplying organs with oxygen and food;
stomach — digestive — digestion;
sex organs — reproductive — reproduction;
kidneys — excretory — excretion–removing waste;
lungs — respiratory — breathing and gas exchange.

A7 **1 heart; arteries 2 support; protect 3 digestion 4 kidneys 5 brain; nerves 6 lungs; oxygen 7 ovaries; sperm.**

A8

enable the plant to reproduce

carry out photosynthesis

support leaves and flowers

anchor plant in soil

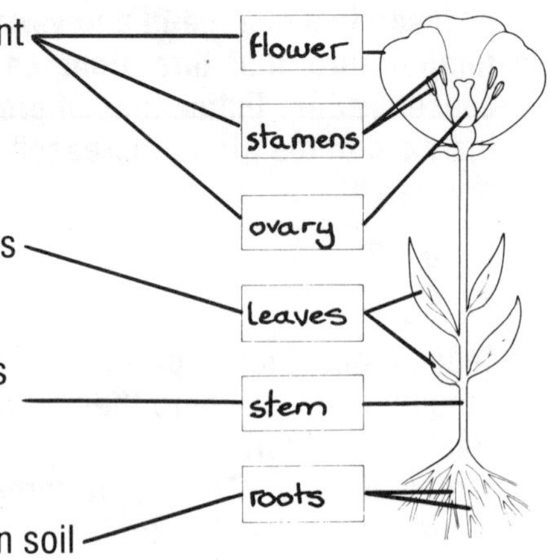

A9

human nerve cell (neurone)	head part holding genetic material, tail part for movement
human sperm cell	long cylinder shape, lots of chloroplasts
leaf palisade cell	long thin cell covered in insulating substance

B1, B2 vertebrate animals:

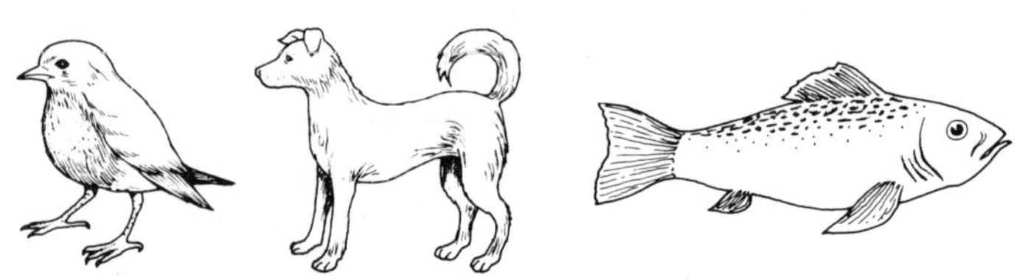

invertebrate animals:

B3

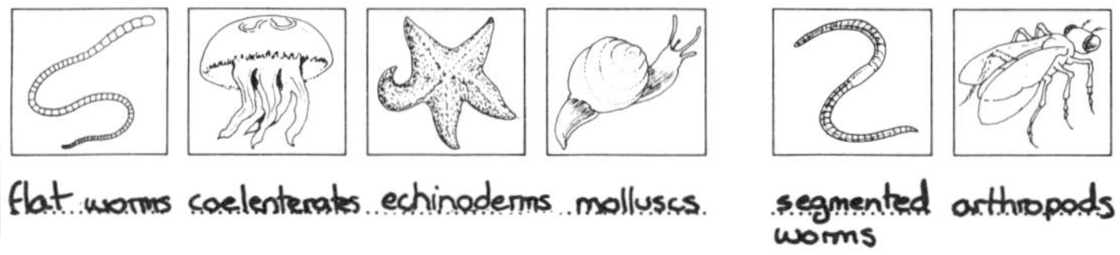

B4 2 Animals with live birth — Name **mammals** Examples **horse, cat, human**

Egg-laying animals — Name **birds** Examples **robin, hawk, penguin**

3 Moist skin — Name **amphibians** Examples **frog, toad, newt**

4 Breathe using lungs — Name **reptiles** Examples **snake, crocodile, turtle**

Breathe using gills — Name **fish** Examples **pike, trout, salmon**

B5 Example:

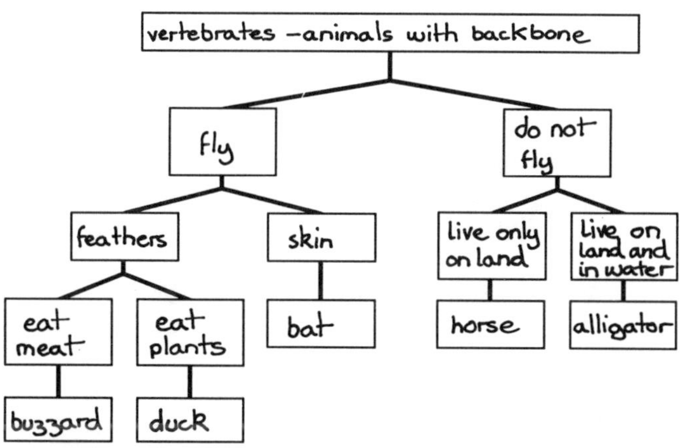

1 wings — **go to 2**
no wings — **go to 4**

2 have hair — **bat**
have feathers — **go to 3**

3 curved beak — **buzzard**
flat beak — **mallard**

4 have hair — **horse**
have scales — **alligator**

Or anything similar.

B6

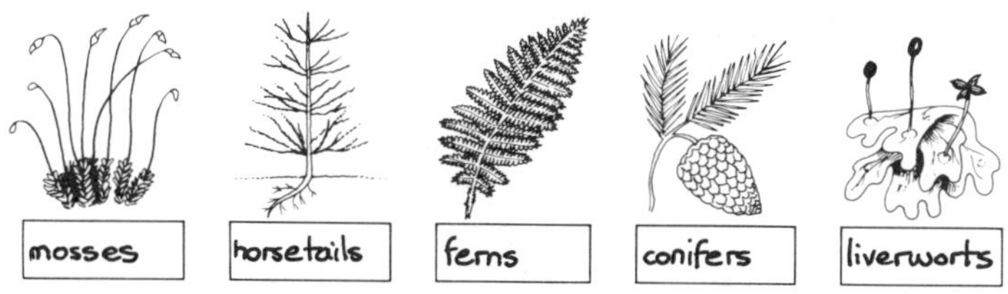

B7, B8, B9, B10

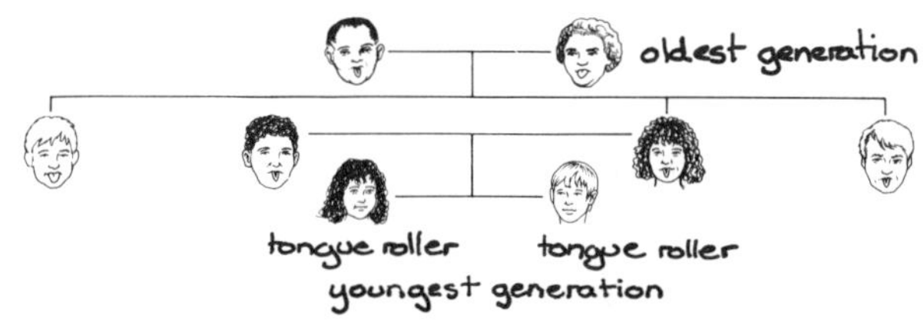

B11 Both parents short **genetic** mother smoked during pregnancy **environmental** mother ate healthy diet while pregnant **environmental** low light intensity **environmental** acid soil **environmental** parent plants tall **genetic.**

C1 light space water.

C2 a) water gain b) absorb c) external d) streamlined e) reduced.

C3 large small large.

C4 air pollution soil pollution water pollution.
Two further examples of pollution: **fertilisers leaching out of soil into rivers exhaust fumes from cars.**
Or anything suitable.

C5, D1, D2 herbivores:

carnivores:

producers: **grass; pondweed**
consumers**: other members of chains**

D3, D4 less; decrease less; increase; herbivores.

D5, D6, D7 photosynthesis

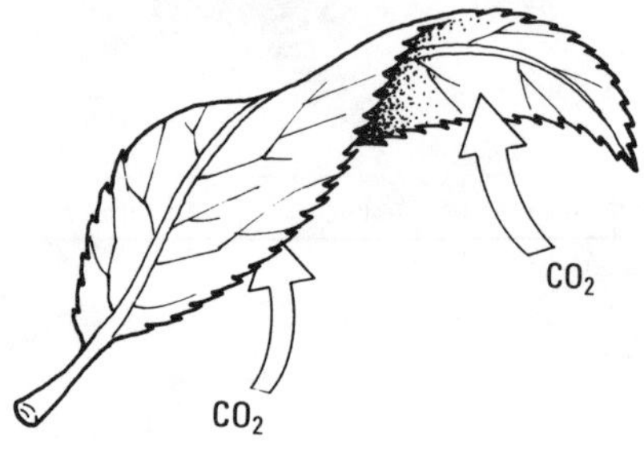

respiration

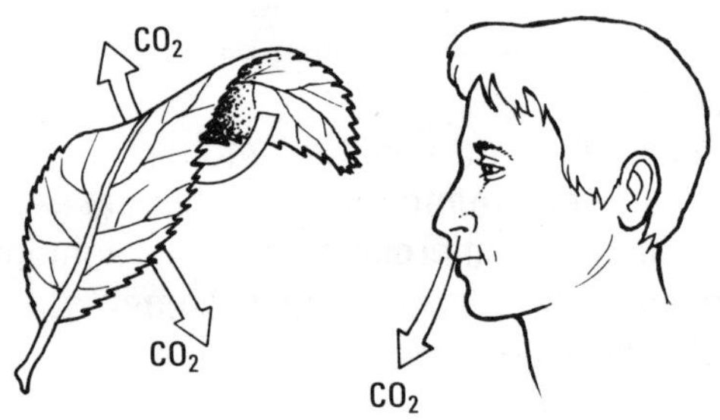

D8

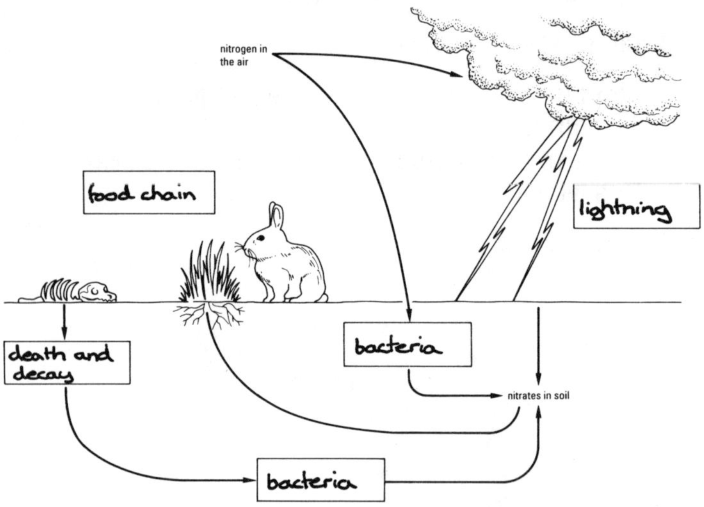

AT2 Levels 7 & 8 (pages 26–38)

A1

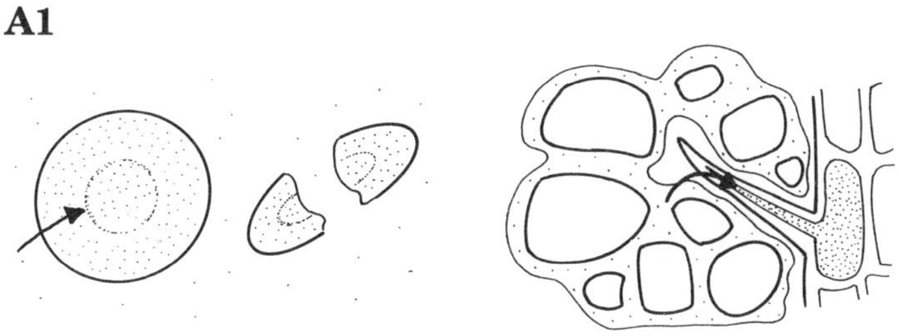

A2

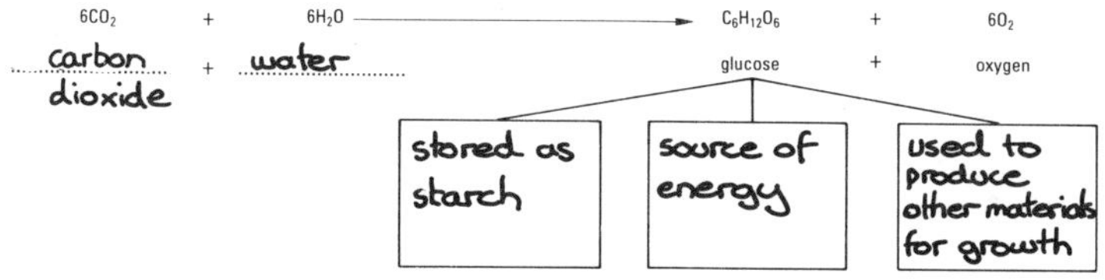

A3, A4 oxygen + glucose → carbon dioxide + water + energy

A5 daytime gas exchange

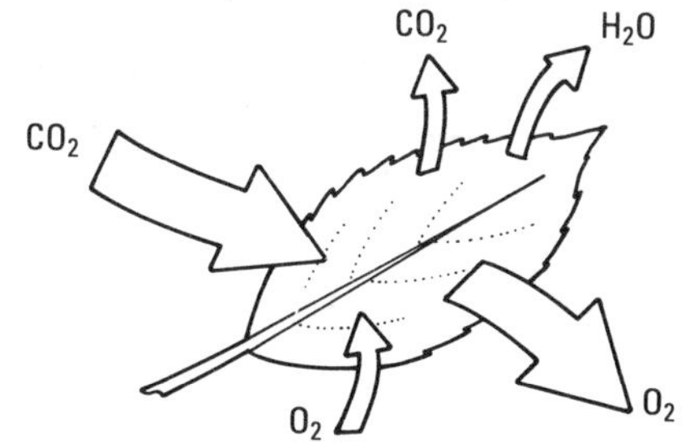

night-time gas exchange

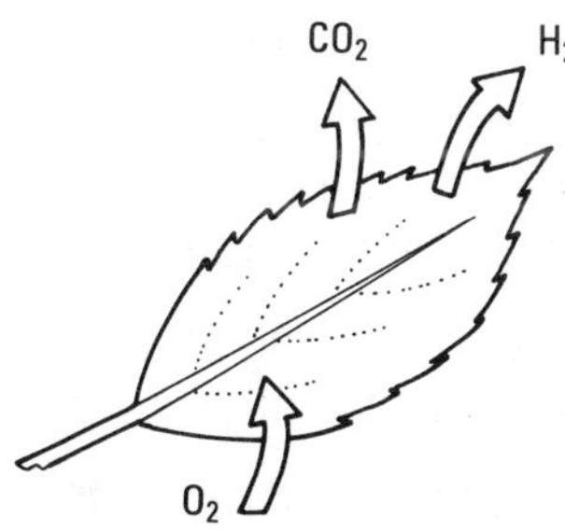

A6, A7

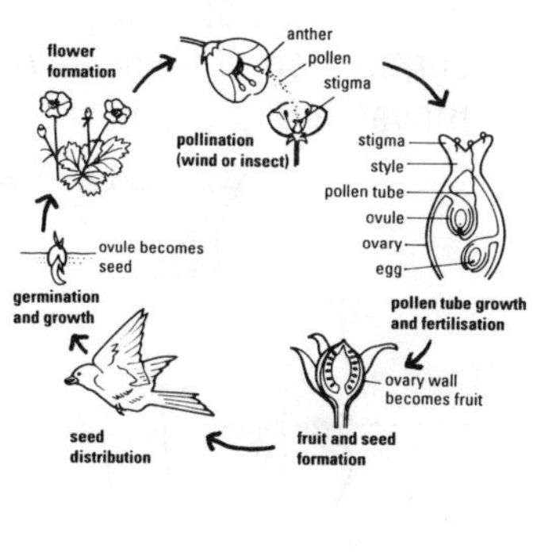

A8, A9

wind:

carriage on an animal:

being eaten by an animal:

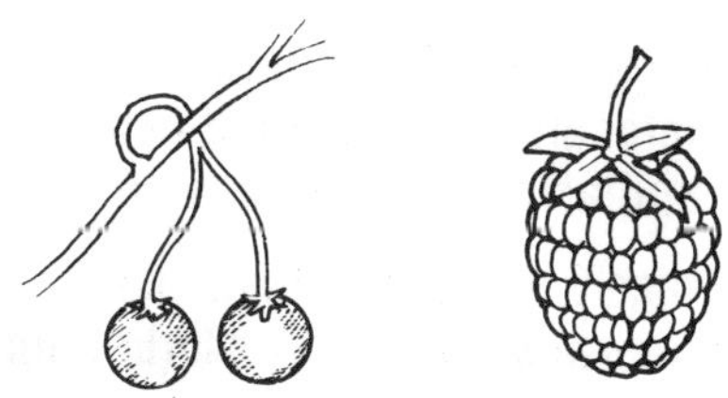

A10, A11

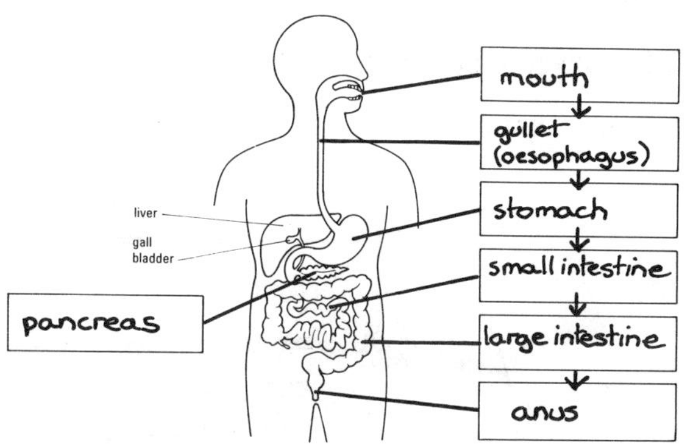

A12 starch → glucose
protein → amino acids
fat → fatty acids and glycerol.

A13, A14

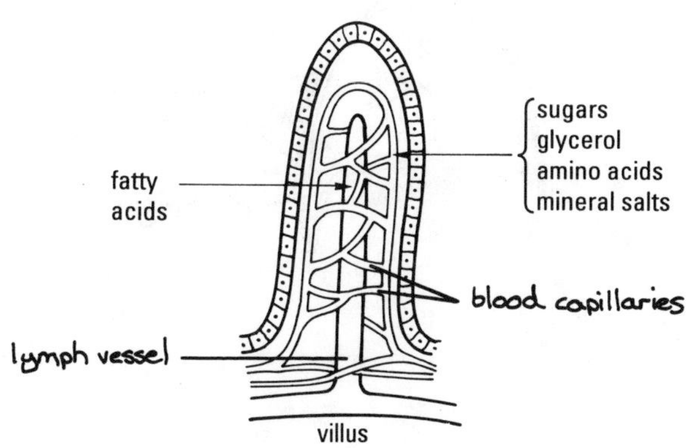

A15

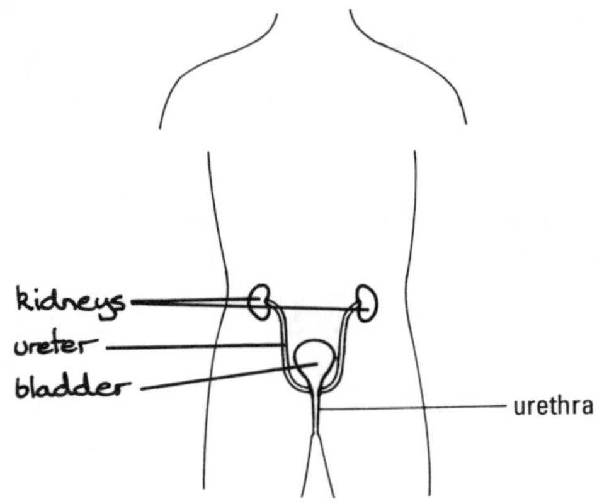

Stage 1 **liquid containing urea and other small molecules is forced out of a group of narrow blood capillaries into the capsule of the kidney nephron.**

Stage 2 **valuable substances such as water and mineral salts are reabsorbed into blood capillaries.**

A16 More water is reabsorbed by the kidney nephrons. A small volume of more concentrated urine is produced.

A17, A18 oxygen; carbon dioxide.

A19 inhaled exhaled

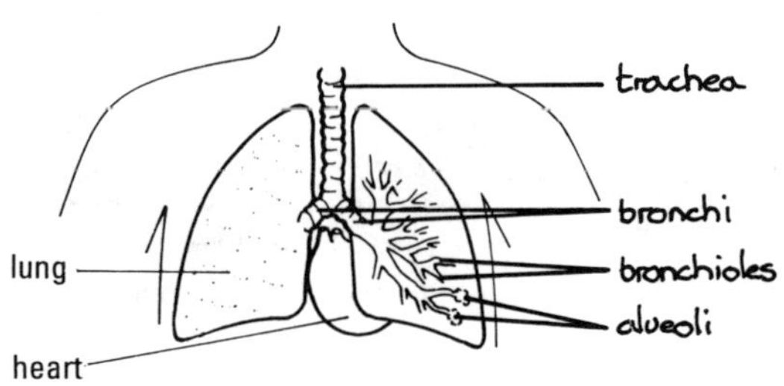

A20, A21 exhaling inhaling

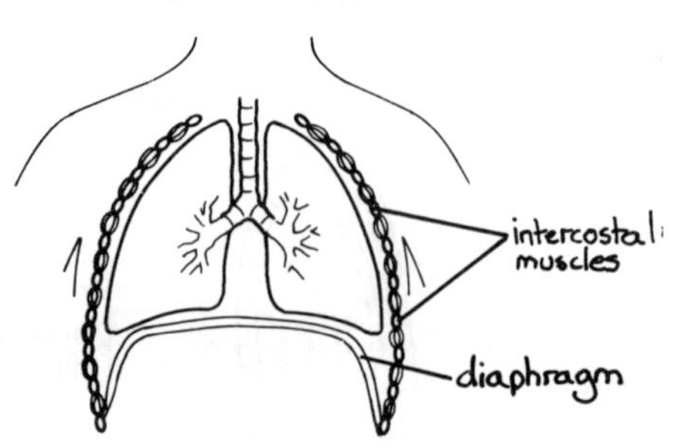

A22 male

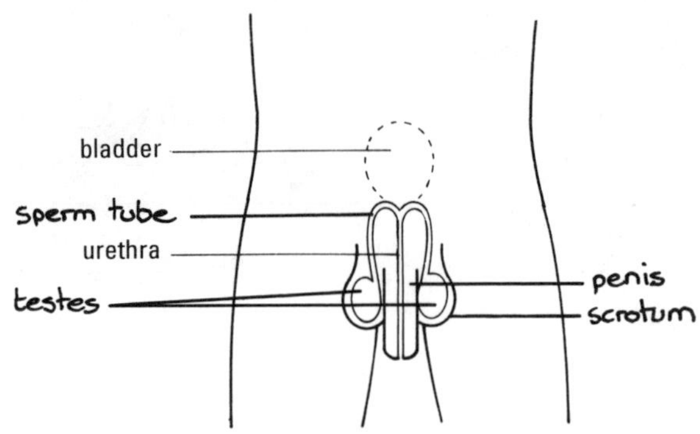

female

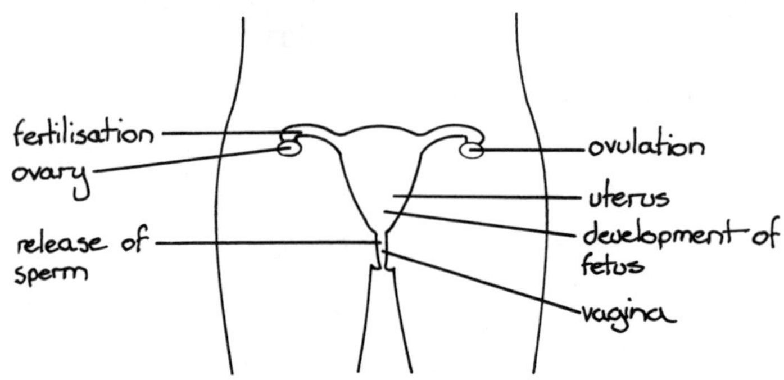

A23, A24 A reflex action, for example, pin prick.

stimulus →	receptor →	co-ordinator →
pin in finger	**nerves in skin**	**CNS**

effector →	response
arm muscles	**move finger away**

A25

bones	act in opposing or antagonistic pairs – when one contracts the other relaxes
muscles	bring nerve impulses from the central nervous system to stimulate muscle contraction
nerves	muscles are attached to these – contraction of muscles results in movement at a joint

A26, A27

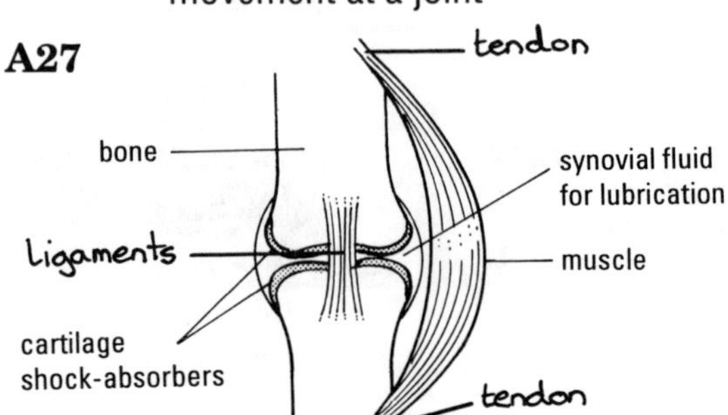

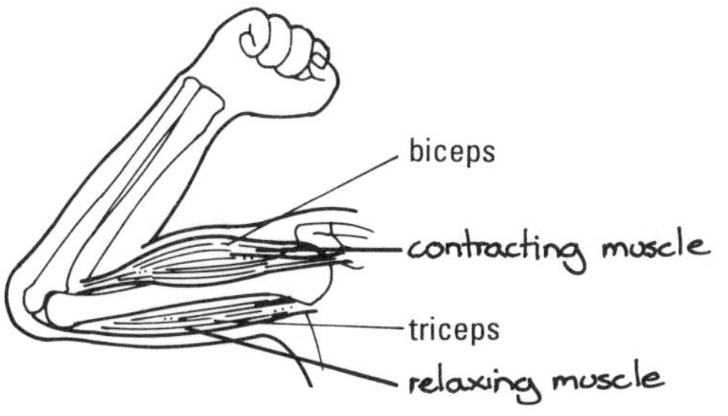

B1, B2

	Mitosis	Meiosis
Function	increases number of cells for growth and tissue repair	produces sex cells for reproduction

B3

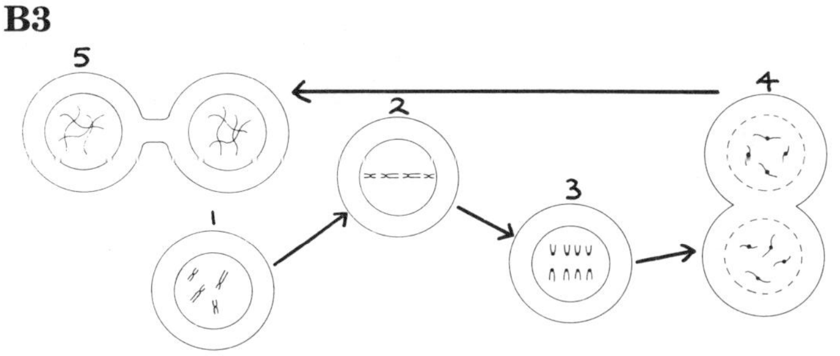

B4, B5, B6, B7, B8

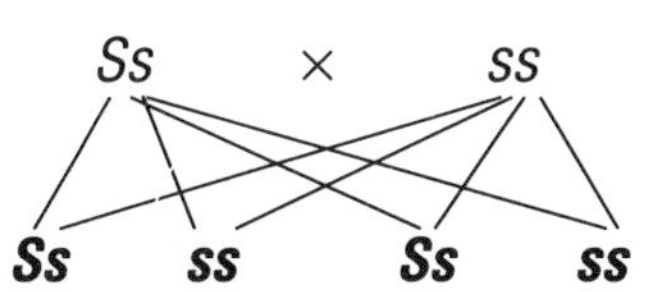

phenotypic ratio; 2 straight wing: 2 curly wing
genotypic ratio; 2 heterozygous: 2 homozygous recessive.

B9 Any two suitable examples: **pea plants with more peas in a pod; tomato plants that produce larger fruits; pigs that lay down less fat; cows that produce higher milk yields**, etc.

C1

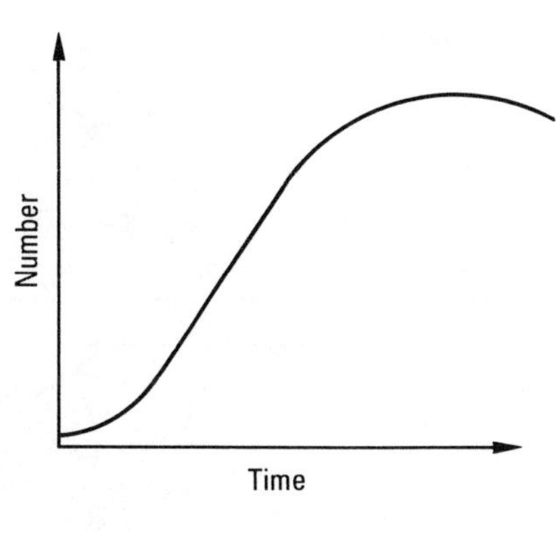

C2, C3

obtaining and burning fossil fuels	over-use of fertilisers causing water pollution
	formation of spoil tips causing land pollution
producing food	release of greenhouse gases and creation of acid rain
	destruction of habitats for farmland

D1, D2

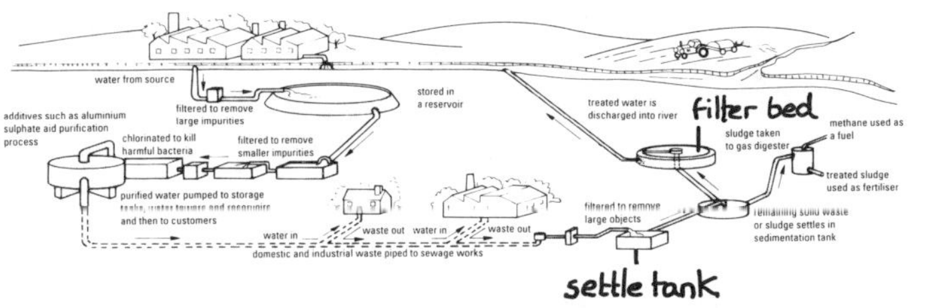

D3

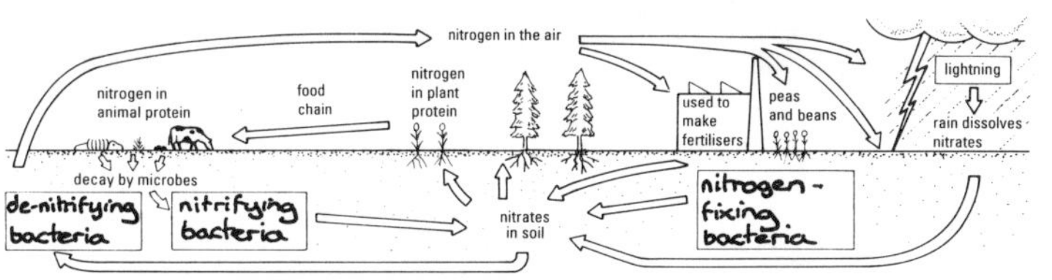

AT2 Levels 9 & 10 (pages 39–46)

A1, A2

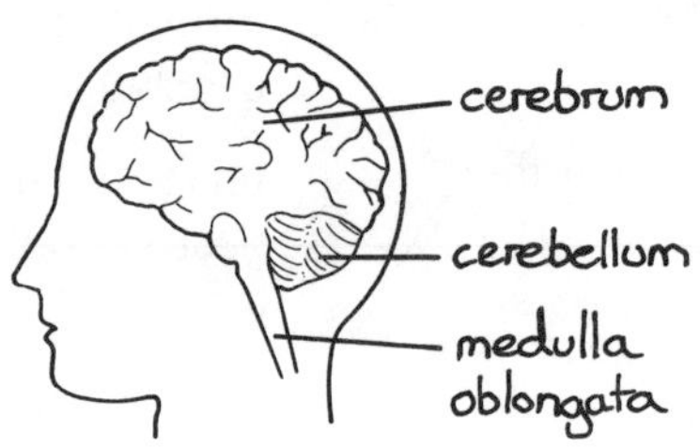

A3

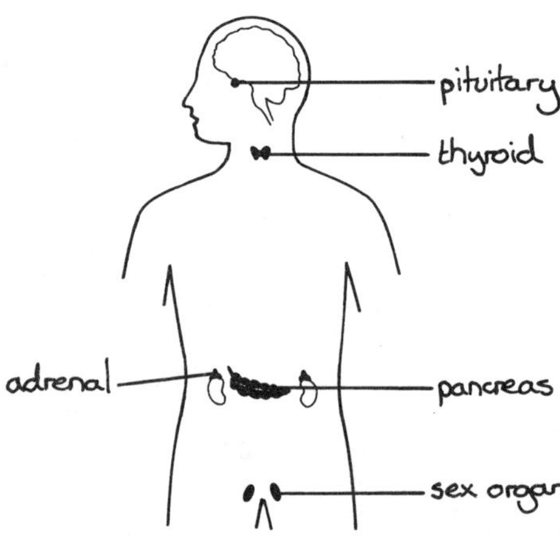

A4 **Adrenaline increases the heart beat rate, which increases the supply of blood and therefore oxygen and glucose to the muscles, enabling a rapid 'flight or fight' response. Glycogen in the liver is broken down to glucose which is transported in the blood to the muscle cells.**

A5, A6, A7

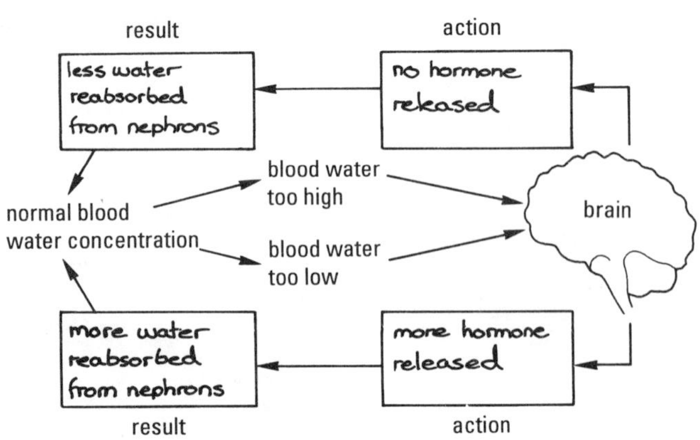

A8

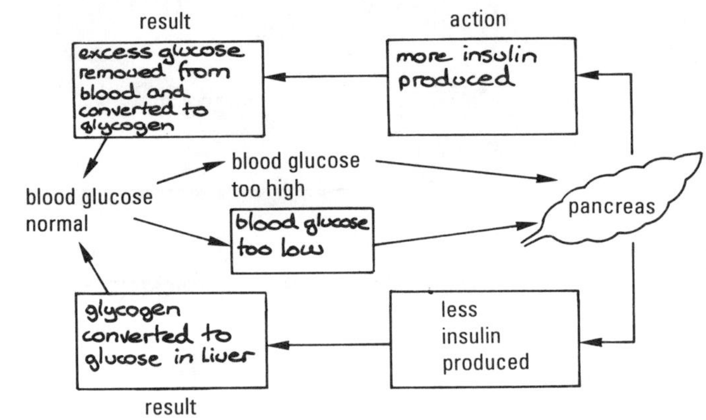

A9 **When it is too hot: the amount of hormone released from the thyroid falls, and metabolic rate slows. Blood flows near the skin surface, body hairs lie flat, and sweating begins.**

A10 **increases decreases.**

B1, B2

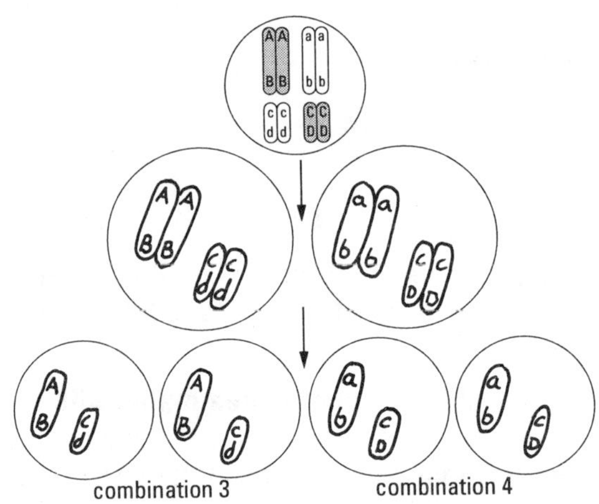

B3, B4

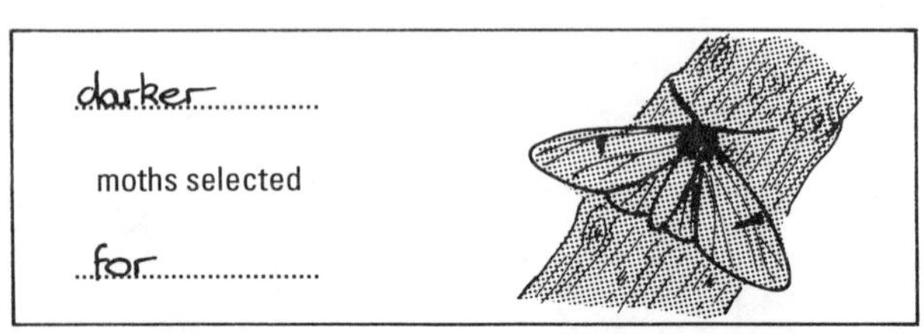

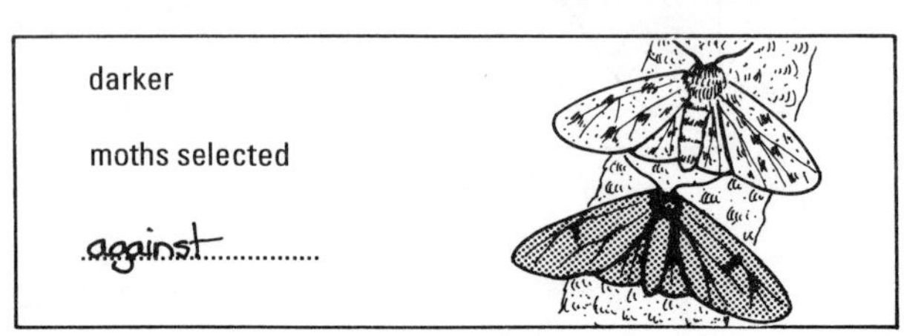

B5, B6, B7, B8

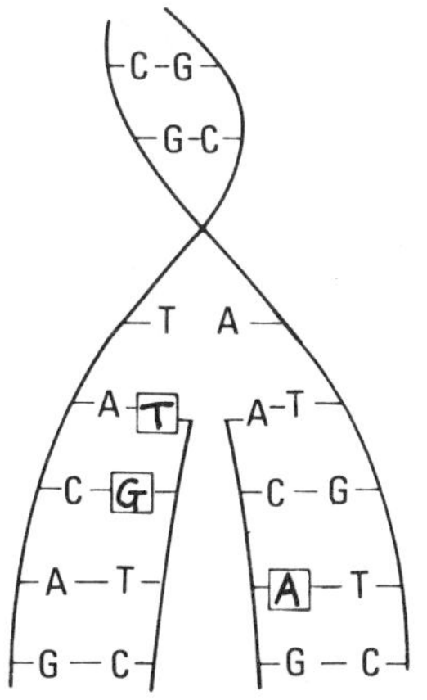

B9, B10

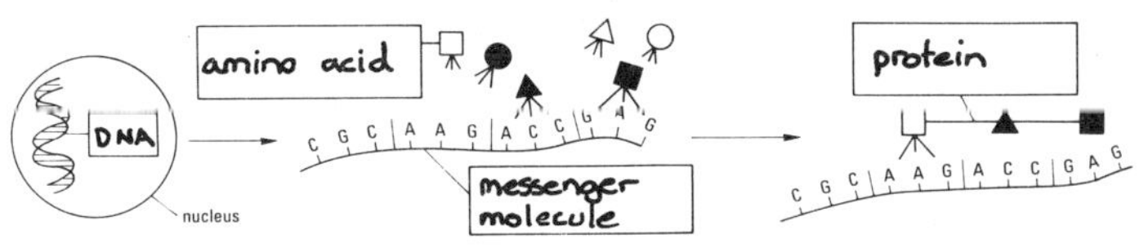

B11, B12, B13

1 **bacterial DNA**
2 **insulin gene**
3 **clones**
4 **extraction and purification.**

B14, C1

deforestation	atmosphere soil organisms	• global warming • organisms must adapt to environmental changes • soil erosion
greenhouse gases from burning fossil fuels	atmosphere organisms	• habitats destroyed • less photosynthesis so more CO_2, less O_2
release of CFC gases	atmosphere organisms	• UV rays damage skin, for example, skin cancers • ozone layer damaged

C2, D1, D2

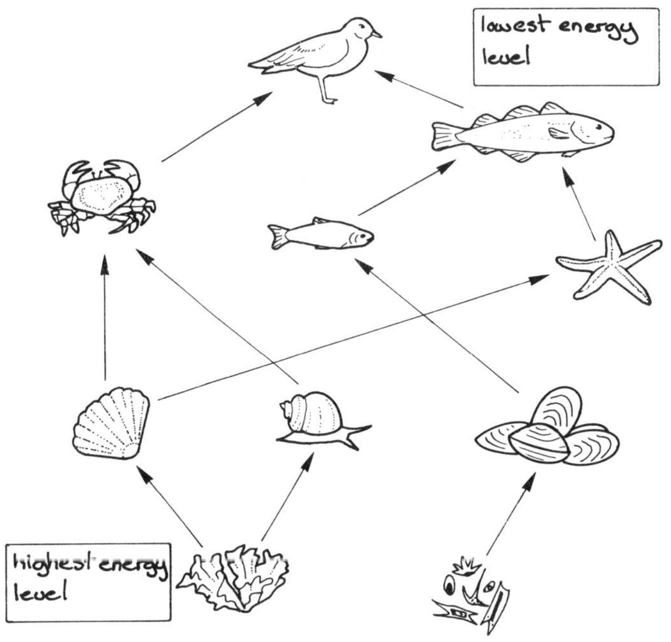

D3, D4

removing hedges to increase area of fields, making ploughing and harvesting easier	rapid spread of disease or pests
adding fertilisers to the soil	destruction of habitats
using insecticides to kill pests	fertilisers leached from soil into waterways causing pollution
growing same plants in huge areas (monocultures)	poisons pass into food chains and concentrated along chain

AT3 Levels 4, 5 & 6 (pages 48–57)

A1 **stone, wool, wood** **bamboo, clay, cotton** **coal, oil, iron ore, wood, sand, salt**

A2 Solids: **wood stone** Liquids: **milk water** Gases: **nitrogen carbon dioxide.**

A3 **gas; solid; liquid.**

A4 **octane; heptane water; salt.**

A5

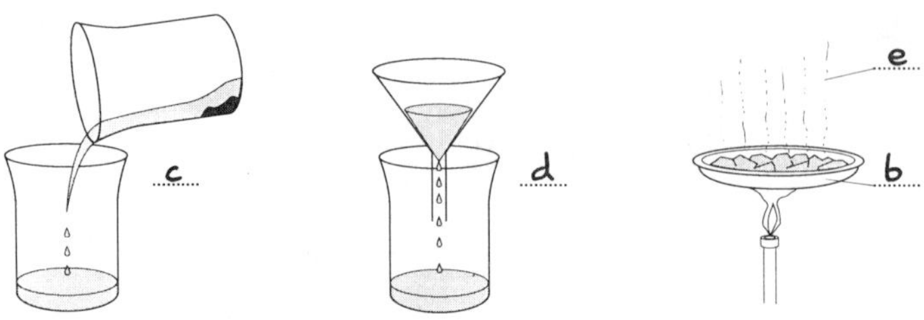

A6 **crystallizing distilling distilling.**

A7

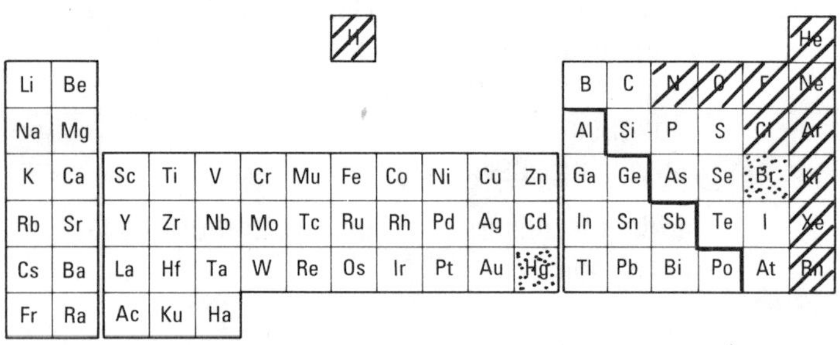

most common non-metal: silicon most common metal: aluminium

A8 copper **bulb lights** magnesium **bulb lights** sulphur and Ag **bulbs light** Ar **bulb does not light** Al **bulb lights.**

A9 **carbon; four sodium; chlorine; oxygen copper sulphate.**

A10 Ionic compounds: **sodium chlorate; copper nitride; copper nitrate; copper sulphate**
Covalent compounds: **carbon tetrachloride; carbon dioxide; sulphur trioxide.**

A11 **low do not conduct.**

A12 **0 °C 100 °C**

A13

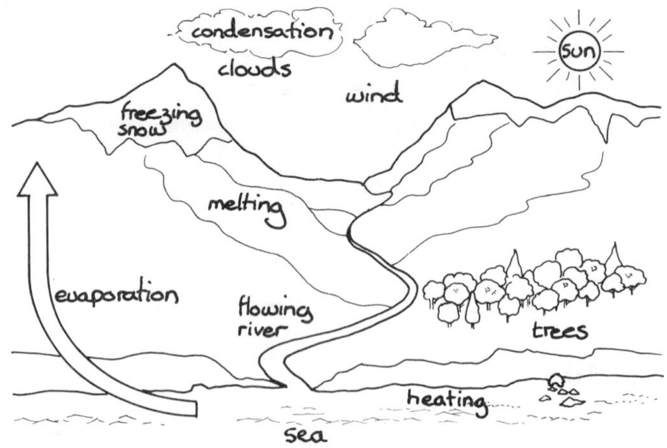

B1

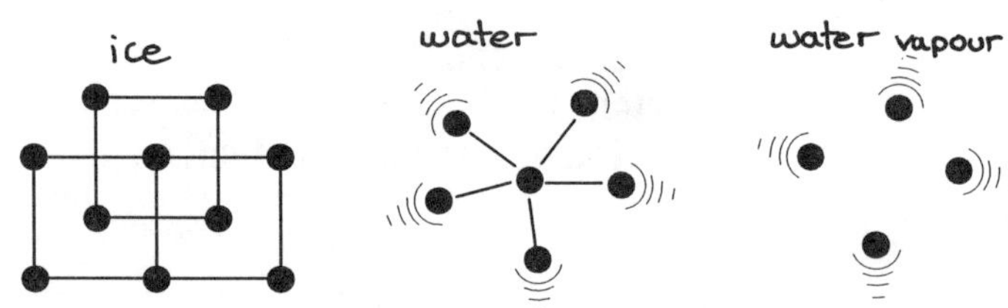

C1 **cheese or yoghurt charcoal copper aluminium alcohol (ethanol).**

C2

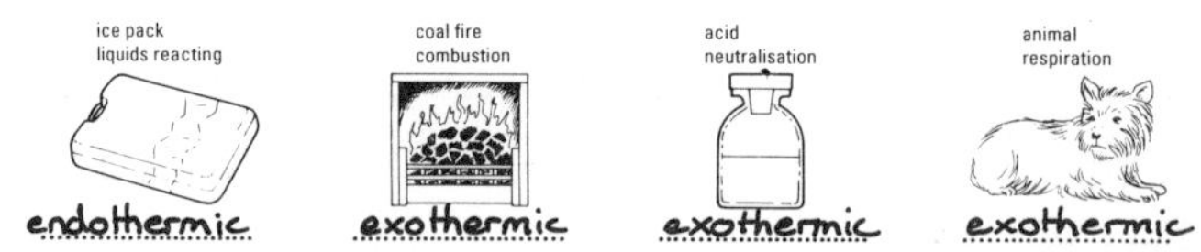

C3

	Metal symbol	Name
Please	K	potassium
Send	Na	sodium
Lord	Li	lithium
Charles	Ca	calcium
McLean	Mg	magnesium
A	Al	aluminium
Zebra	Zn	zinc
If	Fe	iron
The	Sn	tin
Lame	Pb	lead
Horse	H	hydrogen
Cannot	Cu	copper
Munch	Hg	mercury
Sweet	Ag	silver
Grass	Au	gold

Reaction with

water	oxygen	acid
More energy released	More energy released	More energy released

C4 **copper nickel iron.**

C5 **heat; carbon dioxide.**

C6 copper oxide sulphur calcium + oxygen
carbon dioxide + water oxygen; carbon dioxide.

C7 oxygen water.

C8 1 keep oxygen out (by using a fire extinguisher)
2 remove fuel (by chopping down trees in a forest)
3 lower the temperature (by using water).

C9 salt water bath crystals in water.

C10 colour.

C11

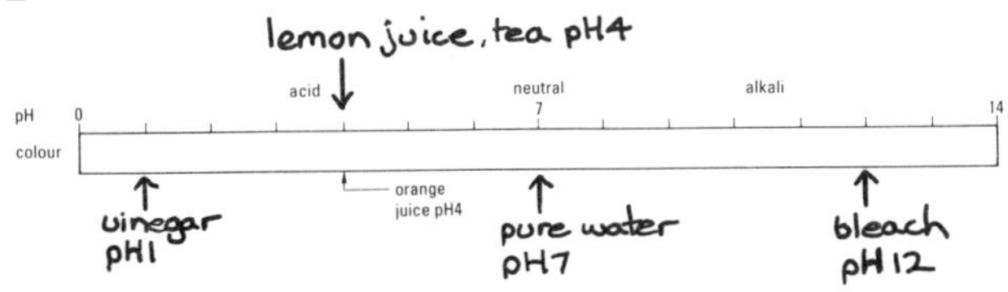

C12 neutralisation.

C13 oxygen gas and copper metal oxygen gas and hydrogen gas.

D1

D2 a) Warm air exerts less pressure than cold air and so winds will blow into a low.
b) Rainfall statistics over a period of years suggest which months will be wettest.

D3 less; rises convection slowly jet streams.

D4

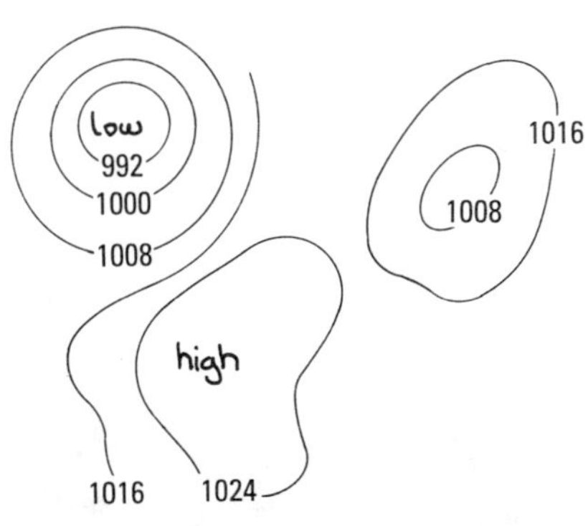

D5

middle of a low	clear day; sunny; frost at night
deep low, moving away to the east	warm cloudless day, hot
middle of a high in summer	'close' day; no rain; no wind; cloudy
middle of a high in winter	heavy rain; gale force winds

D6

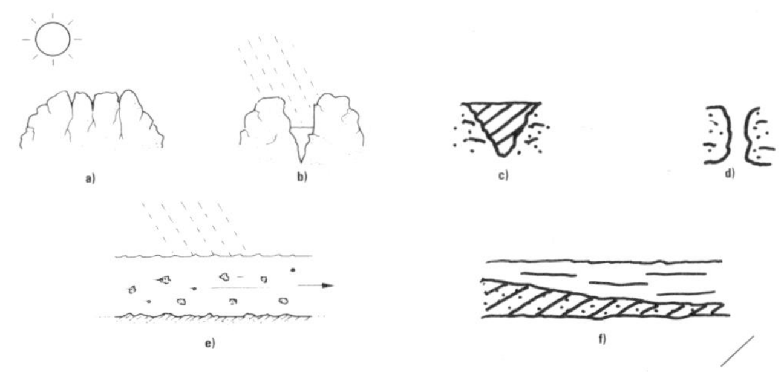

D7 igneous: **basalt, granite** sedimentary: **sandstone, shale** metamorphic: **marble, slate**.

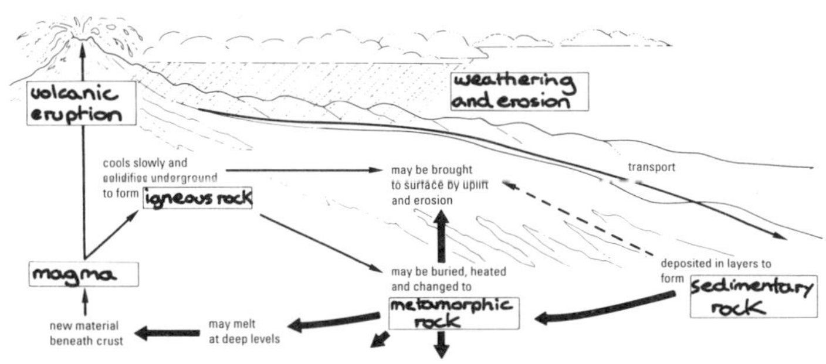

D8 a) Limestone: **sediment, including dead creatures, settled. Everything was squashed and became rock. Some of the creatures had shells which became limestone.**
b) Granite: **molten rock cooled slowly to form an igneous rock with large crystals – granite.**
c) Marble: **limestone was heated quickly underground and changed to the metamorphic rock – marble. All the shells were destroyed by heat and pressure.**

D9

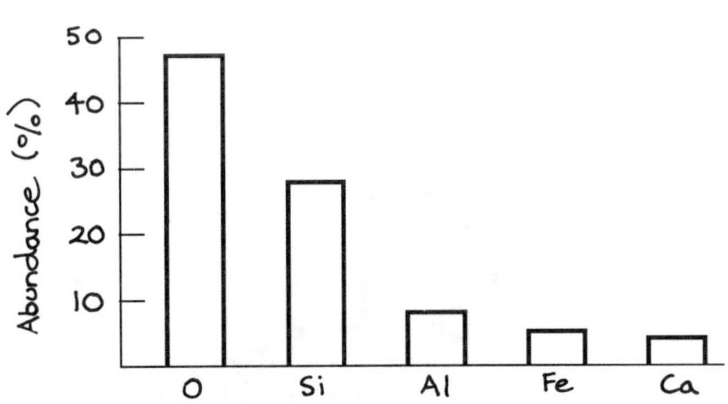

AT3 Levels 7 & 8 (pages 58–71)

A1, A2 a) P b) P c) C d) P e) P f) C g) P h) P.

A3 copper; iron crystal glass; soda glass polyethene; polystyrene brick; china cotton; flax.

A4

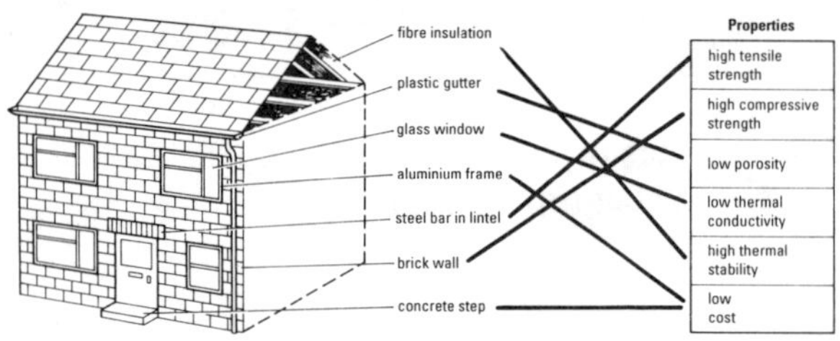

A5

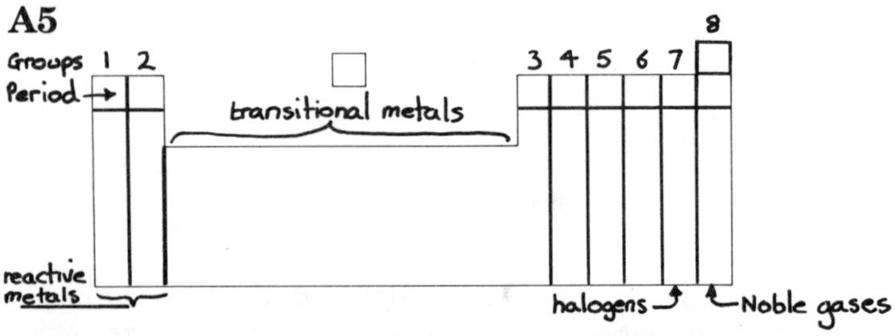

A6, A7, A8 able to be beaten, rolled, etc. into a new shape able to be drawn out into wire without breaking able to be stretched considerably without breaking.

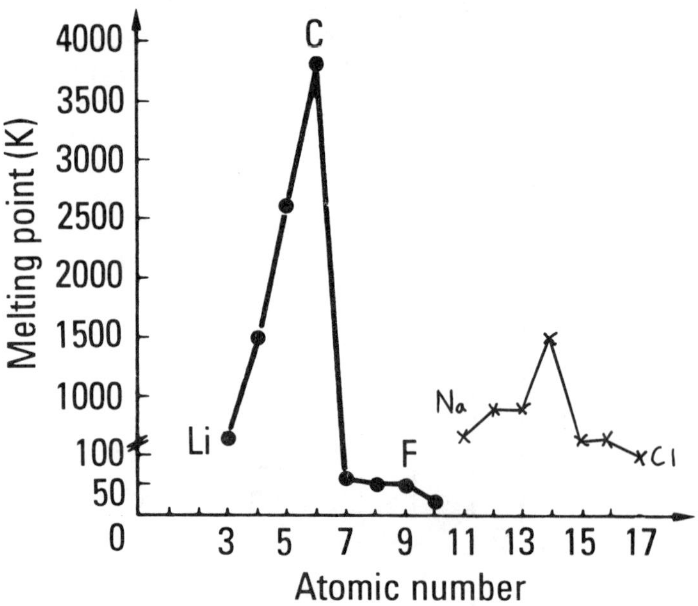

B1

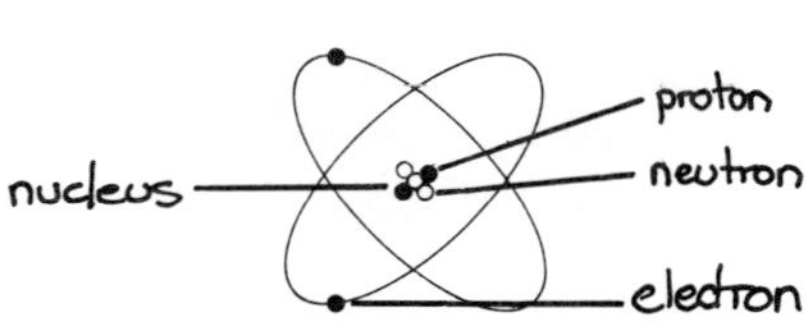

B2 $_6C$: 6 protons
6 electrons

$_{11}Na$: 11 protons
11 electrons

$_{12}Mg$: 12 protons
12 electrons

$_{17}Cl$: 17 protons
17 electrons

B3

Symbol	Number of protons	Number of electrons	Number of neutrons
	13	13	14
	9	9	10
	79	79	118

B4 ^{12}C: $p = 6$; $n = 6$; $e = 6$
^{14}C: $p = 6$; $n = 8$; $e = 6$

B5

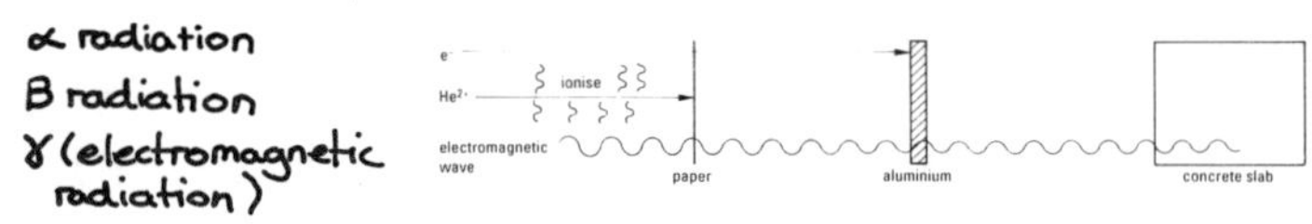

B6

c → f → a → e → b → d

B7, B8 Na^+ 10; Mg^{2+} 10; F^- 10; O^{2-} 10

B9

$_4Be$	4	2, 2
$_{12}Mg$	12	2, 8, 2
$_{20}Ca$	20	2, 8, 8, 2

B10, B11, B12

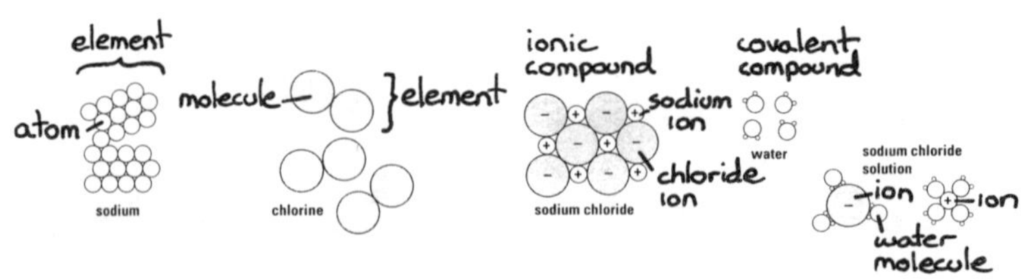

B13, B14, B15

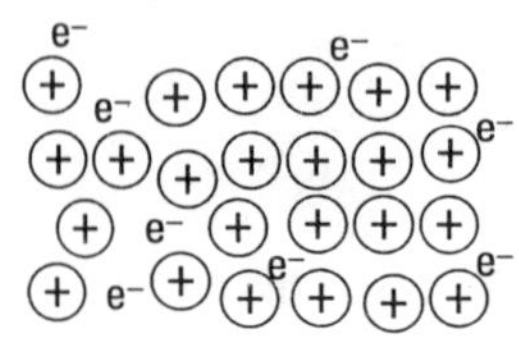
copper

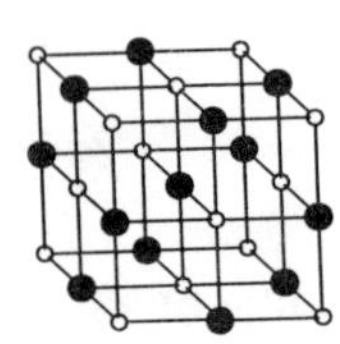
sodium chloride

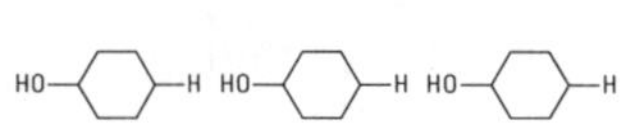
glucose

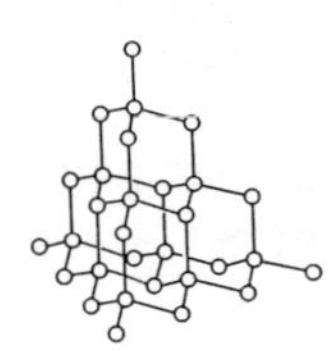
diamond

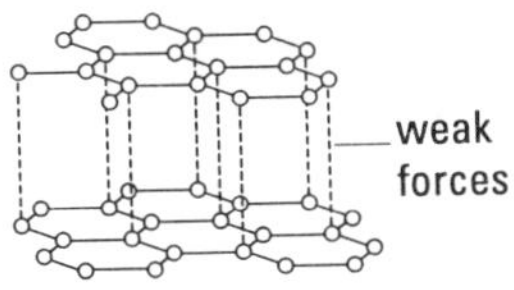

graphite

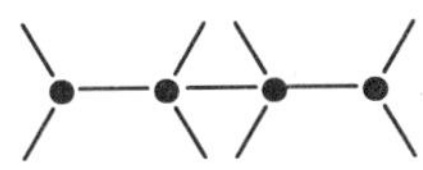

polyethene

B16, B17

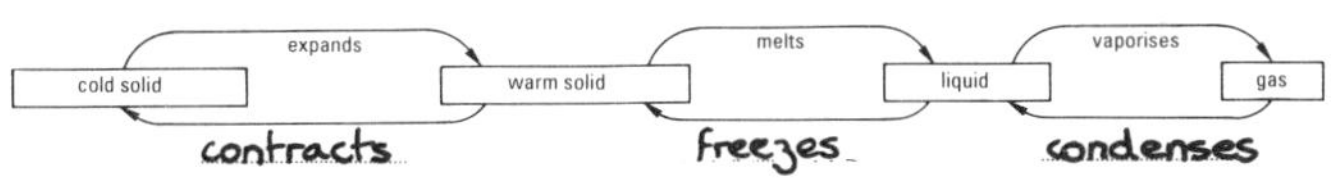

B18 y: $\frac{P_1V_1}{T_1} = \frac{P_2V_2}{T_2}$

$$\frac{1 \times 4}{200} = \frac{3 \times y}{200}$$

$$y = \frac{200 \times 4}{200 \times 3}$$

y = **1.3 litres**

C1, C2

C3

increased temperature	more particles, so more collisions
decreased particle size of reactants	more energy to activate more successful collisions
catalyst present	more particles touching so more collisions
increased concentration of reactants	particles better positioned so more successful collisions

C4 boiling potatoes; cooking toast cutting up vegetables before cooking rennin when making yoghurt adding more coal to a fire.

C5 Haber process: nitrogen gas and hydrogen gas react to make ammonia. Gases passed over an iron catalyst.

Cement manufacture: limestone and shale ground into small pieces. Heated in a kiln.

Oxyacetylene torch: acetylene is burned in a high concentration of oxygen to give greater heat.

C6

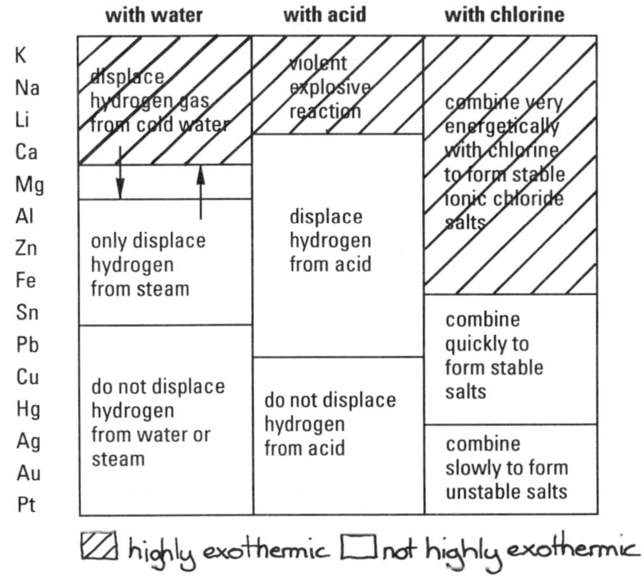

C7, C8, C9, C10

K, Na, Li, Ca, Mg, Al	**melting and then electrolysis**
Zn, Fe, Sn, Pb	**heating with carbon**
Cu, Hg	**strong heating**
Ag, Pt, Au	**gentle heating**

C11

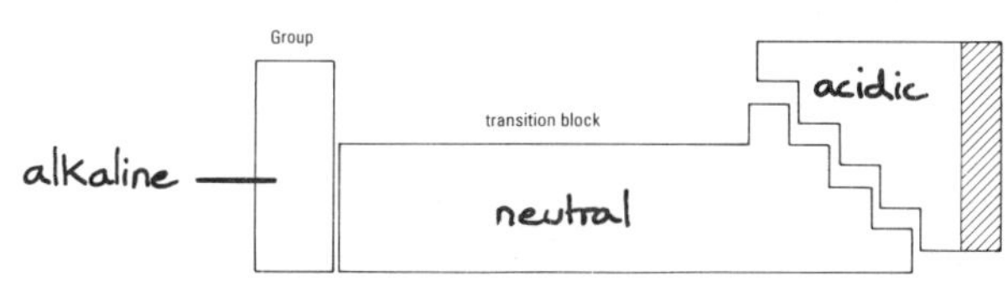

C12, C13 sulphuric acid ($H_2{}^{+}SO_4^{2-}$).

C14 chloride sulphate.

C15 Bases: reactive metal metal oxide metal hydroxide metal carbonate.

C16

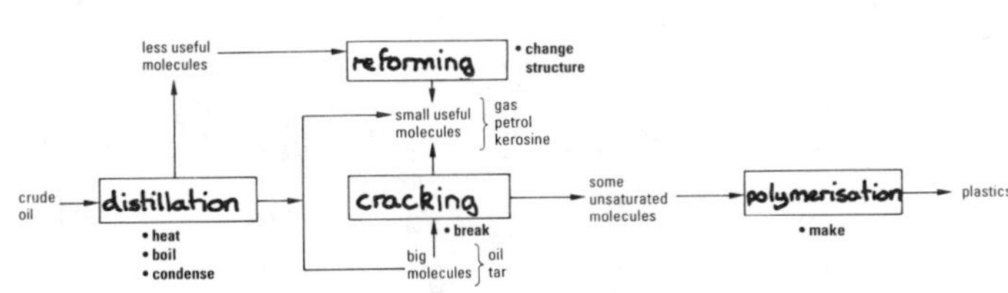

C17

First in series	**ethene**
Molecular formula	**C_2H_4**
Structural formula	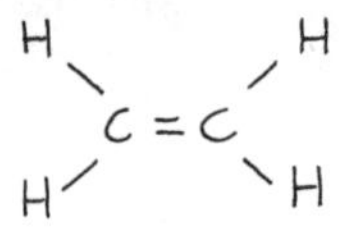
General formula for the series	**C_nH_{2n}**
Trend in physical properties	**boiling point and viscosity increase as molecules get bigger**
Chemical properties	**small ones burn well; decolorise bromine water very fast; double c=c bonds so reactive**

C18, C19

CO_2	acid rain
CO	brain damage
NO_2	greenhouse gas
lead compounds	poisonous

C20

Group	1	2	**3**	**4**	**5**	6	7	8
Valency	1	2	3	4	3	2	**1**	**0**

C21, C22, C23

sodium oxide		hydrogen fluoride	
Na	**O**	**H**	**F**
1	**2**	**1**	**1**
Na_2O		**HF**	
magnesium chloride		silver(I) sulphide	
Mg	**Cl**	**Ag**	**S**
2	**1**	**1**	**2**
$MgCl_2$		**Ag_2S**	
iron(II) chloride		lithium nitrate	
Fe	**Cl**	**Li**	**NO_3**
2	**1**	**1**	**1**
$FeCl_2$		$LiNO_3$	
aluminium phosphate		calcium hydroxide	
Al	**PO_4**	**Ca**	**OH**
3	**3**	**2**	**1**
$AlPO_4$		**$Ca(OH)_2$**	
ammonium carbonate			
NH_4	**CO_3**		
1	**2**		
$(NH_4)_2CO_3$			

C24, C25

a) **hydrochloric acid + calcium carbonate → calcium chloride + carbon dioxide + water**

HCl $CaCO_3$ $CaCl_2$ CO_2 H_2O

$$2HCl + CaCO_3 \rightarrow CaCl_2 + CO_2 + H_2O$$

$$2HCl(aq) + CaCO_3(s) \rightarrow CaCl_2(aq) + CO_2(g) + H_2O(l)$$

b) **copper oxide + carbon → copper + carbon dioxide**

CuO C Cu CO_2

$$2CuO + C \rightarrow 2Cu + CO_2$$

$$2CuO(s) + C(s) \rightarrow 2Cu(s) + CO_2(g)$$

c) **methane + oxygen → carbon dioxide + water**

CH_4 O_2 CO_2 H_2O

$$CH_4 + 2O_2 \rightarrow CO_2 + 2H_2O$$

$$CH_4(g) + 2O_2(g) \rightarrow CO_2(g) + 2H_2O(l)$$

C26, C27 At the negative electrode: **each copper ion gains two electrons and becomes a neutral copper atom.**
At the positive electrode: **each chloride ion loses an electron. Two neutral chlorine atoms join to make a chlorine molecule.**

D1

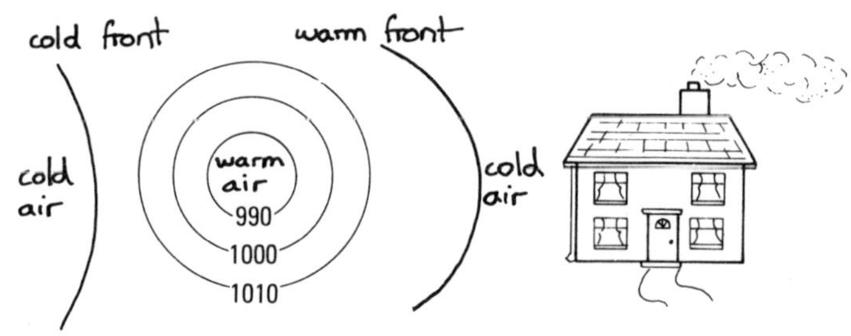

D2

mist and fog	there is a large pressure difference between a deep low and the surrounding area
thunder and lightning	without clouds to retain the heat, the land becomes very cold at night and water condenses and then freezes
frost	the ground is cool. It cools the still warm air above and water droplets condense
summer heat-waves	there is damp warm air near the ground and cold air above it. The warm air rises and the cool air falls, producing ions as they flow past each other
gales	the jet-stream moves north and allows warm tropical air to become established

D3

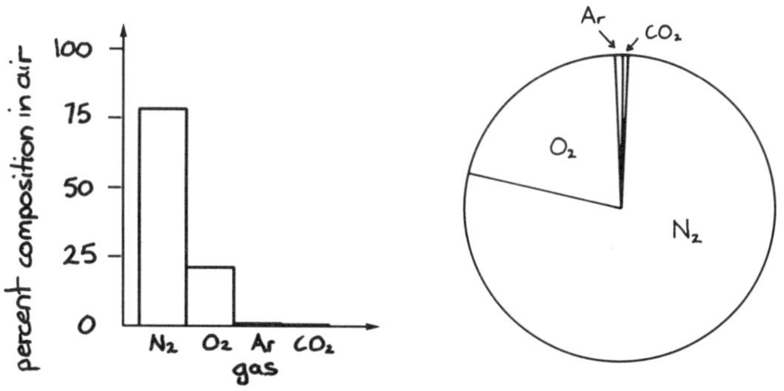

D4 **oxygen nitrogen water.**

D5 **calcite; iron pyrites; fluorite.**

D6, D7

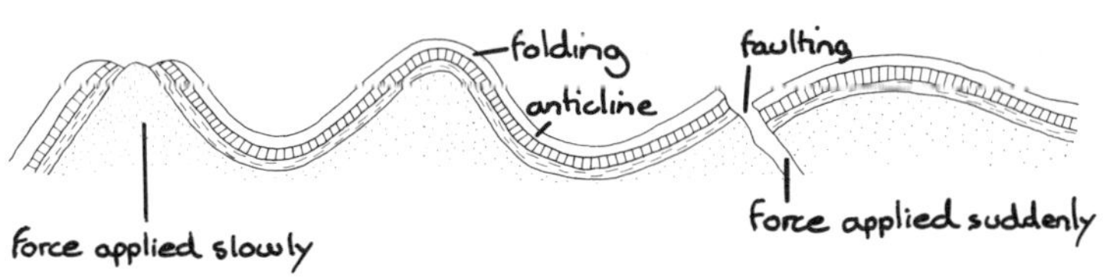

AT3 Levels 9 & 10 (pages 72–84)

A1, A2 addition polymers: **polypropylene; polyvinylchloride; polyethene**

A3

thermal stability:	**very high**
thermal conductivity:	**low**
boiling point:	**above 2500 °C**
solubility in water:	**zero**
compression strength:	**very high**
thermoplasticity:	**zero**
biodegradability:	**zero**

A4, B1, B2

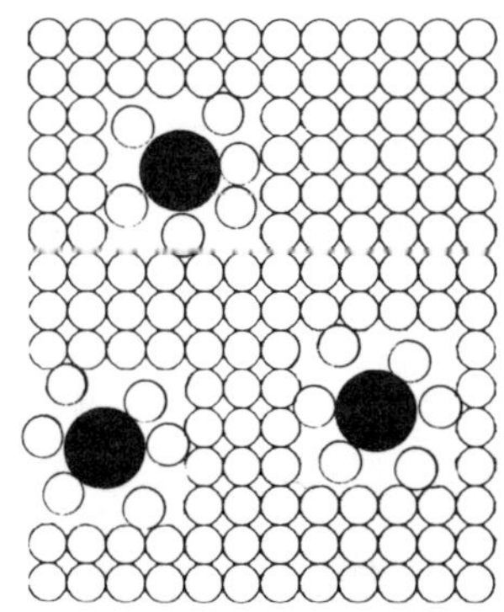

B3 **SiO_2**

B4 no cross-linking: **ductile; weak in compression and tension; low melting and boiling points; malleable; soft** lots of cross-linking: **brittle; stronger in compression and tension; higher melting and boiling points; hard.**

B5

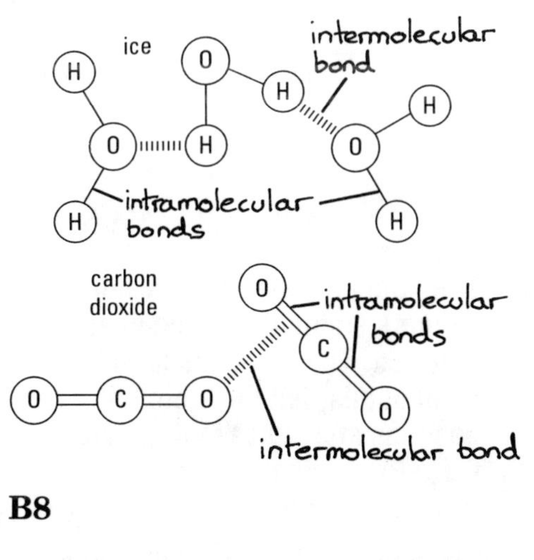

B6, B7, B8

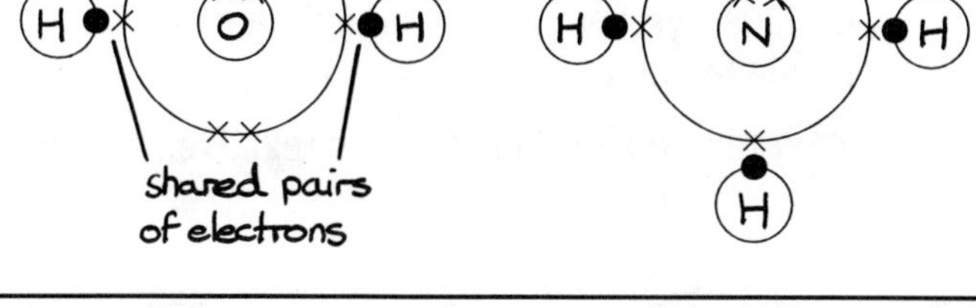

B9

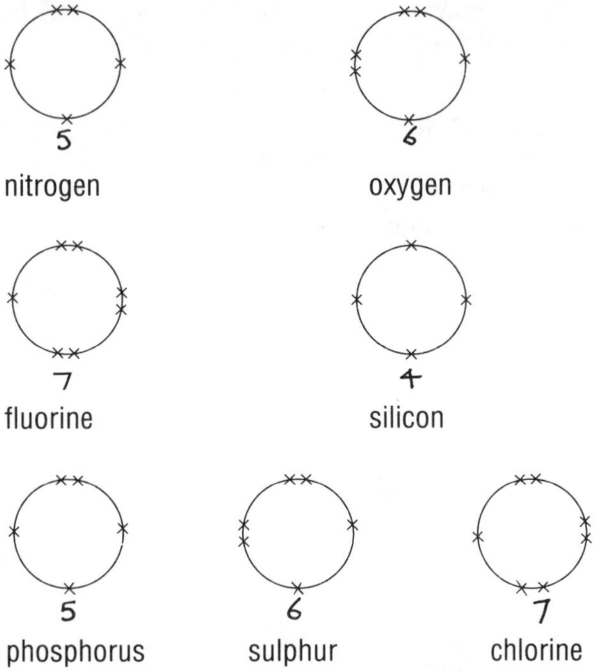

B10

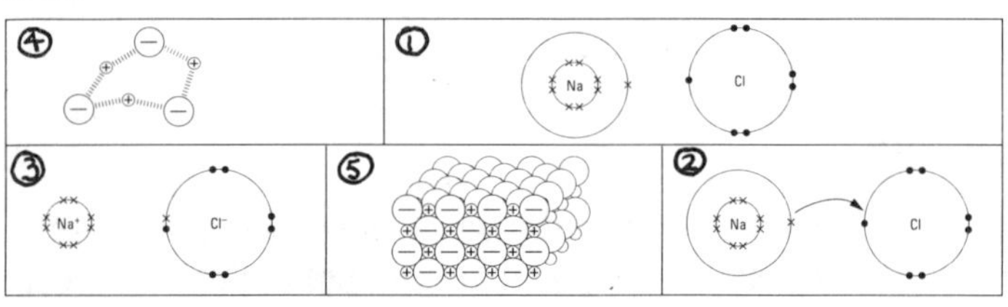

B11

	Metal				Non-metal		
Group	1	2	3	4	5	6	7
Electrons in outer shell	1	**2**	**3**	**4**	5	**6**	**7**
To become stable		lose			gain		
	1	**2**	**3**	**4**	3	**2**	**1**
Ion formed	+	**2+**	**3+**	**4–**	3–	**2–**	**–**
Example	Na^+	Mg^{2+}	Al^{3+}	C^{4-}	N^{3-}	S^{2-}	F^-

B12, B13 **The halogens are all toxic non-metals; to become stable they each need to gain one electron. The halogens form ionic compounds, but the elements exist as gaseous molecules in diatomic state, i.e. $F_{2(g)}$, $Br_{2(g)}$. They all have a valency of 1, and are thus reactive.**

B14 F: **pale greenish-yellow; least dense; very reactive; displaces Cl, Br, I.**

Cl: **greenish-yellow; denser than F; reactive, displaces Br, I.**

Br: **dark red; denser than Cl; less reactive; displaces I.**

I: **black; most dense; much less reactive; is displaced by others.**

B15

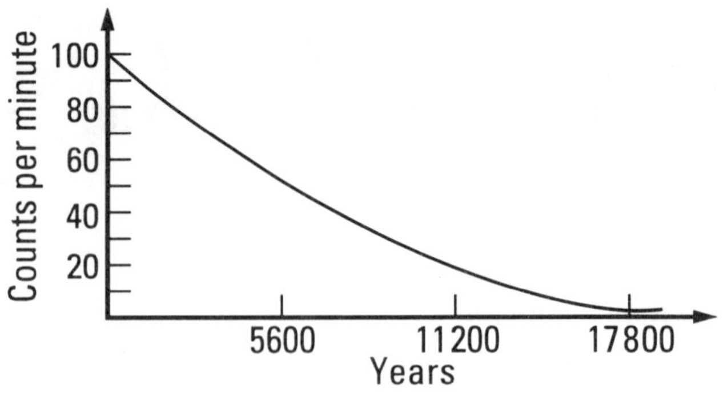

B16 **c → g → e → f → b → a → i → d → h**

B17 **Formation:** $^{14}_{7}N + ^{1}_{0}n \rightarrow ^{14}_{6}C + ^{1}_{1}H$

Decay: $^{14}_{6}C \rightarrow ^{0}_{-1}\beta + ^{14}_{7}N$

C1 **35.5 amu**

C2 $\text{RAM} = \dfrac{(20 \times 90) + (22 \times 10)}{100}$

$= 20.2$ **amu**

C3 hydrogen oxide sodium fluoride calcium carbonate

H_2O NaF $CaCO_3$

RAM: (1)2 + 16 = 18 amu 23 + 19 = 42 amu 40 + 12 + (16)3 = 100 amu

C4

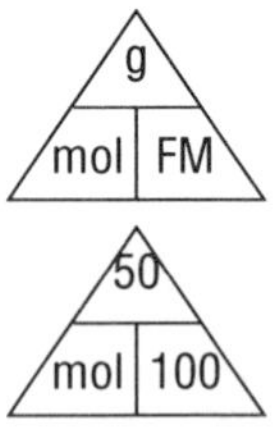

a) **g = 2 × 100 = 200 g**

b) **mole** $= \dfrac{50}{100}$

= 0.5 mol

C5, C6 2 moles of Na need 16 g of oxygen to burn.

10 moles of Na need 80 g of oxygen to burn.

46 g of Na need 16 g of oxygen to burn.

9.2 g of Na need 3.2 g of oxygen to burn.

C7 30 cm^3 of oxygen 15 cm^3 of carbon dioxide.

C8 $2CaCO_3 + 2HNO_3 \rightarrow Ca(NO_3)_2 + CO_2 + H_2O$

$2CaCO_3$	$2HNO_3$	$Ca(NO_3)_2$	CO_2	H_2O
1 mol	**2 mol**	**1 mol**	**1 mol**	**1 mol**
100 g	**126 g**	**164 g**	**44 g**	**18 g**

if 50 g calcium carbonate react, then 22 g carbon dioxide are produced.

C9 ½mole, therefore 12.5 l

C10, C11 electrons on left = gain = reduction
electrons on right = loss = oxidation

C12, C13 *Q:* charge, in coulombs

I: current (i.e. passage of electrons), in amps

t: time, in seconds.

C14, C15, C16

Reactants:

$H_2 + Cl_2$

break 1 H–H = 436

break 1 Cl–Cl = 243

total bond-breaking energy = 679

Products:

2HCl

make 2 H–Cl = 2(431)

= 862

total bond-making energy = 862

overall energy = energy in – energy out = 679 – 862 = –183 kJmol^{-1}.

C17

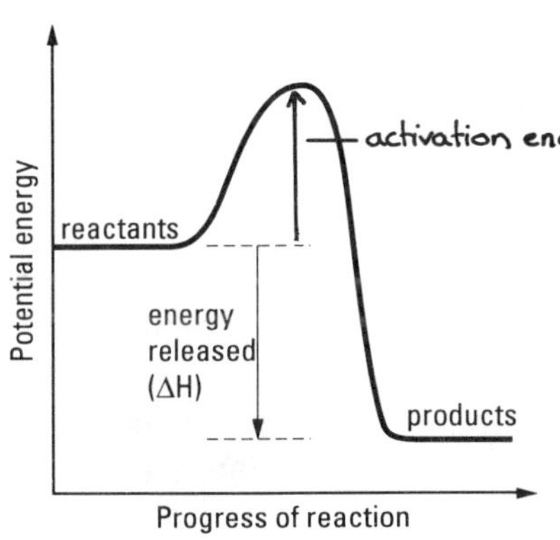

C18, C19

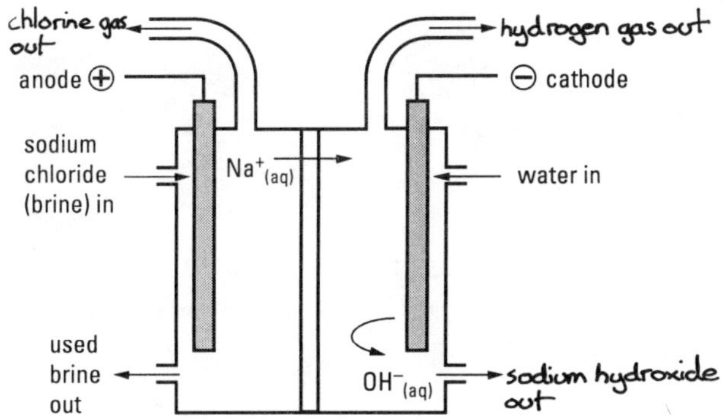

C20

	Products	Sold to make	Benefits	Drawbacks
Cost of process: electricity, **workforce, apparatus**	**chlorine**	pesticides	**increased yields**	**toxic to environment**
		PVC	**long lasting**	**non-bio-degradable**
		bleach	**kills all germs**	**toxic**
		clean water	**reduced disease**	**smell, taste**
	hydrogen	margarine	**substitute to butter**	**fattening**
		hydro-chloric acid	**widely used in industry**	**toxic, acidic**
	sodium hydroxide	paper	**communi-cation**	**loss of trees**
		soaps/ detergents	**cleanse**	**pollution**
		synthetic materials	**ease life**	**non-bio-degradable**

C21 Number **1** is reversible.
High yield by:
1 removing NH_3(g) as it forms (by cooling)
2 using a high pressure
3 using a moderate temperature which speeds up the reaction without destroying the ammonia.

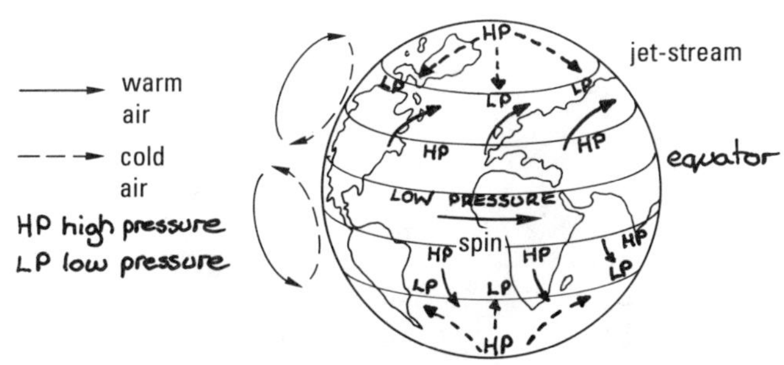

D1 **1 sun (infra-red radiation) 2 moving Earth (energy of motion) 3 latent heat (energy of evaporation).**

D2, D3

D4

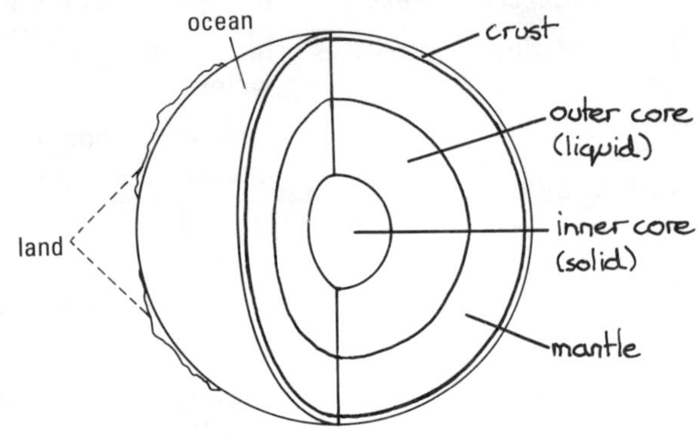

D5, D6

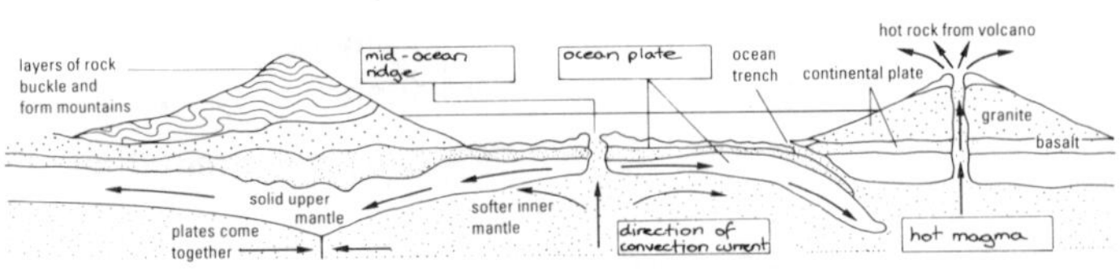

D7

plates slide past one another	fold mountains and trenches
plates collide and crumple at the edges	mid-ocean ridges
plates separate as new material is extruded	fault lines which are susceptible to earthquakes

AT4 Levels 4, 5 & 6 (pages 86–95)

A1

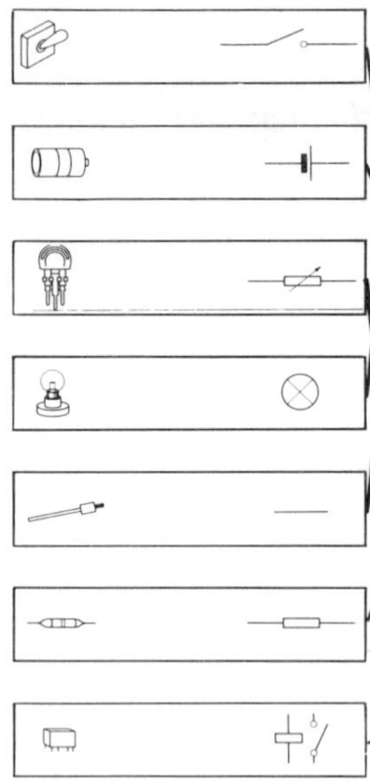

changes electrical energy into light (and heat) energy

conducts electrical charges around a circuit

provides the energy to push the electrical charges round a circuit

opens or closes a circuit to stop or start the flow of electric charges

reduces the electric current by a fixed amount

varies the size of electric current as it is adjusted

a switch turned on or off by an electric current

A2

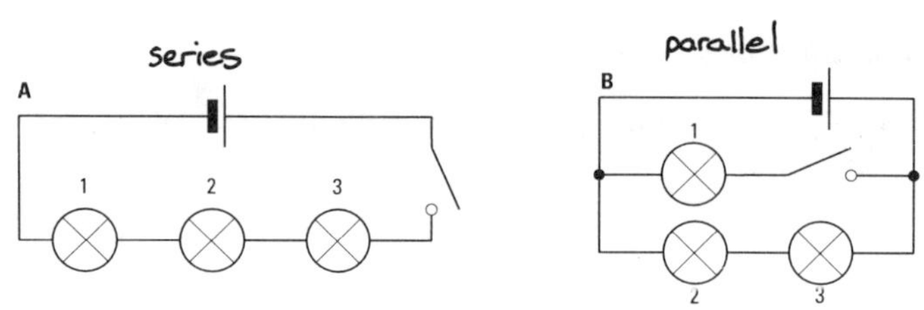

A3 **All the bulbs in each circuit light.**
In circuit A: **bulbs 2 and 3 do not light** In circuit B: **bulbs 2 and 3 light.**

A4, A5, A6 Increase the current by adding **another battery or stronger battery**; or by removing **1 light bulb, or both bulbs.** Decrease the current by **replacing with a weaker battery** or by **adding another bulb.**

A7, A8

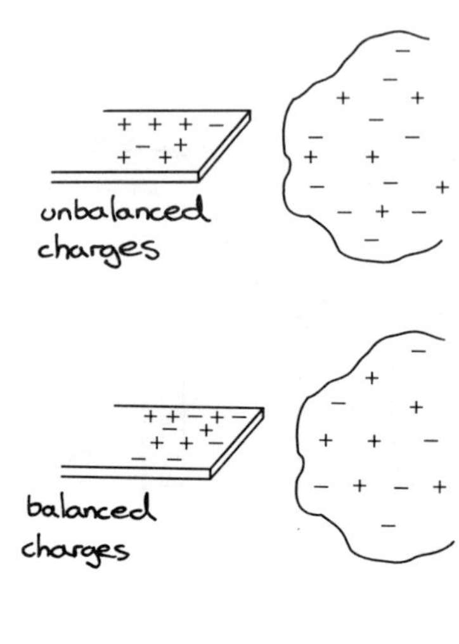

A9 1 **removal of acrylic pullover over hair** 2 **lightning touching television screen.** Or anything suitable.

A10

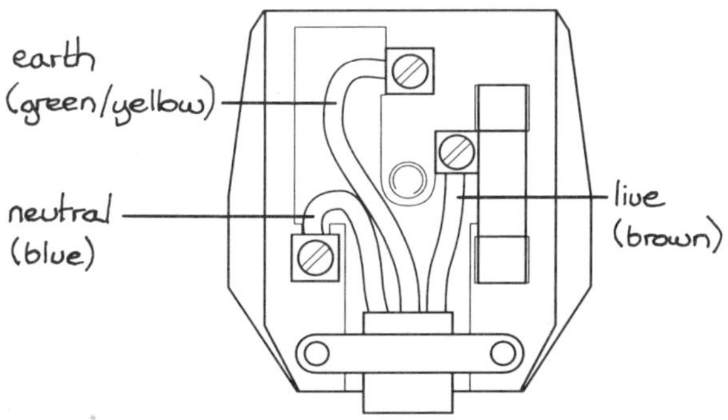

A11 Circuit 1:

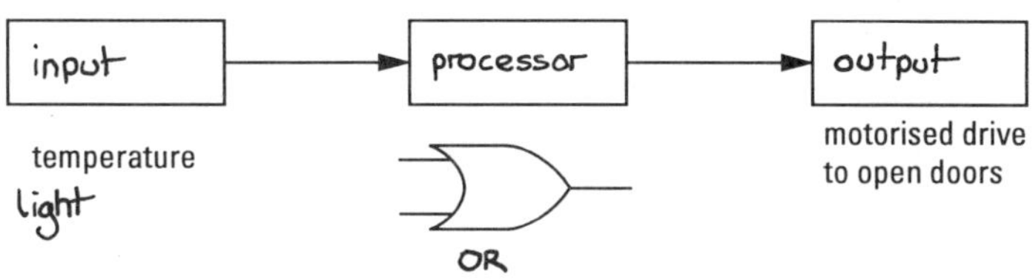

Circuit 2:

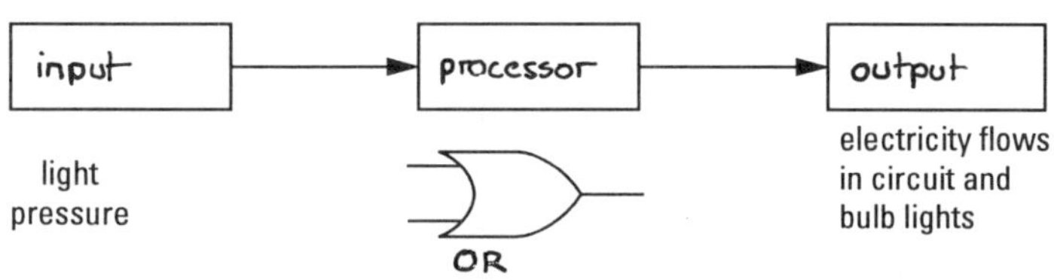

A12

Electronic component	Symbol	Function in electronic circuits
capacitor		**delay processing part of a system**
transistor		**acts as a switch or amplifier**

B1 1 **electrical** to **heat** 2 **light** to **chemical** 3 **radio, television, tape recorder or CD player** 4 **motor or dynamo.**

B2 **chemical → heat → movement → electrical.**

B3 **1** light and sound
2 heat

1 electrical → sound + **heat** **2** electrical → kinetic + **heat**.

B4 **non-renewable** coal; gas; oil; nuclear fuel
renewable wind; sunshine; water; waves.

B5

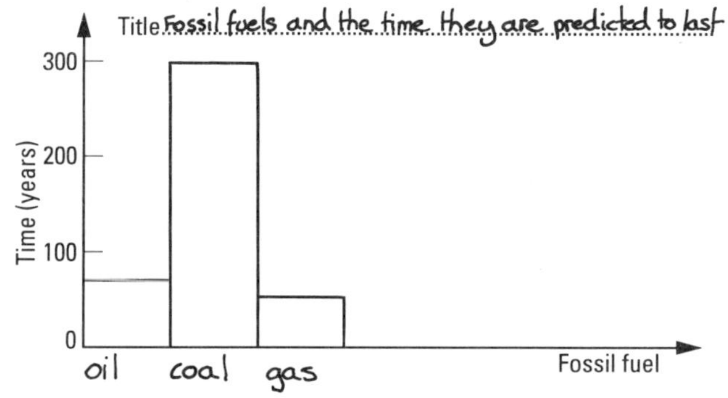

B6, B7, C1, C2

pushing	**pushing**
squashing	**pulling**
pulling	**tearing**
twisting	**pulling**

C3, C4 **bending/pushing** **squashing** **pulling.**

C5, C6 **accelerate** **change direction** **decelerate.**

C7 time taken, $t = \frac{\mathbf{s}}{\mathbf{v}}$

distance travelled, $s = \mathbf{t} \times \mathbf{v}$

average speed of car $v = \frac{s}{t} = \frac{720}{4.8}$

$= 150$ km/hr

C8, C9 pressure = ~~force~~ × area

pressure = ~~$\frac{\text{area}}{\text{force}}$~~

pressure $= \frac{\textbf{force}}{\textbf{area}} = \frac{\mathbf{80}}{\mathbf{0.3}} = $ **266.7 Pa**

D1, D2 a) and b) **Because light (a) reflected from the cricket ball or (b) from the flash travels much faster than sound to a person standing at a distance.**

D3, D4

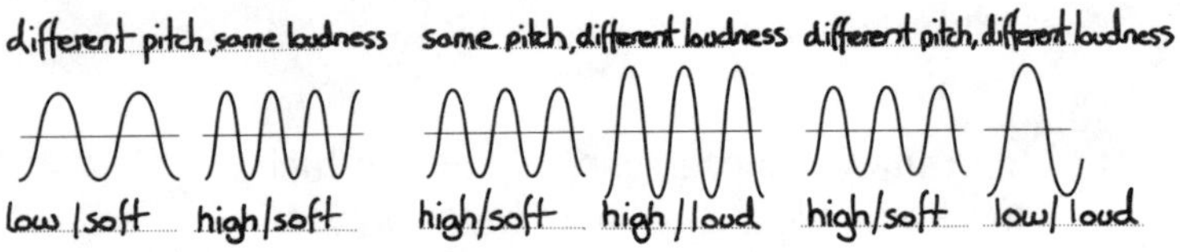

D5

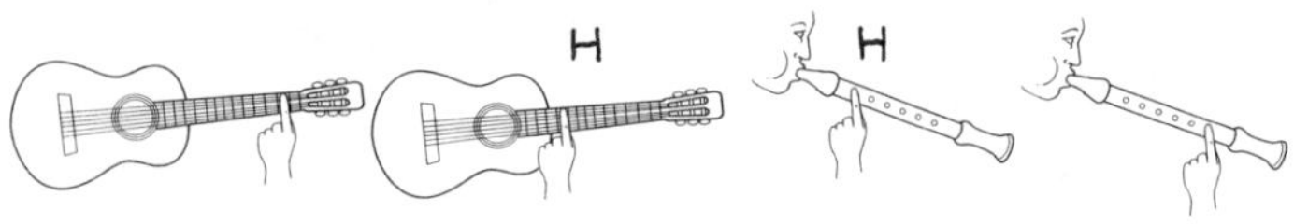

E1 Mercury Venus Earth Mars Jupiter Saturn Uranus Neptune Pluto.

E2

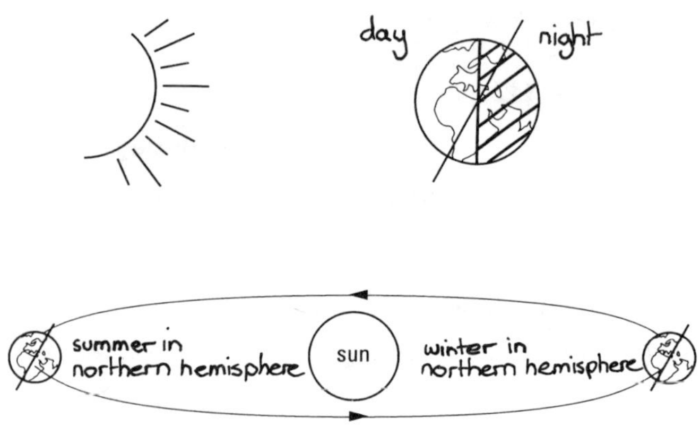

E3 planet; Sun; Solar System; galaxy; universe.

AT4 Levels 7 & 8 (pages 96–107)

A1, A2 current, $I = \frac{V}{R}$

resistance, $R = \frac{V}{I}$

current flowing in circuit:

$$I = \frac{V}{R}$$

$$I = \frac{3}{100}$$

$$I = 0.03\text{ A}$$

A3 $R = R_1 + R_2 + R_3$

$$R = 100 + 200 + 300$$

$$R = 600\,\Omega$$

$$\frac{1}{R} = \frac{1}{R_1} + \frac{1}{R_2} + \frac{1}{R_3}$$

$$\frac{1}{R} = \frac{1}{100} + \frac{1}{100} + \frac{1}{200}$$

$$\frac{1}{R} = \frac{5}{200}$$

$$R = \frac{200}{5} = 40\,\Omega$$

A4, A5 $Q = I \times t$

$$Q = 4 \times (1.5 \times 60 \times 60)$$

$$Q = 4 \times 5400$$

$$Q = 21\,600\text{ Coulombs}$$

A6, A7

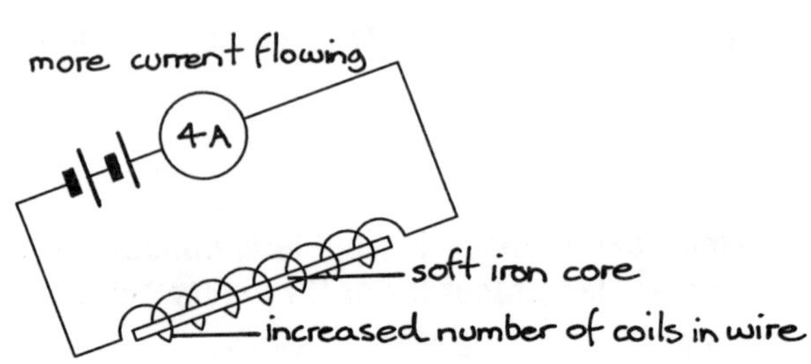

A8

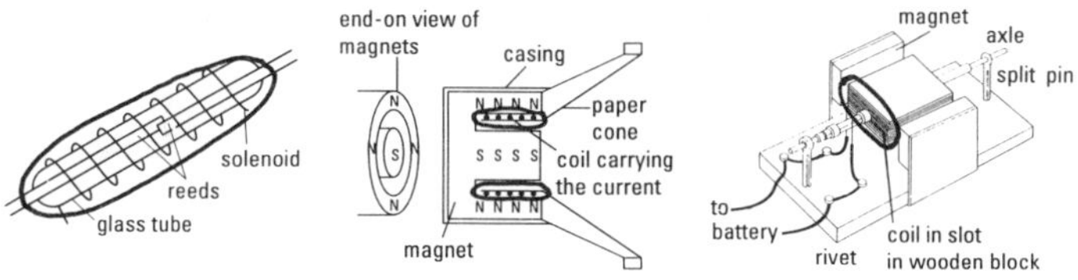

A9

Input A	Input B	Output	Result
0	0	0	nothing happens
1	1	1	door opens
1	0	1	door opens
0	1	1	door opens

A10 The bulb goes on when it is cold and dark. Or when it is cold and light; or when it is warm and dark.

A11, B1

	Radiation	Convection	Conduction
Heat transfer through	through air or space	liquids/gases	through solids
Heat transfer by	vibrating particles transmit some of their heat energy in form of waves	convection currents	passing vibrations through neighbouring particles
One example	heat from Sun on Earth	local winds in weather systems	soldering iron

B2

B3 % muscle efficiency $= \dfrac{\text{energy output}}{\text{energy input}} \times 100$

$$E = \frac{1120}{2800} \times 100 = 40\%$$

$$\%\ \text{electric fire efficiency} = \frac{1425}{1500} \times 100 = 95\%$$

B4, B5, B6 $I = \dfrac{P}{V}$

$$V = \frac{P}{I}$$

$$P = V \times I$$

Power rating of electric kettle, $P = 240 \times 9.6 = 2304$ W

Power of 3-bar electric fire $= 240 \times 12.5 = 3000$ W or 3 kW

Current flowing in refrigerator, $I = \dfrac{P}{V} = \dfrac{120}{240} = 0.5$ A

B7, B8 $t = \dfrac{E}{ms}$

$$m = \frac{E}{st}$$

B9 Energy transferred in 5 minutes $= 2500 \times 60 \times 5$ joules

$$\text{mass of water} = \frac{E}{ts} = \frac{2500 \times 60 \times 5}{10 \times 4200} = \frac{125}{7}$$

$$= 17.86 \text{ kg}$$

C1 work done = force × distance

$$w = 5 \times 1.2$$

$$w = 6 \text{ joules}$$

$$\text{power} = \frac{\text{work done}}{\text{time}}$$

$$p = \frac{6}{6} = 1 \text{ W}$$

C2, C3

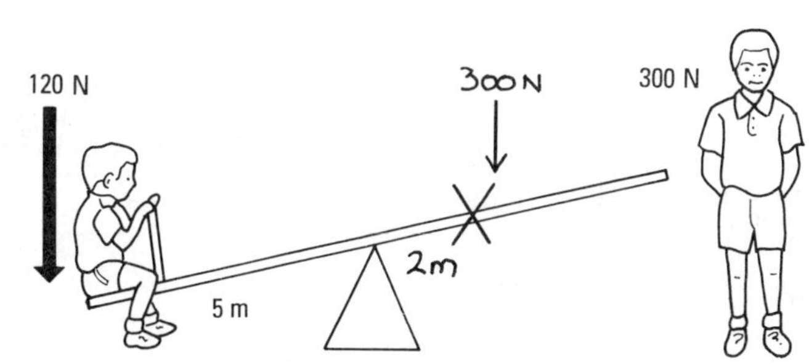

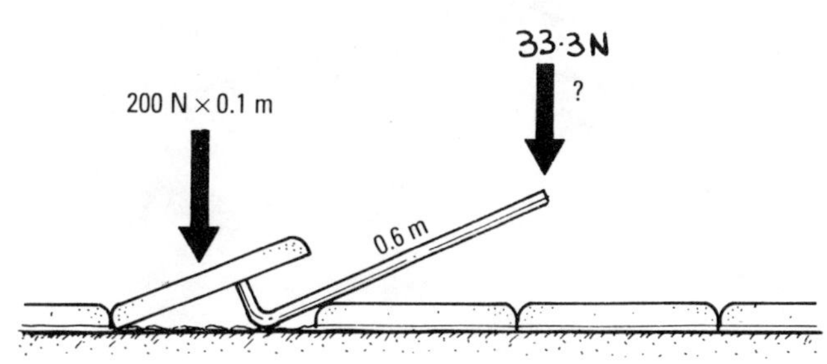

C4, C5

$$\text{acceleration} = \frac{\text{final velocity} - \text{starting velocity}}{\text{time taken}}$$

$$\text{acceleration} = \frac{12 - 0}{10}$$

$$a = 1.2 \text{ m/s/s}$$

C6, C7 60 kg parachutist

force acting = 600 N

mass = 60 kg

$$a = \frac{F}{m} = 10 \text{ m/s/s}$$

30 kg parachutist

force acting = 300 N

mass = 30 kg

$$a = \frac{F}{m} = 10 \text{ m/s/s}$$

C8, C9, C10 stopping force $= \dfrac{m\ (v-u)}{t}$

$$= \frac{1000\ (0-30)}{0.1} = 300\,000 \text{ N}$$

stopping force $= \dfrac{m\ (v-u)}{t}$

$$= \frac{1000\ (0-30)}{0.15} = 200\,000 \text{ N}$$

D1, D2 $f = v/\lambda$ formula for frequency $\lambda = v/f$ formula for wavelength

D3

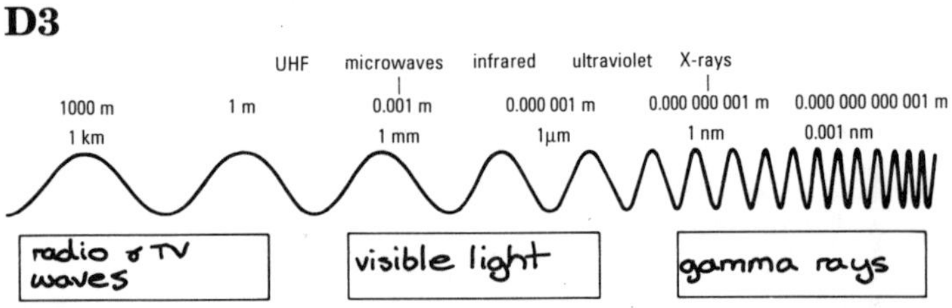

D4

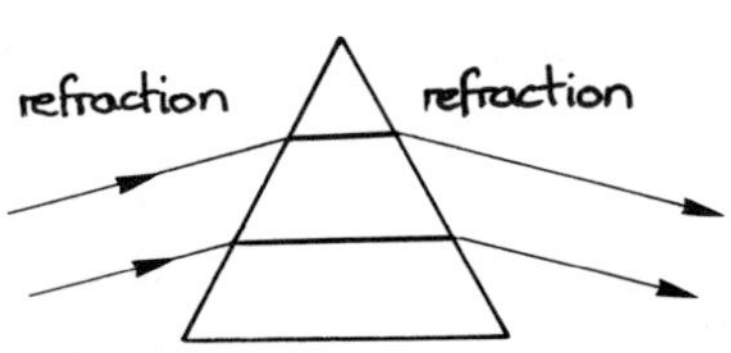

D5, D6

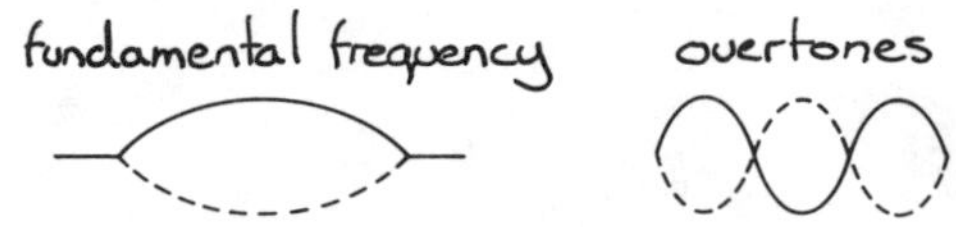

D7, D8, D9, D10, E1 increases; decreases.

E2, E3, E4

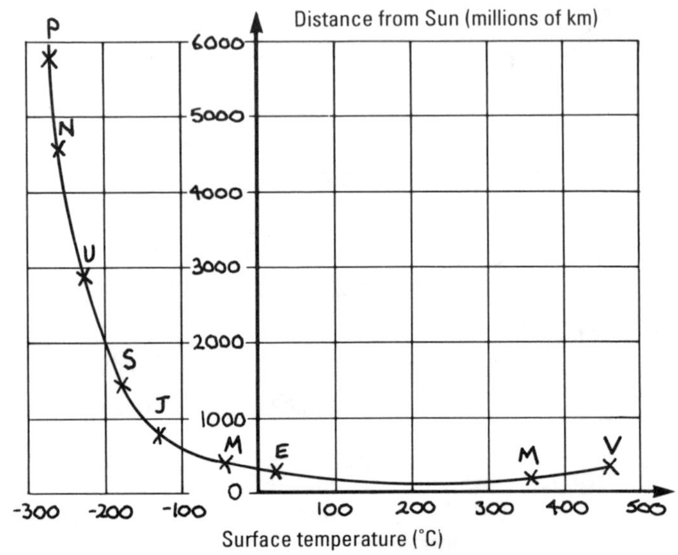

E5 Four inner planets: **Mercury; Venus; Earth; Mars**
Four outer planets: **Jupiter; Saturn; Uranus; Neptune.**

E6 Ohm's law $V = IR$

resistance in parallel circuit $\dfrac{1}{R} = \dfrac{1}{R_1} + \dfrac{1}{R_2} + \dfrac{1}{R_3}$

resistance in series circuit $R = R_1 + R_2 + R_3$

electric charge or coulombs in a circuit $Q = It$

$$\%\ \text{energy efficiency} = \frac{\text{energy output}}{\text{energy input}} \times 100$$

$$\text{power} = \frac{\text{energy transferred}}{\text{time}}$$

power = VI

energy transferred in heating water = mass × specific heat capacity × rise in temperature

work done = force × distance, $w = Fd$

$$\text{power} = \frac{\text{work done}}{\text{time taken}} \quad P = \frac{w}{t}$$

law of moments:

force × distance from pivot on left = force × distance from pivot on right

$$\text{acceleration} = \frac{\text{final velocity} - \text{starting velocity}}{\text{time taken}}$$

$$a = \frac{v-u}{t}$$

force = mass × acceleration, $F = ma$

$$\text{stopping force} = \frac{m(v-u)}{t}$$

AT4 Levels 9 & 10 (pages 108–117)

A1

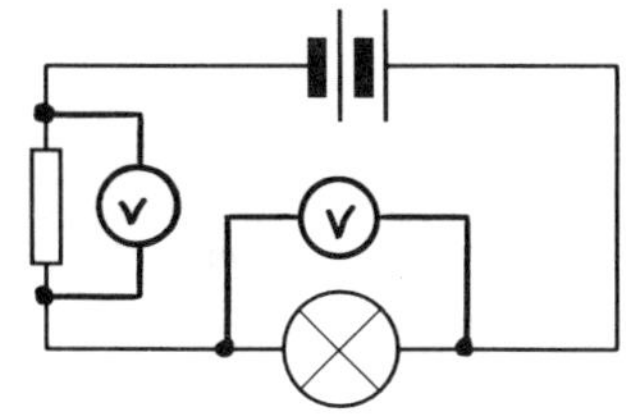

A2

Appliance	Power rating	Voltage	Current	Resistance
car headlamp	**36 watts**	12 volts	3 amps	**4 ohms**
electric drill	240 watts	240 volts	**1 amp**	**240 ohms**

A3, A4, A5

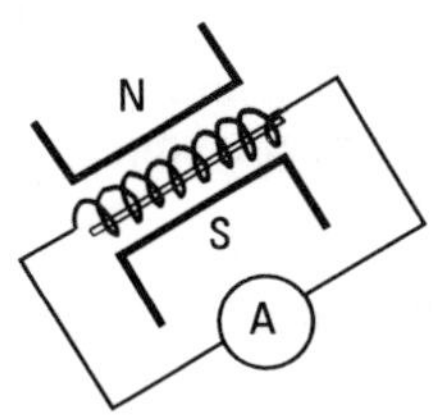

A6

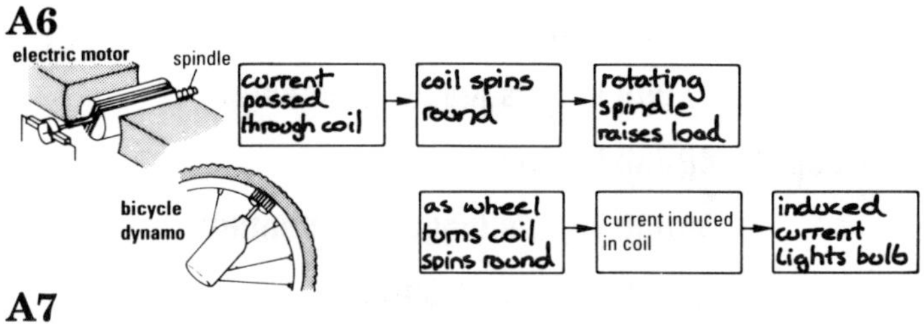

A7

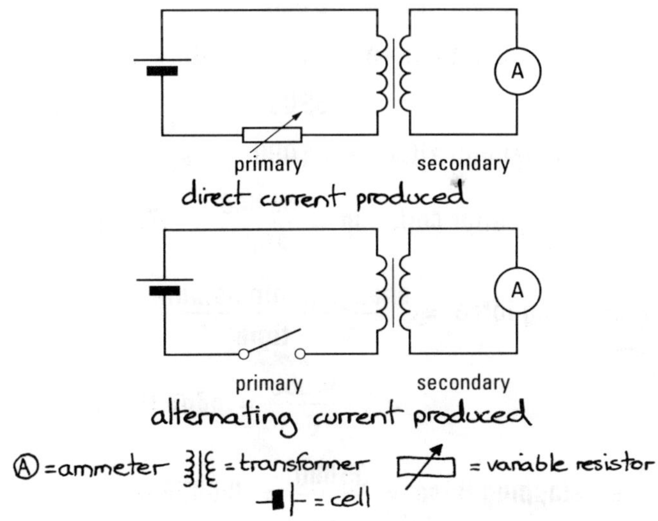

A8 When the voltage is stepped **up the current is stepped down** and vice versa.

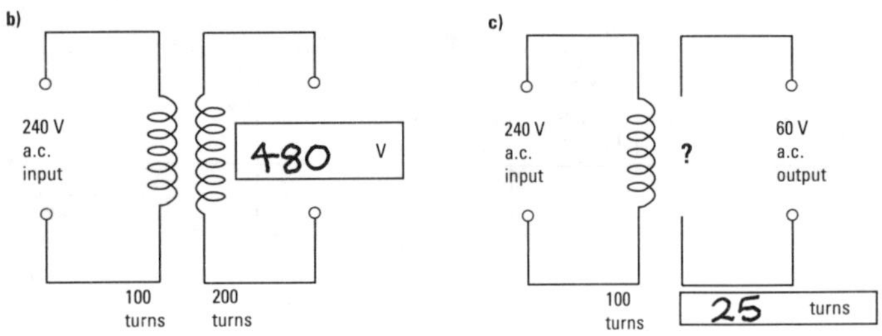

A9, A10

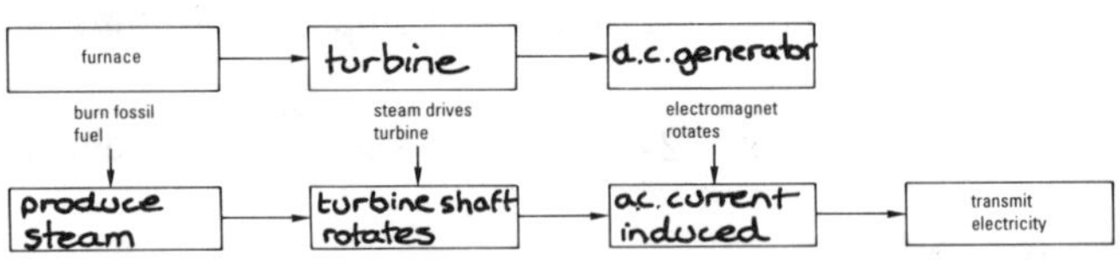

A11, B1 a) **unemployment** b) **slag heaps, pollution of atmosphere when burned** c) **non-renewable energy source, limited supply of coal.**

B2, B3 Advantages Disadvantages

C1 momentum = mass × velocity
(kg) (m/s)

Pair 1: **30 000 kg/m/s**

35 000 kg/m/s bigger momentum

Pair 2: **40 000 kg/m/s**

48 000 kg/m/s bigger momentum

C2 b) **momentum before = 30 000**

momentum after = 30 000

c) **momentum before = (1000 × 30) + (1000 × 25)**

= 55 000

momentum after = 55 000

$$\text{speed after collision} = \frac{55\,000}{2000} = 27.5\text{ m/s}$$

$$\textbf{C3}\ \text{stopping force} = \frac{\text{change in momentum}}{\text{time}}$$

$$= \frac{0 - 35\,000}{6} = 5833\text{ N}$$

$$\text{b) stopping force} = \frac{35\,000}{0.1} = 350000\text{ N}$$

C4 thrust = change in momentum/time

$$\text{thrust} = \frac{mv_{end} - mv_{start}}{\text{time}} = \frac{3 \times 10^6 \times 30}{50}$$

$$= 1.8 \times 10^6\text{ N}$$

C5 potential energy = mgh

$E = 0.5 \times g \times 0.5$ **where** $g = 10$ **N/kg**

$E = 0.25 \times g$

$E = 2.5$

C6, C7 a) $E = mgh$

$E = 2.5 \times 10 \times 2$

Potential energy, $E = 50$

b) **kinetic energy when hitting ground = potential energy lost = 50**

c) $v = \sqrt{2gh}$

$v = \sqrt{2 \times 10 \times 1}$

$v = \sqrt{20}$

$v = 4.4$ **m/s**

C8, D1 **radio waves; microwaves; infra-red; visible light; ultra-violet; X-rays; gamma rays.**

D2, D3

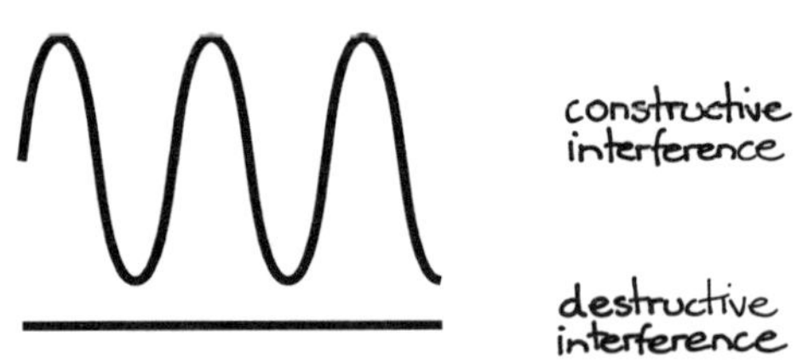

D4, D5, E1, E2, E3

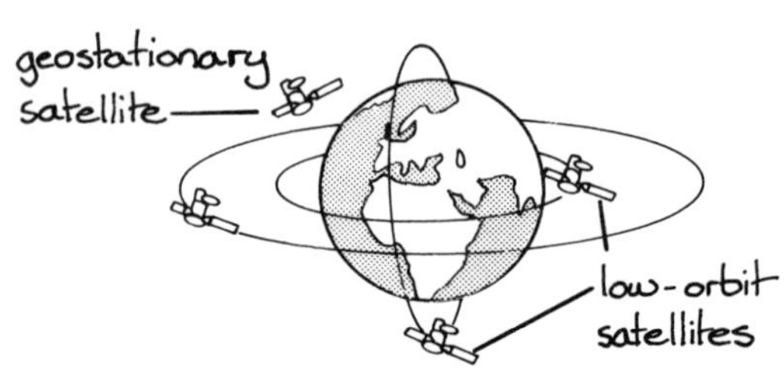

E4, E5, E6, E7

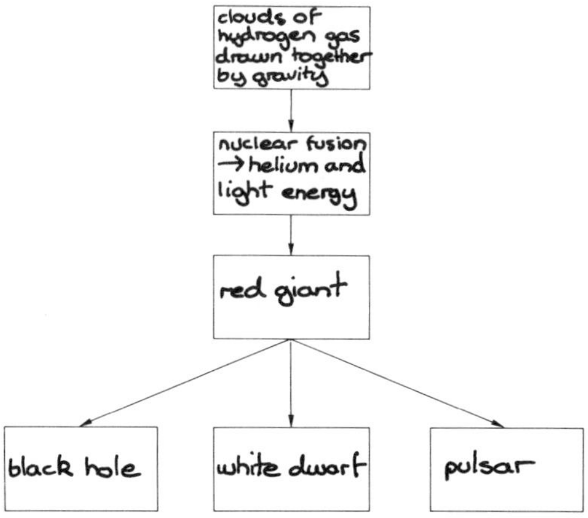

Electrical formulae:

power = voltage × current, $P = VI$

$P = I^2R$

$$P = \frac{V^2}{R}$$

In a transformer,

$V_{primary} \times I_{primary} = V_{secondary} \times I_{secondary}$

Energy and movement formulae:

momentum = mass × velocity

$= mv$

momentum before collision = momentum after collision

impulse = change in momentum

$F \times t = mv_{end} - mv_{start}$

$$\text{thrust} = \frac{\text{change in momentum}}{\text{time}}$$

$$F = \frac{mv_{end} - mv_{start}}{t}$$

energy transferred as potential energy, $E = mgh$

kinetic energy $= \frac{1}{2}mv^2$

In a falling object, potential energy lost = kinetic energy gained

$mgh = \frac{1}{2}mv^2$

$v = \sqrt{2gh}$

NOTES

NOTES

NOTES

NOTES

NOTES